Engaging China

ASIA IN WORLD POLITICS

Series Editor: Samuel S. Kim

Engaging China

Rebuilding
Sino-American Relations

Mel Gurtov

ROWMAN & LITTLEFIELD
Lanham • Boulder • New York • London

Published by Rowman & Littlefield
An imprint of The Rowman & Littlefield Publishing Group, Inc.
4501 Forbes Boulevard, Suite 200, Lanham, Maryland 20706
www.rowman.com
86-90 Paul Street, London EC2A 4NE

British Library Cataloguing in Publication Information Available

Library of Congress Cataloging-in-Publication Data
Names: Gurtov, Melvin, author.
Title: Engaging China: rebuilding Sino-American relations / Mel Gurtov.
Description: Lanham: Rowman & Littlefield, [2022] | Series: Asia in world
  politics | Includes bibliographical references and index.
Identifiers: LCCN 2022027277 (print) | LCCN 2022027278 (ebook) | ISBN
  9781538172186 (cloth) | ISBN 9781538172193 (paperback) | ISBN
  9781538172209 (epub)
Subjects: LCSH: United States–Foreign relations–China. | China–Foreign
  relations–United States. | United States–Foreign relations–21st
  century. | China–Foreign relations–21st century.
Classification: LCC E183.8.C5 G878 2022 (print) | LCC E183.8.C5 (ebook) |
  DDC 327.73051–dc23/eng/20220707
LC record available at https://lccn.loc.gov/2022027277
LC ebook record available at https://lccn.loc.gov/2022027278

∞™ The paper used in this publication meets the minimum requirements of American
National Standard for Information Sciences—Permanence of Paper for Printed Library
Materials, ANSI/NISO Z39.48-1992.

For Jodi, with all my love

Contents

Preface

As a China specialist, I have been disheartened by the dramatic shift in official and public perceptions of China. China's rise has been greeted with fear and trepidation, in sharp contrast with the positive reception that greeted China's "opening to the outside world" in the 1980s. I write at a time when the clock has turned back—when, once again, the United States and China are at loggerheads, with few voices rising in either country on behalf of resetting relations. I'm one of those voices.

Demonizing China could not have come at a worse time, with the world reeling from Russia's invasion of Ukraine, the COVID-19 pandemic, and the climate crisis. It ought to be possible to rediscover common ground in US-China relations, and in this book I offer reasons and ways to do that. Rebuilding the relationship is in the national interest of both countries, and in the global and human interest as well.

I wish to thank several friends whose comments and suggestions have greatly improved my book. Carla Freeman, George Guess, Larry Kirsch, Gil Latz, Paul Marantz, Joe Parker, and Mark Selden all read the entire manuscript and offered many helpful ideas. John Badgley, Walter Clemens, and Peter Van Ness also provided good thoughts and support. I'm especially grateful to Sam Kim, editor of this series, for enthusiastically embracing the book and supporting its publication. As he has done for many years, Milton Leitenberg sent me articles and reports that I would have missed. Thanks for support also to Michael Bloom, Dean Ouellette, and Dali Yang. Finally, I greatly appreciate the editorial and production staff at Rowman & Littlefield for all their help: Ashley Dodge, Haley White, Felicity Tucker, and the editor of this book, Kate Hertzog.

Finally, I thank my wonderful wife, Jodi, for letting me off the hook on farm work so that I could concentrate on writing. It is fitting that I dedicate this last book of mine—or so I keep saying—to her. Thank you, sweetie.

Deadwood, Oregon, April 1, 2022

Chapter 1

What Engagement Means and Why It Matters

WHY ENGAGEMENT?

We live in dangerous times, and the parlous state of US-China relations is a major reason why. United Nations secretary-general Antonio Guterres expressed his concern in the fall of 2021 when he said: "We need to re-establish a functional relationship between the two powers," pointing specifically to "the problems of vaccination, the problems of climate change and many other global challenges that cannot be solved without constructive relations within the international community and mainly among the super-powers." Otherwise, he said, we will face a new Cold War that is "probably more dangerous and more difficult to manage" than the previous one.[1]

If anything, the secretary-general's comment understates the danger—and the common responsibility of great powers. The United States and the People's Republic of China (PRC) have the strongest, most technologically advanced economies. They are also the principal greenhouse gas produc-ers, the major military powers, and nuclear-weapon states. Violent conflict between them is unthinkable but possible. Thus, they have a responsibility to the planet not only to find a path to coexistence but also to lead by example in the resolution of the most pressing global problems, starting with climate change. Hence the reason for this book: to make the case, while there is still time, for "constructive relations" via deep engagement between the United States and China.

These days, US-China relations are generally being portrayed as a clash of titans in a contest for global leadership that could slide into another Cold War or worse. Each country sees the other as the principal obstacle to its preferred world order. As I see it, the need is urgent for ramping up bilateral,

1

multilateral, and unofficial forms of contact rather than (as is presently the case) looking for ways to decouple their economies and form competing geostrategic coalitions. Leaders in Washington and Beijing say they want to avoid another Cold War, yet neither seems interested in taking meaningful steps to defuse tensions—more so the United States, as I will contend in subsequent chapters. These two great powers thus are at a pivotal juncture, where policy choices will shape not just the future of their relations but also the prospects for peace and security in much of the rest of the world.

My argument for US engagement with China urges a policy of competitive coexistence rather than what seem to be the three most popular ideas today: managed competition, containment, and outright confrontation. The book is not a full-blown treatment of US-China relations. Nor does it propose a universal US policy of engagement, since one size doesn't fit all circumstances. Instead, I examine those elements of Chinese and US politics and international policies that either lend themselves to engagement or detract from it. I am critical of both countries' behavior and intentions, placing emphasis on each leadership's insecurity, which frames much of their policy making. In the first two chapters, I define engagement, explore departures from it in recent US administrations, and critique the bipartisan anti-China consensus that now prevails in US politics. I propose ways to interpret China's intentions and objectives that depart from that consensus and from mainstream American views of China. Chapters 3 and 4 cast a critical eye on Chinese domestic and foreign policies, pointing to elements of insecurity and vulnerability that are often overlooked. I then move to the specifics of US-China relations today: major issues in conflict (chapter 5), the Joseph R. Biden administration's China policy and the Chinese response (chapter 6), and four cases of US-China competition that could become cases of cooperation (chapter 7). I summarize my argument on competitive coexistence and provide a US-China engagement menu in chapter 8.

THE STRATEGY OF ENGAGEMENT

In the United States, finding ways to engage China more deeply was once toasted by officials in both countries as a path in their common interest. Engagement efforts evolved from an initial common objective to deter the Soviet Union—the so-called strategic triangle in the Richard Nixon–Henry Kissinger era—to building a commercial relationship in the Jimmy Carter–Deng Xiaoping years in support of China's modernization. Thereafter, from George W. Bush to Barack Obama, the two countries established a web of nonofficial ties that sprang largely from private-sector initiatives and flourished with support from both governments.[2] The administrations of Donald

Trump and Joe Biden have rejected engagement, however, regarding it either as capitulation (under Trump) or bad judgment (under Biden). Two senior officials under Biden wrote the following about engaging China before their appointments:

> The basic mistake of engagement [under Obama] was to assume that it could bring about fundamental changes to China's political system, economy, and foreign policy. Washington risks making a similar mistake today, by assuming that competition can succeed in transforming China where engagement failed—this time forcing capitulation or even collapse.[3]

The authors went on to say that "the avoidance of friction, in the service of positive ties, was an objective unto itself."

In the next chapter I take issue with the "basic mistake" assessment, but here I will argue that those two officials—Kurt Campbell, the White House coordinator for Asian affairs in the National Security Council, and Jake Sullivan, the National Security Advisor—misconstrue the meaning of engagement, perhaps to justify restoration of a hard line in US relations with China. In the first place, engagement is not "an objective unto itself." In my book *Engaging Adversaries*, I make the case for engagement as a *strategy*, distinct from (but inclusive of) occasional transactions such as diplomatic talks and people-to-people exchanges. Deep engagement is not simply about having friendly relations. It is a systematic, consistent, sustained, and sincere effort to find common ground with an adversary, with the aim to reduce tensions and avoid violent outcomes. The strategy utilizes incentives for peace and defensive deterrence to reach accommodation where possible—peaceful coexistence, in short. The strategy does not call for sacrificing basic principles, such as on human rights, or papering over policy differences. Friction in the relationship is a given, not to be avoided but also not to be taken as the defining element in the relationship. Both sides acknowledge their differences but seek mutually beneficial ways to cooperate—as the Chinese saying goes, *qu chang bu duan* (取长补短), usually rendered as "learning from each other's strong points to offset weaknesses." The ultimate ambition of engagement, I wrote, is *transformation* of a relationship: "to create an environment conducive to changes of perspective and behavior on *all* sides by focusing on actions . . . that will move the parties away from destructive conflict."[4]

In an engagement strategy, the search for common ground has priority. Of course, it takes two to tango: China must be as committed as the United States to finding common ground. Avoiding high-risk confrontation, chiefly by promoting dialogue and mutually beneficial exchanges, is a priority of policy making—a process that incorporates regular interactions and that may lead to any of a number of concrete political, economic, military, or other agreements

that foster mutual understanding and respect. Trust is not *essential* to engagement; identifying and fulfilling common interests is. That is what made the
Nixon-Mao opening to China work. I'm reminded of a statement by Iran's
foreign minister to the effect that "mutual *lack* of confidence" led to the Iran
nuclear deal in 2015. But *building* trust through mutual respect and agreements that work *was* essential, as the foreign minister also said.[5] That meant
taking risks and undertaking verifiable tasks, which is what the eventual
nuclear deal encompassed.[6]

Trust building is especially difficult between the United States and China,
and not only because of numerous policy and ideological differences and
a violent history. There are two other obstacles: different interpretations of
basic principles and different ideas about how to reach agreement.

As an example of the first matter, take noninterference, the first of China's
so-called five principles of peaceful coexistence, which have been regularly
recited since the 1950s. (The other principles are nonaggression, equality,
mutual benefit, and peaceful coexistence.) Agreement on mutual noninterference in each other's internal affairs could be the starting point for a broader
acceptance of common principles such as President Nixon and Soviet communist party General Secretary Leonid Brezhnev reached in the 1970s. But
Chinese and American diplomacy poses difficulties. Chinese officials argue
that any criticism of China's human rights or territorial claims is foreign
interference. They ignore or defend other countries where repression is systematic and has drawn international condemnation. The United States often
downgrades repression of human rights abroad when its strategic or economic
interests are at stake. When they are not, the United States reserves the right
to comment, and sanction, governments whose behavior toward their own
citizens does not square with certain "universal values," notwithstanding US
violations of those values with its own citizens. Both China and the United
States regularly interfere in the internal affairs of other states, in defiance of
self-determination and state sovereignty—for example, by supplying authoritarian regimes with weapons used for domestic repression, by pressuring
governments to alter their foreign policy stances in return for aid, and by
deploying troops, ships, or planes across boundaries in the name of national
security. What, therefore, constitutes principled behavior on noninterference
is a matter worth pursuing in the interest of common security.

Insight into the second obstacle, reaching agreement, comes from China's
leading America watcher, Wang Jisi, who is dean of Beijing University's
Institute of International Strategic Studies. He writes that trust between the
People's Republic of China (PRC) and the United States cannot come until
different "mind-sets" converge:

Whereas the Chinese insist on identifying principles, the Americans want action on immediate issues. The Chinese believe in first "finding common ground while reserving differences" [求同存异], which means agreement on a set of principles, including mutual respect and win-win cooperation. Americans, by contrast, tend to focus on hard issues, such as tensions over Taiwan and the South China Sea. So it appears that the Chinese want to set up principles before trying to solve specific problems, but the Americans are eager to address the problems before they are ready to improve the relationship.[7]

Neither government has proven very good at overcoming these obstacles. The Chinese never acknowledge their violations or ignoring of their five principles, simply dismissing evidence to the contrary. That happened most recently in the 2022 Ukraine crisis. American leaders accept criticism of US violations of professed principles from left and right, but—guided by the notion of exceptionalism—rarely change their behavior. Often they will fail to perceive their double standard, as when Jake Sullivan wrote in 2019:

At a gathering of Asian nations in 2011, I heard the Chinese foreign minister address the issue of Beijing's ambitions in the South China Sea this way: "China is a big country, and other countries here are small countries. Think hard about that." This is China's way, and Russia's way. It generally has not been America's way.[8]

Sullivan was correct to criticize the Chinese foreign minister's bluster, but he was disingenuous in dismissing the idea that America doesn't "generally" have aggressive ambitions. That pretense, common among US officials—I think of President Ronald Reagan telling the Russians that America never engaged in imperialism, or Secretary of State Antony Blinken lecturing the Russians during the crisis over Ukraine that no country has "the right to exert a sphere of influence," an idea that "should be relegated to the dustbin of history"—does not help advance discussion with China. In fact, what it sometimes does is whitewash one's own history.

ENGAGEMENT BETWEEN INSECURE RIVALS

American and Chinese leaders today operate from insecurity, internally as well as in their foreign relations. US officials may continue to proclaim that their country is still the greatest power on earth, and Chinese officials may insist that this is China's century. International opinion polls point to great admiration for each country on certain matters, such as US universities and China's economic development. But barely beneath the surface are profound concerns at the highest levels in both countries about the long-term stability

of their political and social systems. The United States faces, most fundamentally, a crisis of democracy. Social and political divisions are tearing the
country apart: battles over voting rights, racial inequality, resort to violence
to achieve political ends, culture wars, and widespread questioning of basic
ideas such as the rule of law and adherence to the Constitution. Once an
object of admiration, America's democracy is now judged, by Americans
as well as others, to be in steep decline and in danger of a right-wing coup.[9]
China also has serious governance issues, many of them associated with
its extraordinarily rapid economic rise: for example, official corruption at
every level of government and widening income gaps that exceed those in
the United States.[10] Widespread, systematic repression is taking place not
just around China's rimland but also in the heartland, where the party-state's
absolute authority hangs over intellectuals, lawyers, and civil society groups.
High growth rates mask serious environmental and public health problems
and sharpening social inequality. Chinese society is in flux, increasingly
diverse and increasingly demanding.

Insecure elites present a special challenge for a strategy of engagement.
Mistrust between governments is likely to be higher than usual, driven not
only by the usual disagreements but also by criticisms at home that engagement might exacerbate—charges of conceding too much to the enemy, for
example, or failure to obtain satisfaction on basic interests. Incentives offered
by the adversary might be viewed with suspicion. US-China frictions that
might normally be regarded as amenable to diplomacy now tend to be magni-
fied, whereas issues in the relationship that could be opportunities for consensus are more likely to be shelved. Out of that unsatisfactory situation might
come more aggressive behavior rather than a willingness to compromise. On
the other hand, mutual insecurity might, with appropriate incentives by both
governments, lead to recognition of the necessity for engagement. A government that has to devote attention and resources to domestic problems may
have incentives to engage, if only to neutralize potential external interference
in its affairs. Likewise, a government that must depend on certain imports or
on critical supply chains might look to its own resources, but with appropriate incentives, it might instead choose cooperation with others. So rather than
lashing out when things go badly, an insecure government might be open to
engagement offers that, in better circumstances, it would reject.

Since the early 1980s, even when US-China relations were reasonably
stable compared with the present, leaders in both countries have always
had concerns and suspicions about each other. Friction has been a constant,
cooperation occasional. But the sources of friction were usually amenable
to diplomacy; tensions in relations, both sides agreed, could be *managed*.
Witness, for example, the handling of the Tiananmen crackdown in 1989,
the mistaken bombing of the Chinese embassy in Belgrade in May 1999,

the Chinese missile exercises near Taiwan in 1996, and the 2001 fatal air collision between a Chinese jet and a US intelligence-gathering plane near Hainan. All of these incidents could have ended in a serious confrontation, but deft high-level intervention, bolstered by expansive economic, political, and cultural relations, enabled them to be overcome. Indeed, the US-China relationship before Donald Trump and Xi Jinping looked from afar like a textbook model of the liberal school's approach to conflict: an ever-growing web of transactions—governmental, nongovernmental, business, and people-to-people—would lessen the possibility of overt conflict and might motivate greater cooperation.

Identifying exactly when the knot in the US-China relationship began to unwind is not so easy to determine. When expectations are not met, when "incidents" arise, when cooperation does not bear fruit, leaders who have invested in a relationship must answer to those who questioned its value in the first place. Trump certainly accelerated the unwinding by blaming China for the trade deficit and then for COVID-19, but most observers agree it started earlier, with the 2008 global financial crisis. That event tarnished the US image in China as a responsible economic power and emboldened Chinese leaders to pursue self-reliance to some degree.[11] The crisis catalyzed the now-prevailing view among Chinese analysts, official and nonofficial, that America is in decline and China should seize on the opportunity to promote its own version of national greatness—hence, Xi Jinping, who came to power as party general secretary in 2012 and shortly after began promoting a "great national rejuvenation" (中华民族伟大复兴) and the "Chinese Dream" (中國夢). But the timing was not quite right for a Chinese takeoff: Official corruption was endemic, economic problems loomed large, and China was facing what some Chinese called a "crisis of values" brought on by materialism, uncertainty about the future, and ideological decay. Xi may have faced opposition, perhaps constraining any plan to take a more assertive stance in foreign affairs.

That was then. In the present moment, with Europe at war and the global economy in turmoil, Xi Jinping faces crucial decisions on how to position China as a great power. Relations with the United States have deteriorated, but the possibility of mending them remains open. In a call with President Biden, Xi Jinping observed that "China-US relations still haven't escaped from the dilemma created by the previous administration, and instead have encountered more and more challenges."[12] The two leaders agreed that regular communications are very important given their joint responsibility for world peace. But how to improve understanding of each other's motives and intentions remains among their greatest "challenges." As Xi said, "the US side has misread and misjudged China's strategic intentions." Biden could easily have said the same about China's America watchers.

Chapter 2

Understanding and Misunderstanding China

SOURCING CHINA'S BEHAVIOR

The typical US government analysis of China's international strategy these days makes several time-worn presumptions about motivations. Chinese leaders are said to be most influenced by Marxist-Leninist-Maoist ideology, the party-state's unquestioned authority, opportunism (taking advantage of US retreat from Asia, for instance), a militant nationalism, and the personal ambitions of Xi Jinping and those around him. Employing only these factors goes far toward ensuring a threat-based strategic assessment that is often alarmist and, consequently, prioritizes military power over diplomacy in the US response. An example is the argument of Rush Doshi, who became director for China in Biden's National Security Council. His book purports to identify the elements of China's "grand strategy," but it reads like an update of the old "two steps forward, one step back" idea that many analysts in Cold War days said characterized Russian and Chinese strategy. Doshi depicts a China doggedly marching forward, its grand strategy perfectly attuned and in sharp contrast with American actions that are unprovocative and well-intentioned.[1] He never mentions the variety of domestic problems Chinese leaders face when making foreign policy decisions.

Foreign policy making does not take place in a political vacuum, and China is no exception. Yet most American analyses give scant attention to the relationship between China's domestic and international affairs.[2] Chinese leaders and senior officials have consistently said that the chief purpose of foreign policy is to create a safe international environment for the flourishing of China's economy and the advancement of China's international status. In a word, national security for China begins at home—which, importantly, is Joe Biden's mantra too. Again, Wang Jisi makes the point:

> There seems to be a consensus among Chinese social elites that domestic problems, rather than challenges from abroad, are posing greater threats to China's political order, social cohesion, national unity, sustainable economic growth, financial stability, individual livelihood, morality and the natural environment. However, it is hard to find a consensus on what constitutes the root causes of these domestic problems, not to mention solutions to them.[3]

What Wang Jisi was careful not to mention is that all these factors are subordinate to an even higher purpose of foreign policy: preservation of the party-state system and the primacy of the Chinese Communist Party (CCP). Foreign Minister Wang Yi did say as much: "The leadership of the [CCP] is the greatest political strength of China's diplomacy. It is the root of the major-country diplomacy with Chinese characteristics and the institutional guarantee for all our achievements."[4]

Granted, "domestic factors" embrace a wide variety of issues that may influence China's foreign and national security policies. Among these factors are leadership questions (such as debate over policy and the concentration of power), party rectitude, bureaucratic politics (such as bargaining and groupthink), military priorities, budgetary concerns and their implications for economic development goals, political dissidence, social and cultural friction, educational conformity, public opinion, and the impact of economic and other reforms on local and national interests. On that last point, Wang Jisi draws attention to "the diversity of interests in China among regions, localities, industrial sectors, government agencies and social spectra." Studies by China scholars confirm his observation.[5] Conflict between local and central leadership is fairly common—as a Chinese saying goes, at the top there is policy, but those below have countermeasures: *shang you zhengce, xia you duice* (上 有政策□下有对策), and although foreign policy is usually not the issue, it may well be affected.

All these domestic issues touch on unity and disunity at home, which relates to the main worries of Chinese leaders: how to maintain social order and party discipline while building a strong China, or what the Chinese call comprehensive national strength (*zonghe guoli*, 综合国力). When and under what circumstances domestic affairs come into play is the analytical challenge, but this much is certain: No assessment of China's foreign policy is complete without taking account of the possible ways that the state of the nation affects Chinese worldviews, intentions, and capabilities.

For China as for other countries, domestic strength undergirds initiatives in foreign affairs, whereas serious domestic problems siphon attention and resources as well as create potential vulnerabilities that an adversary can exploit. That is why, for instance, Chinese leaders pay attention to public opinion, not just as a useful tool to undergird a foreign policy, such as by cultivating or containing nationalist sentiment, but also as a barometer of its "performance legitimacy."[6] Weaknesses and conflicts at home can make China far less secure than its official rhetoric or its think-tank analyses suggest, and therefore may make China far less of a threat to US security interests than official studies propose. Chinese public sources rarely address domestic problems as a source of foreign policy uncertainty or report on internal debate over a foreign policy or national security issue.[7] Typically, only when identifying enemies of the state, such as ethnic minority "separatists" and political activists, do we get a peek into internal insecurity. The official press and officials don't talk about budget battles over military spending, power struggles among leaders, the possible impact of repression in Xinjiang (the Xinjiang Uyghur Autonomous Region, XUAR) or Hong Kong on China's reputation, or the leadership's fretting over the fraying of society over income gaps or official corruption. Nevertheless, it seems reasonable to conclude that domestic policy debates, inequities, and opposition *constrain* policy making on international questions, possibly even when it comes to decision making on China's core interests, such as Taiwan and Tibet.

Dogmatic assessments of the China threat are grist for the mill of the US military-industrial complex—arguments for still larger military budgets, more deployments to Asia, and tighter security partnerships. They are also arguments to justify containing or constraining China rather than engaging it with the goal of seeking common ground. Such is the case today. To be clear, engaging China does not preclude having a strong US military. But an engagement strategy would shape decisions about funding and deploying the military: Less becomes more, as reduced numbers invite reciprocation by adversaries. Presumed threats to national security, of which there are always many, would become less of a factor in government budgets. Instead, *collective security* concerns, such as nuclear weapons, pandemics, and climate change, would have priority, and *cooperative security* thinking would guide security policies. The security agenda for all the major powers would focus on those and other global issues such as energy conservation, cyberwarfare, economic inequality, the role of multilateral organizations, adherence to international law, and terrorism.

ASSESSING CHINA'S AMBITIONS

What does China want? Security and respect? Primacy in Asia? Displacement of the United States as the global hegemon? Economic domination? China's ultimate ambitions are a matter of great dispute among China watchers and US officials alike. Most everyone can agree that Beijing wants regime security and a stable order under communist party leadership, but the scope and limits of its international aims remain a matter of intense debate. Analysts make *presumptions*, influenced far more by China's rapid economic rise and fervid nationalism than by the domestic factors mentioned earlier. The problem for American analysts is not just to be able to view the world through Chinese eyes and to avoid conflating China's greater capabilities with its intentions. They must also filter political influences at home that may skew interpretations, such as a rising sense of threat and China's global economic reach. America watchers in China surely have to deal with the same kinds of influences.

The US bipartisan consensus on China until roughly the second Obama administration was that China's rise, thanks in large part to the scope of its dealings with the United States, made it less threatening. Differences between the two countries, such as on trade and human rights, could be managed through quiet diplomacy. As Bill Clinton remarked, better to have a China focused on rapid growth than a China in chaos, as happened in the Cultural Revolution. In Obama's time, although new issues with China arose to complicate the relationship—such as over China's military buildup on islands in the South China Sea—US and Chinese representatives met in as many as ninety bilateral forums for discussion of everything from the environment to military affairs, capped by an annual Security and Economic Dialogue. But the honeymoon ended when China's economic and commercial rise no longer seemed, to increasing numbers of policy makers, to have benign intent. "Strategic distrust" between the two countries, two prominent American and Chinese analysts agreed, had become the chief characteristic of US-China relations.[8] Official views saw China as more rival than partner; the conflation of capability with intentions dominated US assessments, a classic error in foreign policy analysis. Some Americans went further on intent, seeing China as the inheritor of the Russian threat—the only country that really could challenge US leadership, at least in Asia. Now, the China challenge is global and strategic in the eyes of many US analysts—the mirror image of the widespread Chinese belief that the United States is the one power that stands in the way of completion of national unification and China's economic and technological rise. Therein lies the danger facing US and Chinese leaders and, for that matter, the world.

OBAMA'S CHINA POLICY AND AMERICA'S
DISAPPOINTMENT WITH CHINA

When it comes to China, Campbell and Sullivan are correct to criticize a policy that banks on China's economic rise to morph into some form of political liberalism. During the early post–Cold War euphoria over communism's demise in Europe, some US opinion leaders may have held that view. But China's transition away from authoritarianism was never the basis of US policy, and it had no chance of happening in China, especially after the Tiananmen protests and the collapse of the Soviet Union soon after. The Tiananmen uprising reaffirmed Deng Xiaoping's warning to his party colleagues about liberalism's danger to the CCP. And the experiment with *glasnost* and *perestroika* in Russia under Mikhail Gorbachev after the USSR's collapse convinced China's leaders that socialist market economics had to be entirely separate from political liberalization, a view held just as strongly today. "A fortress can be most easily captured from within," as Chinese analysts were fond of saying, meaning that the party's authority was most likely to be challenged by liberal sympathizers inside the party.[9] Thus, even as Xi Jinping's "socialism with Chinese characteristics" embraced economic globalization, it also meant preventing certain dangerous features of Western politics from infecting China. CCP Document No. 9 in 2013, reflecting Xi Jinping's perspective, identified "seven proscribed" (*qi buzhun*, 七不准) ideas that are threats to party control, including "Western constitutional democracy," human rights, pro-market "neoliberalism," and Western-inspired ideas of media independence and civic participation.

Like all his predecessors, Obama certainly hoped that China's integration in the global economy would help open up China's social order and moderate its external behavior. China's involvement in multilateral organizations, economic (such as the World Trade Organization, WTO) and military (the Nuclear Nonproliferation Treaty, for example), the thinking went, would give China prestige, wealth, and influence, but it would also provide a means of punishing China for breaking the rules.[10] Chinese society did become more fluid, with more lifestyle and economic choices, as Alastair Iain Johnston has argued.[11] But China's *political* liberalization, from the Clinton to the Obama administrations, was not considered the inexorable outcome of Beijing's expanding external involvements. Pessimism about China in US administrations focused on China's lack of progress on human rights, yet even that issue got relatively less attention than did China's rapid advances in economic, technological, and military modernization. Clinton's *National Security Strategy for a New Century*, for instance, released in October 1998, listed six objectives in China policy, not one of which was to transform China's political system. All had to do with security issues, such as stability in the Taiwan Strait and "strengthening China's adherence to international nonproliferation norms."[12] As Evan Medeiros observes, US security concerns led to a strategic reappraisal of China in the mid-1990s that would carry over into the Obama years:

> Beginning in the early 1990s, engagement worked well as Washington sought to draw China into the evolving post–Cold War order and Beijing sought to break out of its post-Tiananmen isolation. Washington largely set the terms for that process. After the Taiwan Strait crisis of 1995–96 and the acceleration of Chinese military modernization, however, U.S. policymakers began pursuing security balancing and binding strategies more deliberately, as the downside risks of a rising China started to become more apparent. The renovation of the U.S.-Japanese alliance in the late 1990s, Chinese accession to the World Trade Organization in 2001, and updates to the U.S. defense posture in Asia in the 2010s are notable examples of this [balancing].[13]

Obama's China policy amounted to what I have called "halfway" engagement.[14] To the extent the policy sought to engage China, it was based on promoting US security interests, chiefly by seeking to reduce the risk of war.[15] Obama did not seriously entertain Xi Jinping's proposal in 2013 for a "new type of great-power relationship" (*xin xing de daguo guanxi*, 新型的大国关系). Obama evidently could not, for domestic political as much as for international reasons, acknowledge China's equal standing, though at a summit meeting in June of that year, Obama agreed with Xi that "working together cooperatively" and bringing US-China relations "to a new level" were sound ideas.[16] When the G-20 countries convened at St. Petersburg in September, Obama repeated these diplomatic niceties, saying of Xi's proposed new model: "we agreed to continue to build a new model of great power relations based on practical cooperation and constructively managing our differences." But he added that "significant differences and sources of tension" remain with China, implying that the United States remained to be convinced that China was "playing a stable and prosperous and peaceful role" in world affairs.[17]

The two countries were far apart in their understanding of each other and of global affairs in general.[18] Obama showed as much by pushing for congressional approval of the Trans-Pacific Partnership on trade, which he saw as "the centerpiece of our broader regional strategy, one in which the United States and not China, would write the rules of international trade."[19] He also ordered US air and naval power shifted to Asia and challenged China's militarization of the South China Sea islets that it occupied, in line with his National Security Council's worrisome assessment of China.[20]

Gaining China's commitment to the "rules of the international trading system," as Bill Clinton put it, did work for a time. China's growing trade and investment network, and the relocation of multinational manufacturing plants to China, showed that China was embracing the market. But all that was not enough to satisfy *either* Chinese reformers *or* Western governments. Much of the reason for the limits to China's "reform and opening" had to do with its politics. As China got stronger, it set out to create its own regional economic institutions as well as be more assertive about its strategic interests. Moreover, as described by Yeling Tan, joining the WTO in 2001 gave Chinese reformers the opportunity to make significant changes in domestic institutions and the role of the market, in conformity with WTO rules. As with any major policy decision, WTO membership produced winners and losers in China's economy at every level, from state to local. However, those officials who favored the state and resisted the intrusion of globalization due, for example, to foreign competition and free-trade rules, would have their day. Under Xi, state capitalism has won out, though "despite Xi's efforts, China's global economic posture remains mostly the product of the country's messy internal politics and not the result of a coordinated master plan."[21]

Nevertheless, in the United States the story line persists that US policy toward China was lenient, dependent on China's evolving into a democracy and oblivious to the threat it might one day pose. The eminent political scientist John J. Mearsheimer has written, for example, that the United States failed to apply fundamental realism by widening the power gap with China while China was weak. "Washington promoted investment in China and welcomed the country into the global trading system, thinking it would become a peace-loving democracy and a responsible stakeholder in a U.S.-led international order."[22] Greg Sargent, writing for the *Washington Post* on November 30, 2018, references "the theory that including China in a U.S.-led global system would induce Beijing's Communist rulers to open their economy and, over time, political system as well. By now, it is abundantly clear to people across the political spectrum that this bet has not paid off." Some academics may have embraced that "theory," but not Obama or other US presidents. They understood the blowback that would result from trying to keep China down.

None of the critics of US policy mentions actions taken by Obama, as well as by his predecessors, that were *not* in China's interest, such as those in the Medeiros quote above. Nor do the critics mention how American missteps and weaknesses, such as military intervention in Libya and avoidance of involvement in Syria, influenced Chinese policy choices and perceptions of the United States. Last, as Thomas Fingar's review of engagement with China makes clear, there was no US grand strategy for transforming China. Once official relations were established under Carter in 1979, the "underlying logic" on the US side was that the greater the number and scope of contacts with China, especially in the nongovernmental sector, the better the chance of avoiding a breakdown.[23] Normalization was the essence of US policy toward China, premised on the expectation that China would play by the rules governing trade, human rights, and the use of force. That expectation proved overoptimistic, yet normalization—that is, a reasonable degree of predictability, but with acceptance of occasional friction—did prevail in US-China relations until Trump took over.

Where US administrations before Trump, as well as the press and some intellectuals, might be faulted is for their misreading of the intent behind China's economic reforms. For Chinese leaders during and after Mao's time, the chief purpose of economic strengthening has been to promote social order and elevate China's influence in world affairs, including its ability to stand up to the United States as a great power deserving of respect. It was one thing to invite Western investments and rely on Western technology, quite another to sacrifice national interests such as reuniting with Taiwan or forgoing military modernization. Chinese economic reforms have always served *national security*, by both preserving the party's absolute rule and safeguarding China's sovereign interests. US leaders concerned about competition from China have never quite grasped that security dimension and how it would lead to China's becoming (in the Pentagon's language) a "peer competitor."

TRUMP'S LEGACY

Donald Trump, on the other hand, was never in the least concerned about China's politics. He just wanted to outduel the Chinese on trade, having lambasted Beijing years before his election over the trade surplus with the United States. No other issue seemed to matter. The Chinese were initially optimistic about dealing with a businessman-turned-president, reflected in Xi Jinping's visit to Trump in 2017 at his Mar-a-Lago estate, where he said: "There are a thousand reasons to make the China-US relationship a success and not a single reason to break it."[24] But reality set in not long after, when the Chinese realized the ineptness of Trump and his inner circle of advisers, and the danger they posed to a manageable relationship with the United States. From Trump on down, there was an appalling superficiality in understanding China and its international outlook—a failure to understand that the Chinese are realists who can't be won over by friendly gestures such as Trump's chocolate cake offering at Mar-a-Lago. The rapid fraying of US-China relations could have been avoided had Trump not been so suspicious of the "deep state" he believed dominated in the State Department and intelligence community. But area expertise was more a target than a resource under Trump.

Trump's central demand was that China significantly increase purchases of US goods and lower trade barriers; otherwise, it would face punitive tariffs. (He once called himself "Tariff Man.") This "America First" approach got nowhere with the Chinese, who answered every US tariff increase with one of their own. Both economies suffered in the process.[25] Under Trump the United States retreated from the world and from Asia, leaving the field to China and no doubt convincing the Chinese that they had a once-in-a-lifetime opportunity to expand their economic and political influence at America's expense. Thus, Trump withdrew from the Paris accord on climate change, downgraded (and even hoped to have the United States leave) the North Atlantic Treaty Organization (NATO), demanded more rent for the US military presence from security allies in Asia, and reduced US foreign aid. Beijing took full advantage, initiating formation of banking and trade institutions with wide international participation and expanding development loans under the Belt and Road Initiative (BRI), including to US allies in Europe such as Greece and Italy.

In Asia, Trump abandoned the Trans-Pacific Partnership, called for the WTO to remove China as a developing country, and rarely attended multilateral meetings in Asia after his first year in office. US strategy relocated from the Middle East to cover a "free and open Indo-Pacific," stretching from Japan and Australia to India. Confronting China was the key—a country that the Pentagon decided "undermines the international system from within by exploiting its benefits while simultaneously eroding the values and principles of the rules-based order."[26] When the successor to the Trans-Pacific Partnership was formed in 2018 without the United States—the Comprehensive and Progressive Agreement for Trans-Pacific Partnership (CPTPP)—China expressed the hope of joining, sensing the opportunity to crash a party that brings together not only the major US trade partners in East Asia but also countries in Europe and Latin America. Trump also abandoned China itself. Gone were the compliments of Xi's leadership. Trump terminated the Fulbright and Peace Corps programs in China. He cut US ties with China's Center for Disease Control, essentially ending years of mutually beneficial research cooperation on infectious diseases. The Chinese matched each of his other decoupling moves, such as restricting visas, closing a consulate, pressuring journalists, and blocking US-based social media.

Unlike Trump, whose singular focus was sanctions, his top advisers on China were ideologues, led by Secretary of State Mike Pompeo, Vice President Mike Pence, and advisers Stephen Bannon and Peter Navarro (*Death by China* and *The Coming China Wars* are among Navarro's books). They viewed the US-China relationship as an apocalyptic struggle between good and evil, hence the chief threat to US national security, surpassing Russia.[27] They portrayed the competition with China in the most expansive terms. As a State Department publication on China in November 2020 said: "The CCP aims not merely at preeminence within the established world order—an order that is grounded in free and sovereign nation-states, flows from the universal principles on which America was founded, and advances U.S. national interests—but to fundamentally revise world order, placing the People's Republic of China (PRC) at the center and serving Beijing's authoritarian goals and hegemonic ambitions."[28]

The ideologues directed their outrage at the CCP rather than merely at "China." Pompeo led the charge, situating the struggle in a Cold War context and portraying China as an ideological enemy and a fundamental threat to US global supremacy. He said, for example:

> If we want to have a free 21st century and not the Chinese century of which Xi Jinping dreams, the old paradigm of blind engagement with China simply won't get it done. The free world must triumph over this new tyranny. . . . we have to keep in mind that the CCP regime is a Marxist-Leninist regime. General Secretary Xi Jinping is a true believer in a bankrupt totalitarian ideology. It's this ideology that informs his decades-long desire for global hegemony of Chinese communism. America can no longer ignore the fundamental political and ideological differences between our countries, just as the CCP has never ignored them.[29]

"If we bend the knee now," Pompeo railed, "our children's children may be at the mercy of the Chinese Communist Party, whose actions are the primary challenge today in the free world. General Secretary Xi is not destined to tyrannize inside and outside of China forever unless we allow it. The old paradigm of blind engagement with China simply won't get it done. We must not continue it and we must not return to it."[30] Beijing, he proposed, represents "a new kind of challenge; an authoritarian regime that's integrated economically into the West in ways that the Soviet Union never was."[31] But Pompeo forgot that China's embrace of globalization had been a fond wish of US leaders, and a core dimension of US foreign policy, for decades. Such amnesia led him at times to denounce the "corporate appeasement" of some US investors in China.

Pompeo's belligerent speeches made him the bête noir of the official PRC press, which responded to him with epithets such as "enemy of humankind" and "super spreader" of a "political virus."[32] But he had plenty of company. The national security adviser, Robert O'Brien, said "The Party General Secretary Xi Jinping sees himself as Josef Stalin's successor." In a speech devoted entirely to China's ideological threat, O'Brien accused China of an "effort to control thought beyond the borders of China."[33] Pence described China as a "whole-of-government" threat in a major speech in October 2019 that was full of historical inaccuracies about the US-China relationship, including the notion that the United States was mainly responsible for China's rise. He also said that China can't be treated "as a normal country" and that "the Chinese Communist Party continues to resist a true opening or a convergence with global norms."[34] Kiron Skinner, the director of policy planning at the State Department, viewed the China rivalry, strangely, as a "fight with a really different civilization and a different ideology."[35] The departing director of national intelligence, John Ratcliffe, went further in an op-ed, not only calling China America's number-one enemy, but also saying that China posed "the greatest threat to America today, and the greatest threat to democracy and freedom worldwide since World War II."[36] Ratcliffe painted a picture of a duplicitous government whose economic, social, and military policies threatened US interests. Great power competition, he wrote, is the necessary US policy because China has chosen to make it so—an extraordinary evasion of any US responsibility for things gone wrong.

The White House 2020 strategy paper on China avoided rhetorical excess. While emphasizing tough actions on China, the paper also reassured China that the Trump administration did not seek to contain it or stop mutually beneficial cooperation. But, in line with Pompeo and other officials, the paper contended that trust had vanished, casting China as an unfair player in international trade, oppressor of its people, and political and military threat to its Asian neighbors. "Great power competition," the paper said, borrowing Ratcliffe's language, was the only available choice in relations with China.[37] (That view, as I will discuss later, has held fast in the Biden administration.) Demonizing China became the new political sport, especially (though not exclusively) for Republicans as the November 2020 elections approached. Republican senators with a shaky hold on their seat had a fallback strategy: "Don't defend Trump, other than the China travel ban [as the pandemic hit]—attack China."[38] As an electoral strategy, however, China bashing did not work. There is no evidence that blaming China for the COVID-19 virus or the trade war resonated with American voters.

Trump's administration gave China new reasons to claim victimization, promote nationalism, and proclaim resistance to US pressure. *Renmin Ribao* (*People's Daily*, the official newspaper) published numerous public comments on the theme of the strength of China's economy and resistance to outside pressure.[39] The official Xinhua News Agency denounced American "bullying" and reminded Washington that this was not the old China—a "soft persimmon that can be kneaded at will."[40] Various editorials made reference to China's military successes in Korea, India, and Vietnam, with one ending: "We advise the U.S. side not to underestimate the Chinese side's ability to safeguard its development rights and interests. Don't say we didn't warn you!"[41] The "beautiful country" view of the United States gave way to a belief that the United States now was a major threat to China.[42] While a number of Chinese commentators insisted a trade deal would eventually be reached, Xi Jinping told the Chinese people to be ready for a "new Long March." Pompeo was accused of "launching a new crusade against China in a globalized world."[43] There was an overall downturn in people-to-people contact, specifically Chinese students and tourists. Xi exuded confidence: "What is most important is still that we do our own things well." Party cadres should keep two things in mind: "the overall strategic situation of the Chinese people's great rejuvenation" and "the great transformation in the world's coming century."[44]

Then the COVID-19 pandemic hit China and the world, overshadowing the trade issue and bringing relations with the United States to a new low.

THE NEW US CONSENSUS ON CHINA

Demonizing China became a rare bipartisan pursuit in the Trump era—an opportunity for lawmakers to outdo one another in calling China to account. Bipartisan criticism of China has always existed over trade, human rights, and territorial issues, but it has not prevented presidents of both parties and a bipartisan coalition favoring strong relations with China from wanting to preserve the relationship on commercial and national-security grounds.[45] The new bipartisan consensus on China has gone in the opposite direction, holding that China is untrustworthy and aggressive, since it rejects the "rules-based international order" that the United States built in service of its own interests after World War II. The fact that China's current leader has restored some features of Mao-era repression is proof to the critics that the communist regime is inherently threatening. In their view, China's cyberhacking, repression of dissent, modernizing military, and aggressiveness in Asia make it a dangerous adversary.

The anti-China consensus has three prongs: Democrats and Republicans in Congress and elsewhere in government, the mainstream media, and interest groups, including nongovernmental organizations (NGOs) and some academic specialists on China.[46] Liberals are nearly as numerous as conservatives in the overall grouping, though each has its own emphasis. Liberals are mainly concerned about China's repression of human rights, its advances in high technology, and its presumed threat to the Asia balance of power. Liberal congressman Adam Schiff of California, for example, sees a China threat everywhere: "At present, it appears that China has determined to be increasingly aggressive and bellicose in the [Asia-Pacific] region. China is projecting its power around the world and seeks to change international institutions, moving them away from a law-based, rules-based order to one where 'might makes right.'"[47] Robert Kuttner argued in the progressive *The American Prospect*: "There has never been a threat to U.S. well-being comparable to China. Its rapid global expansion challenges America's economic and geopolitical security, as well as basic democratic values and the rule of law."[48] Thomas Friedman of the *New York Times* believes China has been cheating in order to become a great economic and technological power.[49]

Conservatives focus more on China's trade practices, its communist ideology, and its threat to US national security from without *and* within. Right-wing senators such as Ted Cruz, Tom Cotton, and Marco Rubio regularly harp on the China threat to American institutions and the economy. Cotton, for example, offers a "Beat China" strategy based on economic decoupling, with the ultimate aim of bringing about the demise of the CCP.[50] Senator Chuck Grassley of Iowa, following classified briefings by the FBI, said that the Beijing-funded Confucius Institutes on US campuses "are an arm of the Chinese Government . . . The activities of Confucius Institutes are inherently political in nature and intended to influence U.S. policy and public opinion."[51] Both a liberal and a conservative senator sponsored a bill to deny Confucius Institutes federal funding, arguing (incorrectly, as I discuss in chapter 5) that the institutes are CCP propaganda organs.[52]

The bipartisan consensus sees the China threat mainly stemming from the CCP's subversions, China's predatory economic and technology practices, and China's growing military capabilities and assertiveness. As Democratic and Republican members of the congressionally appointed U.S.-China Economic and Security Commission concluded in its 2021 report:

> Both the CCP's confidence and its insecurity have contributed to an uncompromising approach domestically and to the outside world. *Regardless of how China's internal and external environments develop*, the CCP's aggressive posture will likely harden further as Chinese leaders confront the tensions between their rhetoric and their challenges. The CCP is now likely to react in an aggressive manner either in order to defend itself against perceived threats or to press perceived advantages.[53] (*Italics mine.*)

Such a conclusion leaves little room for contestation. China specialists once could be counted among China's best friends—not as fellow travelers but as people knowledgeable enough about the country to understand the difference between aggressive and defensive behavior, the importance of seeing the world through Chinese eyes (its history in particular), and a balanced view of China's domestic reforms. China specialists consistently in the decades following the US-China opening warned against confusing China's intentions with its capabilities, pointed to the need to maintain active engagement at every level with Chinese counterparts, and drew a line between the repressive state and an increasingly mobile, market-oriented, and freer people. But now the China critics include a fair number of specialists who see China as a threat. Some of them participated, for instance, in the conservative Hoover Institution's publication, edited by Larry Diamond and Orville Schell, that counseled vigilance against Chinese influence campaigns to undermine democracy and economic espionage to acquire the latest technology.[54]

Organizations left, right, and center have joined the "China threat" chorus. The American Association of University Professors, Human Rights Watch, the National Association of Scholars, the Federation for American Immigration Reform, the (reconstituted) Committee on the Present Danger, the *New York Times*, the *Washington Post*, labor unions, and numerous NGOs and media outlets have all been highly critical of China and urged various forms of counteraction. Language is important here: The media, for instance, regularly refers to Chinese "aggression," either failing to specify when and where, or mistakenly characterizing a pressure tactic as aggression—for example, against Taiwan. It denounces China's failure to play by "the rules" without explaining which (and whose) rules. Such language used to be the peculiar province of the right wing, part of its traditional anti-communism. Now, however, we have the *Washington Post*'s editorial board saying, on October 13, 2021: "A hegemonic China would menace Japan, Australia and the Philippines, destabilizing the entire Indo-Pacific region. . . . The urgent question, for Taipei and for Washington, is not how to verbalize opposition to Beijing's ambitions, but how to back it up in terms of military deterrence." American public opinion has followed along. A Pew Research poll in March 2020 found that 66 percent of Americans—including 62 percent of Democrats and 72 percent of Republicans—held a negative view of China, and 62 percent regarded its "power and influence" as a "major threat."[55] Those figures represent a remarkable shift from the early Obama years when views of China were more than 50 percent favorable. But increasingly unfavorable views of China began about 2013 and accelerated in 2019, tracking Trump's own hostile views.

Chapter 3

China's World

XI'S SEARCH FOR "STABILITY"

Understanding where China is headed must start from the inside, with Xi Jinping's political leadership. He's a man in a hurry to consolidate personal and party power, one scholar has written, while also taking advantage of US and Western retreat from global leadership to claim top rank for China.[1] Once regarded by China watchers as a modest reformer in the tradition of Deng Xiaoping, Xi has turned out to be an ambitious authoritarian with bold visions for China and himself as the CCP passes its one-hundredth anniversary. None of Deng's advice to "hide your ambitions, bide your time" for Xi! In this respect, Xi has far more in common with Mao than any post-Mao leader—a throwback to personalist, highly centralized rule after roughly four decades of collective, decentralized governing.[2]

Ambition is often tempered by political realism. Xi Jinping must meet challenges faced by all his predecessors: simultaneously maintaining economic growth, social order, and the absolute authority and internal discipline of the CCP. Pragmatism ("market socialism") coexists with ideology: Xi's "obsession with Party control."[3] Thus, rule number one in Beijing is "stability maintenance" (*wei wen*: 维稳). It has deep roots in the thinking of China's supreme leaders. Mao Zedong and Deng Xiaoping were equally determined to maintain party-state supremacy despite their differences over economic strategy and a cult of personality. Deng, for instance, will long be remembered as the power behind China's "opening to the outside world." But he also authored the "four cardinal principles" (in 1979): keep to the socialist road and uphold the dictatorship of the proletariat, communist party leadership, and Marxism-Leninism-Mao Zedong Thought. Deng frequently referred to "stability and unity" as essential preconditions, not just for successful party control but also for keeping foreign powers at bay. "We must show foreigners that China's political situation is stable," he said in a 1986 talk. "If our country were plunged into disorder and our nation reduced to a heap of loose sand, how could we ever prosper? The reason the imperialists were able to bully us in the past was precisely that we were a heap of loose sand."[4] "A heap of loose sand," "sick man of Asia"—these metaphors reminded the Chinese people of the country's historic weakness and vulnerability, but they have also been justifications for permanent party-state rule.

Mao's answer to the stability problem was constant (and destabilizing) ideological mass movements designed to purify and revitalize the top-heavy bureaucratic system and purge his critics. Deng, witness to the disastrous Great Leap Forward (1958–1962) and a victim of the Cultural Revolution (1966–1976), rejected Mao's approach in favor of economic reform and bureaucratic streamlining. Xi has used elements of both approaches, emphasizing reform—that is, sustained economic growth and rising incomes—and punishment, that is, defeating challenges to the party's "concentrated, unified leadership" that he heads. Xi has also reinstalled the social contract that Deng Xiaoping originated when the economic reforms began in 1978. The contract is this: So long as you, the Chinese people, don't make trouble, we leaders will continue to improve the quality of life. It's a trade-off: There must be no challenge to the CCP's monopoly of power, and one-man rule demands absolute loyalty. But in return, citizens are free to make money and enjoy material benefits similar to those in other market economies. Social stability and free markets in return for surrender of some basic human rights and limits on decentralized authority.

This duality is not, however, an exercise in balance. Stability, which entails political and personal survival, always comes first for Xi. That means responding to forces and practices that might threaten the one-party state, disrupt economic plans, and unravel the myth of the unified multinational state—hence the necessity of repression to enforce social stability. Out of that objective has come the surveillance state. As my discussion of mass internment of Chinese Muslims later in this book makes clear, Xi is determined to wipe out all sources of resistance and disloyalty, actual and potential. He has added to the "three evils" that the Chinese authorities consider threatening to social order: separatism, terrorism, and extremism. Now other evils have come to the fore: organized religion, protest demonstrations, cultural autonomy, activist lawyers, independent journalists, professors, and environmental organizations.

THE STATE OF XI

Chinese society is drifting toward becoming a full-fledged Orwellian state. The population is under constant surveillance by the world's most advanced facial-recognition technology; communities are patrolled by the public security bureau's regular police and the people's armed police under the People's Liberation Army (PLA); the cyber world is subject to the internet police, who belong to a little-known cybersecurity force within the public security bureau, searching for and nabbing regime critics.[5] In many countries, even undemocratic ones, one would expect signs of opposition when a leader personally authorizes crackdowns on political protests (as in Hong Kong), on ethnic minorities (Xinjiang and Tibet), and on appeals for more responsible government (from journalists, lawyers, and academicians). Even the Taliban have faced protest marches in Afghanistan. But not in Xi's China where, with few exceptions, legal scholars, fearful of protesting and in some cases hopeful of advancement, cravenly support the Xi cult[6] and the jailing of journalists is (in 2021) the highest in the world for the third straight year.[7]

Even billionaires cannot rest easy: They were added to the target list in mid-2021 when Xi, as part of a bewildering crackdown on certain un-socialist practices—everything from private tutoring and outsize media personalities to online gaming and ride-hailing services—sought to cut big-time entrepreneurs down to size as well. This new class of the super-rich may now have party membership, but many have evidently become too high-profile and present an image at odds with the one Xi prefers: a China increasingly self-reliant, determined to root out corruption, and capable of renewal in the spirit of "common prosperity" (*gongtong fuyu*: 共同富裕). China's largest firms, which prospered in a "Gilded Age" of unregulated growth, now have to bend to that new slogan. Heads of companies have been arrested and others humiliated—a time-honored way to cut rivals down to size. Some observers were reminded of a Maoist rectification campaign, but Xi's motives are entirely different. He was preparing for his unopposed reappointment as party general secretary in 2022. Playing the populist—the "people's leader" (*renmin lingxiu*: 人民领袖)—would cement his place in the pantheon of modern Chinese leaders. Xi may lose more than he gains by appealing to smaller businesses, consumers, and poor villagers while corporate leaders, intellectuals, and professionals are ignored or worse.[8] But business leaders who "abuse" the market are the perfect foil.

Xi's boldness, however, masks numerous sources of insecurity that may go beyond domestic and international problems. His sense of urgency identified by some foreign observers may stem from fears about the future, reflected not only in his newfound populism but also in the personality cult that now surrounds him. The constant references to his words and wishes in the media and official pronouncements, the grant of lifetime tenure to Xi in March 2018, the insertion of "Xi Jinping Thought" into the PRC constitution alongside Mao's thoughts, and the official elevation of Xi to the pantheon of Chinese historical figures at a CCP central committee meeting in November 2021[9]— all these actions put Xi on par with Mao and Deng as transformative forces in the country's history. All institutions now must "fully integrate" Xi's thoughts just as they once had to integrate Mao's.[10]

Authoritarianism in China is now again deeply entrenched, and the "dictatorship of the proletariat" that seemed to vanish with Mao's death remains alive, though tempered, importantly, by materialism and opportunities for personal advancement and overcoming poverty. There is, however, an emerging counter-trend: Many people are using social media to defy party censorship and vent their anger.[11] In a way, they are merely following Mao's prescription: to rebel is justified (*zao fan you li*, 造反有理). Indeed, a good deal of the grousing stems from the Maoist left, pushing Xi to crack down on corporations, entertainers, and others who have gained the most from the socialist market economy. For now, however, the party's control remains firm, and there is no evidence of elite dissatisfaction with Xi even though, in 2022, war in Ukraine, the resurfacing of the COVID pandemic, and rising prices were testing "common prosperity."

Rebelling often comes at a high price, moreover, as several well-known critics found out before and during the pandemic. They include the eminent law professor Xu Zhangrun, the Hong Kong book publisher Gui Minhai, the legal activist Xu Zhiyong, and the real estate mogul Ren Zhiqiang. All of them were jailed, some multiple times, for their advocacy of human rights and democracy. Xu Zhangrun was removed from his teaching position at Qinghua University for his pro-democracy writings and arrested in 2020. His dissidence led to the destruction of his career and official attempts to stop his writing.[12] Gui Minhai is a Swedish citizen who was abducted by Chinese officials while on vacation in Thailand in October 2015. Gui was released in 2017 and then arrested again and secretly tried for giving foreigners state secrets. In February 2020 he was sentenced to ten years in prison following a forced confession that was televised by a Chinese television news station in Britain.[13] Xu Zhiyong, a founder of the New Citizens' Movement for legal reform, continued his criticisms of the Xi regime and Xi personally while in hiding, notably the early cover-up of the Wuhan pandemic outbreak—until, that is, mid-February 2020 when he was arrested for subversion along with Ding Jiaxi, a cofounder of the movement.[14] As for Ren Zhiqiang, his whereabouts are reportedly unknown, but it appears that he has been seized by the police and taken away after offering constant criticism of the party leaders.

To summarize, Xi Jinping's concerns about and ambitions for China come down to this:

- Social order and uninterrupted economic growth are essential both to system maintenance and national security.
- Any attempt to challenge the power and authority of the party-state and its leaders will be ruthlessly suppressed.
- China's authoritarian nationalism and high level of economic development are a model of great-power governance.
- The world should look to China for leadership on climate change, advanced technologies, social stability, and development strategies (as under the Belt and Road Initiative), all of which challenge the declining US hegemon.
- International institutions and economic globalization should be used to advance Chinese interests. But China first: promote self-reliance wherever possible to guard against undue reliance on foreign (especially American) sources and markets.

PANDEMIC POLITICS IN
SINO-AMERICAN RELATIONS

All of these elements in Xi Jinping's thinking came to light when the COVID-19 pandemic appeared in China late in 2019 and then spread throughout the world. US-China relations were particularly impacted by China's handling of the pandemic and Trump's attempt to use it for domestic and international political advantage.

Both China and the United States displayed failures of leadership in dealing with the COVID-19 crisis. Donald Trump, who promised to make America "great again," wound up underwriting national disgrace. The pandemic took a huge toll in American lives and economic and social well-being, yet Trump was oblivious, trying to talk down the costs ("It is what it is") and pretend that normal life was one vaccine away. Ignoring science by then was well ingrained in his administration. Trump was told by many within his inner circle that he needed to take the lead on preventive steps to stop the virus from spreading. But he *decided* not to act, confiding to the journalist Bob Woodward he was well aware that COVID-19 posed a serious health menace but chose to "downplay" the danger with the presidential election upcoming. Trump thought the virus would pass without causing political harm; and he made matters worse by spreading false information about treatments while refusing to accept the commonsensical advice of the medical specialists around him who were calling for universal vaccination and quarantining. Trump's inaction set the stage for the world's worst pandemic casualties.[15]

Rather than face the facts, which included more than 200,000 American dead by late in 2020, Trump decided he was "just done with Covid."[16] He found it easier to accuse China of responsibility not just for being the pandemic's starting point but also for scheming to use it to undermine America. First it was China hampering his reelection bid: "China will do anything they can to have me lose this race," he told Reuters April 29—this from the man who, according to John Bolton, asked for Xi's help in winning the election. Then it was China spreading the virus: "We will find ways to show the Chinese that their actions are completely reprehensible," said a White House official in a CNN report of April 30 that also quoted Pompeo insisting that the CCP will "pay a price for what they did here"—as though the virus was a planned Chinese attack on the United States. And then there was China's responsibility for the US economy's slide, because "all of a sudden I have to close the economy" (April 30), raising the question "did somebody [in China] do something on purpose." On cue, Peter Navarro suggested that China "seeded" the US virus crisis. These were extraordinary words from an administration whose president often flaunted his friendship with Xi Jinping, earlier complimented Xi for his great job handling the coronavirus outbreak in Wuhan, and once called Xi the greatest leader in China's history. The accolades soon gave way to constant blaming for what Trump called "China's plague."[17] The shift to a blame model caused bitterness and resentment among China's leaders.[18]

For China, the failure in dealing with the pandemic was of an entirely different order. It lay in not quickly accepting and acting on scientific evidence of a looming pandemic, and instead imposing strict social controls to prevent the spread of reliable information that could have resulted in many fewer deaths outside China. Studies of the pandemic's origins make plain that the Chinese authorities knew as early as October–November 2019 that cases of infection in Wuhan posed a major public health threat—whether that came from bat-to-human transmission or a laboratory leak.[19] It appears that the Chinese leadership sat for weeks on awareness of COVID-19's lethality before it reported to the World Health Organization (WHO) at the end of December 2019 that it was dealing with a highly contagious disease. It was another month before Beijing said the coronavirus could be passed between humans.[20]

Instead, the bureaucracy responded in ways predictable in an authoritarian state: Don't transmit bad news to the top, prevent bad news (especially from medical specialists) from spreading at the bottom, arrest citizens and journalists who are troublemakers, control scientific findings. Xi admitted at a politburo meeting that COVID-19 was "a major test of China's system and capacity for governance."[21] When Dr. Li Wenliang, one of the first to warn of COVID's transmissibility, then died of it, the resounding anger of people over the official lies about the virus danger and the harassment of Li led to a massive coverup operation by China's censorate. Internal documents reveal orders from on high to control internet opinion and prevent critical views of the CCP—in short, turn "the spearhead" of public hostility into admiration of the party's efforts to contain the disease.[22] Even after the pandemic had been brought largely under control, internal documents obtained by an Associated Press team "shows the Chinese government is strictly controlling all research into its origins, clamping down on some while actively promoting fringe theories that it could have come from outside China."[23] What this control at the highest level of the party showed is that the leadership was not about to share methods and data, not to mention findings, with outsiders.

Many people in Wuhan and elsewhere nevertheless spoke off the record to foreign journalists about official lies to keep the real story under wraps. Those sources pointed not only to officials' delayed response to the spreading virus but also to the deliberate undercounting of the death toll. The extremely low official toll of about 4,600 deaths and 108,000 cases was probably off by a factor of five to ten, though even that total would represent an extraordinary accomplishment in a population of China's size.[24] Despite the conspiracy of silence, stories emerged from China of personal heroics in response to the official narrative on COVID—for instance, Zhang Xuezhong, a legal scholar who posted a letter to the National People's Congress, China's legislature, on freedom of speech. He was briefly arrested. Zhang wrote of how, before the lockdown, the authorities in Wuhan were "still investigating and punishing citizens who had disclosed the epidemic . . . showing how tight and arbitrary the government's suppression of society is."[25] He was right; China's police arrested citizens—lawyers, journalists, and others—people like Zhang Zhan, who filmed hospital scenes in Wuhan, posted on YouTube, that showed a pandemic not under control.[26] She received a four-year prison sentence. (Her lawyer was prevented by the Chinese authorities in Hong Kong from defending jailed activists there, and some of her mainland supporters apparently have disappeared.[27]) These challenges to the official Beijing narrative revealed the authorities' use of the law as a dragnet, since dissenters like Zhang Zhan are often seized under the omnibus charge of "provoking quarrels" (*xunxin zishi*, 寻衅滋事).

Xi unquestionably performed far better than Trump in dealing with the coronavirus. Having overcome an initial cover-up of the pandemic, Xi's decision to thoroughly isolate residents in Wuhan and other major cities prevented the kind of public health disaster that Trump's inaction brought on. Whereas Xi used control of the virus to fuel nationalistic pride and claims of China's superior governance, Trump abdicated his authority, a decision that helped doom his presidency. And Trump's attempt to depict the disease as a Chinese policy further poisoned US-China relations. Predictably, it led the Chinese to respond in kind by accusing the United States of being the source of the coronavirus. A good example is a ten-question article that appeared in the May 1, 2020, issue of *Renmin Ribao* under the authorship of "Observer," usually indicating a senior official. "Americans Must Answer These 10 Questions" sought to raise suspicions about US civilian and military biological experiments that may have produced the coronavirus.[28] It was only one of many articles in a CCP international propaganda campaign to counter growing anger at Beijing's initial cover-up of the virus.

With the nationwide protests in the United States against police brutality and racism in May and June 2020, Chinese commentators had more opportunities to shift the narrative away from Wuhan. They pointed to the hypocrisy underlying America's support of Hong Kong protesters and its pretensions to put human rights first in foreign policy. Photos of police and military repression in various US states enabled these commentators to make the case for the superiority of China's political model. "The moral ground of the United States is indeed greatly weakened," one Chinese scholar said.[29] But that judgment was also, if not equally, true of China.

CHINA'S UNCERTAIN CONSENSUS ON THE UNITED STATES

How did the pandemic affect US-China relations? Trump's ineptness in handling the pandemic at home became one key element in the Chinese consensus: America was in decline. Failed US interventions in the Middle East, social division, and economic backsliding also contributed to that consensus.[30] Chinese public opinion reflected that assessment, seeing China's stock rising in world affairs while America's role was declining.[31] But, as Michael Swaine cautions, the "declinist" thesis shared by many Chinese analysts has important qualifications. It does not mean that China denigrates US global power. Nor does it mean that the Chinese view America's decline as irreversible. And Chinese analysts—and perhaps China's leaders as well—are by no means united on specific ways China might take advantage of US decline, or how the United States might respond if China tried to take advantage. What does seem clear from Swaine's analysis is that many authoritative Chinese analysts see America as having become its own worst enemy, yet trying to pin the blame for much of the world's troubles on China. Nevertheless, interviews of other Chinese specialists in international relations show that they overwhelmingly favored improving US-China relations and in quite a few cases have actually been critical of the new assertiveness of their own country's foreign policy.[32]

As for Xi Jinping himself, it is probably fair to assume that he shares, and probably is most responsible for shaping, the Chinese view of overall US decline in international influence. He is the focal point of the Chinese decision-making system, as Suisheng Zhao observes: He is his own man, with far greater overseas experience than previous Chinese leaders and an apparent certainty about how to handle the United States.[33] Xi, we may surmise, has come to at least these three conclusions:

- America must understand that China will not kowtow to US pressure, will insist on equal treatment on all international issues, and will not yield an inch on China's "core interests" in sovereignty over its proclaimed border areas: Tibet, Taiwan, Hong Kong, and the South China Sea.
- China has an exceptional opportunity to take advantage of US preoccupation with its domestic problems and challenges abroad (such as with Russia and in the Middle East), by taking leadership on global development, environmental, and energy issues, and even making inroads on US security alliances.
- At the same time, China must find ways to keep relations with the United States from exploding.

Chapter 4

China on the March, Forward and Backward

There is a growing tendency in US politics and journalism to make the same mistake about China that was once made about the USSR: worst-case analysis that inflates threats, fails to consider that Chinese actions may be reactions, confuses assertiveness with aggressiveness, and presumes that China has a master plan for global domination. These errors stem from two others: attributing a certain infallibility and consistency to China's decision making and exaggerating China's strength while minimizing or ignoring its weaknesses. Together, we are presented with a picture of a China on the march, unencumbered by political, social, and economic concerns that other major powers have. Closer analysis reveals a more nuanced story, one that begins—as I tried to convey in an earlier book—with the many social, economic, environmental, and security problems any Chinese leadership faces.[1]

To illustrate, consider China's economy, the world's second largest and undeniably central to China's emergence as a great power. The macro figures, such as gross domestic product (GDP) and growth rates, are invariably impressive. And there are exceptional social accomplishments, such as dramatically reducing poverty and significantly improving overall human development.[2] Xi Jinping is often quoted as saying, "I have spent more energy on poverty alleviation than on anything else," and the results bear that out. According to Chinese sources and the World Bank, government spending on poverty alleviation has been exceptional and the incidence of rural poverty has dropped dramatically.[3]

But serious problems, actual and potential, also must be taken into account. A falling birth rate and aging population, for example, the result of the disastrous one-child family policy only recently ended, mean insufficient labor, reduced tax revenues, and unequal treatment of women, all contributing to slowing growth overall as 2022 began.[4] The omicron virus has caused lockdowns and supply chain problems. Real estate, which accounts for about

14 percent of GDP, is in a debt crisis thanks to overbuilding and the unwarranted largesse of state-run banks, some of which are themselves deeply in debt. Income gaps greatly favor the urban rich. Pollution has always had a significant impact on public health and therefore on the economy, probably (according to the World Bank) lowering the usual official annual growth rate of 6 to 8 percent by a few percentage points.

Rural China is particularly disadvantaged when it comes to other elements of human security. Its workforce has the lowest level of education of workers in any of the world's middle- to low-income countries, making it—and China—ill-equipped to move on to the next stage of economic development. This huge group of unskilled workers—China's "invisible" problem—is returning to the countryside as foreign investment moves to other countries and Chinese employers seek better-educated young people.[5] But what these workers are discovering is limited housing and available arable land, due in large part to climate change.[6] Historically high export levels help the economy look good but actually reflect stagnant wages and consequently low domestic consumption. As one economist based in Beijing writes, "Larger trade surpluses, driven by a declining household share of GDP, allow Chinese manufacturers to absorb weaker domestic demand without reducing output." China's huge trade surpluses thus "are symptoms of deep and persistent imbalances in the domestic distribution of income."[7]

In this chapter I assess another story that has been less successful than is often reported: China's diplomacy. China has adroitly taken advantage of opportunities to advance its influence, such as on the pandemic, in the Middle East, and most recently in the South Pacific; and its increasingly close relations with Russia are a great concern in Washington. But China has also had its share of misjudgments and mistakes, overreaching and suffering blowback. Just as the United States can sometimes be its own worst enemy, so can China.

"Our own worst enemy": Many analysts who are persuaded of China's inexorable rise to global dominance also see America's decline as probable, resulting either in a Cold War–style standoff with China, a world in which China is ascendant, or a leaderless world of competing states. Too often, however, US decline is measured in strategic terms, with little thought to those fundamentally domestic sources of international power and influence that will make or break the US future. While some would therefore take comfort in the gap between US and Chinese military capabilities—in spending, nuclear weapons, bases, and allies—those are not going to determine the two countries' relative competitiveness or underlying strengths as a sociopolitical system. The sources of US shaping and leadership of the post–World War II world lay within, as the war left the American homeland untouched, its enormous economic assets, social cohesion, and political influence in position to exercise hegemony. All those sources of national strength are now badly depleted, not just by foreign interventions but also by political and cultural polarization, divided government, and self-interested opportunism, exposing a leadership vacuum that China seeks to fill. But China's ability to do so is questionable. Concerns about global economic disorder and vulnerability to US sanctions, as happened in China's response to the Ukraine crisis, discussed below, show that China remains a fundamentally reactive power.

CHINA'S COVID POLITICS ABROAD

In the wake of the pandemic, China used the humanitarian crisis to lay claim to being the most "responsible great power." While Trump suspended US contributions to the WHO, stopped US attendance at its meetings, and then threatened a permanent end to US aid to the organization, China took the opposite tack, bidding to become the world leader in combating the pandemic. It followed up on a $20 million grant to WHO with a second donation of $30 million. A foreign ministry statement said it all: "at this crucial moment, supporting WHO is supporting Multilateralism and Global Solidarity." Speaking at a World Health Assembly gathering in May 2020, Xi promised additional global aid to WHO and developing countries to combat the virus.[8]

Trump's incompetent and untruthful handling of the coronavirus, and the administration's effort to militarize the response to nationwide protests for racial justice, gave Chinese propagandists plenty of material to taunt Washington on its human rights and democracy stances. The once-admired United States became an object of mockery on the Chinese *weibo* (the Twitter equivalent) and other social media. It was precisely at this juncture that the phenomenon of nationalistic "wolf warriors" (*zhan lang*, 战狼) in China's foreign ministry and embassies took over the official narrative.[9] But they were not the only ones who perceived a shift in the global political balance. A former Swedish prime minister and diplomat wrote:

> This was the post-American world on display: China assertive and confident. Europe trying to save what can be saved of global cooperation. And the Trump administration mostly outside firing its heavy artillery in all directions, but with limited actual results.[10]

China's gifts of protective supplies turned heads among Chinese and aroused nationalistic pride and even arrogance.[11] According to a Chinese government white paper on COVID-19, apart from the grants to WHO, China provided $2 billion in "international aid" over two years, suspended debt repayment for seventy-seven developing countries, sent medical teams to twenty-seven countries, and "exported protective materials to 200 countries and regions."[12] US humanitarian aid under Trump, on the other hand, was a case of promise over performance: Of $1.59 billion allocated by Congress in March 2020, less than $400 million had actually been delivered to overseas recipients as of June, arousing complaints from nongovernmental relief organizations that, along with UN agencies, were supposed to distribute it.[13] Aid delayed meant increased deaths.

In 2021, China linked its Sinovac and Sinopharm vaccines to the BRI, touting vaccine aid to Southeast Asian countries as a contribution to economic development and (incorrectly) criticizing the United States for not weighing in with vaccine aid. In fact, under Biden, US vaccine aid was distributed to sixty countries, and in quantities claimed to be greater than all other countries combined.[14] The Chinese surely knew this, hence announced further free vaccine deliveries to developing countries in what looked to be an attempt to outdo the Americans. Quite a few of those countries, such as Vietnam, accepted the Chinese vaccines, but a number of others, including Singapore and Malaysia, questioned their efficacy and rejected them.[15] Brazil and Turkey were among more than twenty countries that complained about slow shipment of the Chinese vaccine or about its effectiveness.[16] The head of China's Center for Disease Control admitted that its vaccine was only about 50 percent effective. That was bad news in Brazil, where the COVID infection and death rates were among the world's highest.[17]

Numerous countries challenged the Chinese narrative of unerring success at fighting the virus at home and extending generous help to others abroad. The EU put China in the same boat as Russia for "targeted influence operations and disinformation campaigns [on the virus] in the E.U., its neighborhood, and globally."[18] Calls by Sweden, Australia, and Germany for an independent international investigation of the virus' origin were countered by Beijing's announcement that it would launch its own investigation or be part of one. Later, China agreed to a WHO proposal for a joint investigation, starting with allowing two WHO scientists to visit in July 2020 and then the actual investigation in the new year.

But who could blame the recipients for accepting? China was first in line to offer the vaccine to developing countries, and most of them were happy to accept despite knowing that the Chinese vaccines had lower efficacy rates and that data about them was hard to come by.[19] Africa and Latin America were largely shut out of obtaining vaccines from the major producers, Pfizer and Moderna, most of whose vaccines went to the wealthiest countries. Even where developing countries submitted orders for the vaccine, delays of a year or more were the rule for mass inoculations. But here was China offering the vaccine not only in its backyard but also in America's, where the only other provider was the WHO's Covax program. Even Brazil, once a China critic, tempered its comments once it started to receive the Chinese vaccine.[20]

In retrospect it appears that a key motivation behind China's donations was to bury the fact that Beijing had refused to submit to an "impartial, independent and comprehensive evaluation" even though it had voted for the WHO resolution that called for it. The WHO visit to Wuhan in February 2021 was widely panned for failing to obtain adequate data and dismissing the thesis that the virus resulted from a laboratory leak. Only one American scientist was allowed by Beijing to be part of the WHO group, and he had conflicts of interest that led to questions about his impartiality.[21] The other outside investigators were not allowed the kind of access necessary to reach firm conclusions, as the Chinese authorities not only removed relevant laboratory data but also used a variety of search engines to push conspiracy theories that once again tied the origin of the virus to some external source.[22] WHO bought that line, virtually eliminating the possibility of a lab accident—as the lone American scientist had insisted be excluded—and instead giving credence to the far less likely chance that the virus came from frozen food or a US military lab. Science gave way to propaganda as the Chinese foreign ministry and other officials used the WHO mission to point responsibility for the virus anywhere but to China.

Well into 2022, the question of origin remained unresolved. Numerous scientists embraced the lab accident theory while others pointed to wild animals as the source.[23] But underlying all the explanations is China's failure to share data in a timely manner.[24] Prominent scientists rejected Chinese deflections, instead publishing four open letters that pointed to the WHO mission's numerous shortcomings and suggesting a lengthy list of questions that still needed answering, mainly about missing data.[25] The last of the four letters "encourages China to participate in a comprehensive, science-based, and data-driven investigation" of COVID-19's origins and suggested establishing an alternative to a WHO mission if China declined as expected.[26] China did decline, leaving open the distinct possibility that top Chinese officials *knew the origin all along.*[27]

Disrupted Honeymoons in the Western World

Europe has tried to straddle the line between condemning China on human rights and relying on China's trade and investments to spark their economies. In this weighing of costs and benefits, the fulcrum has swung against China.[28] The European market is important to China, and vice versa, with total imports and exports approaching $800 billion as 2022 began. Though that figure is only a fraction of intra-EU trade, China does loom large as the EU's principal source of imports and third-most-important export market.[29] Some major corporations, mainly German—such as Volkswagen and Siemens—are heavily invested in China, including in Xinjiang. Beijing no doubt sees growing European dependence on the China trade as a wedge opportunity.

But patience wore thin on both sides in the wake of the mass internments in Xinjiang, China's crackdown in Hong Kong, and questions about the origins of the coronavirus. Many in Europe were set to abandon trying to influence developments in China based on "change through trade."[30] Public opinion reflected the shift: In every EU country, opinion of China turned sharply negative, mirroring similar downturns in Australia, Japan, and the United States.[31] Hosting the Winter Olympic Games in 2022 may have heightened China's prestige in many parts of the world, but in the West the games were politicized as Xinjiang became a high-profile topic, with some human rights organizations calling the event the "Genocide Games." Several EU countries responded to the US call for a diplomatic boycott.

Britain took the lead in response to China's imposition of a national security law in Hong Kong (discussed in chapter 5) by opening the door to the more than 350,000 United Kingdom (UK) overseas passport holders in Hong Kong who wished to emigrate. When twelve pro-democracy candidates for Hong Kong's Legislative Council elections in September 2020 were ruled ineligible, London also suspended its extradition treaty with Hong Kong to protect its citizens in the United Kingdom from being sent to China.[32] (Hong Kong's pro-Beijing administration then put off the election for a year and, at the start of 2021, China announced it would not recognize the special British passports granted to Hong Kong citizens.)

In July 2020 the Boris Johnson government reversed a decision on Huawei's 5G wireless network system and followed the US lead in turning to other sources. Cut out of access to US technology by being put on the Commerce Department's entity list, Huawei has essentially been removed from the European market, as well as from Japan and South Korea—a victory for critics who wondered how much longer "European values" would be sacrificed in order to win China's favor.[33] Actually, it was a victory for US pressure tactics. (Huawei turned to Russia, partnering with its engineers to produce an alternative operating system for its smartphones.[34])

Yet London very much wants to remain the key European locale for the Chinese renminbi and a major trade and investment partner of China, mindful of China's major stake in Britain's nuclear power and steel industries. Though Britain's parliament called the Xinjiang repression a genocide, Johnson demurred on sanctioning Chinese officials, perhaps aware of how China punished Australia's export industries over criticism of China's handling of the COVID-19 outbreak. But in mid-2021 the foreign affairs committee of parliament persisted, calling for a partial boycott of the Winter Olympics, forbidding Chinese surveillance companies from operating in Britain, and forming a "coalition of sanctuary states" to grant Uyghurs asylum.[35] A British court levied fines totaling more than $600,000 on CGTN (China Global Television Network) for televising forced confessions of jailed citizens, Chinese and foreign, and for violating the law against political party ownership of a television station.[36] Inquiries into Chinese money in British universities and research organizations turned up tens of millions of pounds invested by Huawei and Chinese state-run companies in return for collaborations that were "concentrated in strategically critical areas such as telecommunications and life science" and sometimes connected with the Chinese military.[37]

Germany was among thirty-nine countries that voted in the General Assembly to "demand that China closes detention camps in Xinjiang, stops tearing down mosques and religious sites, stops forced labor, and stops forced birth control."[38] France turned activist on the Uyghurs, with Foreign Minister Jean-Yves Le Drian telling parliament: "Since [the Chinese] say my statements are baseless, we propose an international mission of independent observers, under the auspices of [UN] rights commissioner Michelle Bachelet, to visit and bear witness."[39] European values also seemed to account for closure of several Confucius Institutes, such as in Germany and Sweden.[40] EU countries also took aim at Chinese disinformation campaigns on social media, closing down tens of thousands of accounts on Twitter, YouTube, and Facebook.

The EU worries that the weak links in Europe's economy, such as Italy, Greece, Portugal, and Serbia, will be vulnerable to Chinese takeovers of key industries and to financial enticements under the BRI that China has used to gain port control in Piraeus, Greece. Rivalry and suspicion contest with the lure of accommodation.[41] China has also aggressively courted European outliers such as the autocratic leader of Turkey, Recep Tayyip Erdogan, and Eurosceptics such as Hungary's Viktor Orbán.[42] Nevertheless, when it came time to finally bring closure to lengthy negotiations on a comprehensive investment deal, the EU failed to ratify it, apparently bowing to pressure from the incoming US administration about adopting a common posture on China before reaching any new agreement.[43]

The Chinese still hoped for approval of the agreement but also sharply attacked the EU's "cognitive dissonance," with Foreign Minister Wang Yi saying: "It is hard to imagine that on one hand, Europe seeks to build a comprehensive strategic partnership with China, and on the other hand, it defines China as a systemic rival."[44] Once war in Ukraine began, rivalry clearly won out over partnership. That became painfully apparent to Beijing when the first EU-China summit in two years was held in April 2022. Any hope in Beijing that it could mend strained relations and move Europe away from the United States was undone by China's unwillingness to distance itself from Russia or take the initiative to bring the fighting in Ukraine to a halt. As Kevin Rudd, the former Australian prime minister, said, there could be no such hope for

China that "the old, comfortable status quo [would be] restored: with Europe divided and deeply hesitant to compromise trade and investment with China in the name of geopolitical security."[45]

When the Biden administration sanctioned Chinese officials in Xinjiang and got applause for the move in the EU, China's aggressive diplomats and Beijing itself responded with sanctions of their own. These crossed a European red line, however, because the sanctions and blacklisting were imposed not only on officials but also on individual critics in universities and private institutes in the EU countries and Britain. Germany led in issuing a Bonn Declaration in support of academic freedom as a core "European value."[46] Numerous EU scholars and research institutes voiced solidarity with European China critics as well as with critical voices inside China.[47] The era of close EU-China relations, a hallmark of Chancellor Angela Merkel's leadership, seemed over. When she stepped down, no other European leader seemed able or willing to rally the EU to her cause. Left unresolved, however, is just how European academia would deal with Chinese pressure tactics other than by protests and increased funding of China studies.

Australia's volte-face in China policy has been more dramatic than the EU's.[48] For many years the dominant thinking about China was reflected in the 2016 Drysdale Report, named for Professor Peter Drysdale of the Australian National University and co-authored with a Chinese economic research center. The bullish report contended that close Australia-China trade and investment relations were essential to Australia's economic prosperity and that concerns about China's growing presence in Australia were overblown. It advocated raising the Australia-China relationship to a "Comprehensive Strategic Partnership for Change."[49] The contrary view was, and is, that China views Australia as a vulnerable influence target, one that could be pried from its tight relationship with the United States and cultivated as a "second France." Whereas the first view welcomed Chinese investments, tourists, immigrants, and students, the second denounced Australia's subservience to China and China's exploitation of its economic power to buy (or silence) business and political leaders.[50] The first view prevailed for several years, but in 2021 the relationship became openly adversarial. There are good reasons for both.

Prime Minister Scott Morrison, who said in 2018 that Australia did not have to choose between China and the United States, unexpectedly took a hard line on China's handling of the coronavirus. China's ambassador not only took umbrage; in November 2020, via the Australian press, the PRC embassy transmitted fourteen grievances that, if satisfied, would improve relations. The grievances included the Morrison government's insistence on an independent investigation of COVID's origins and its banning of the Huawei 5G network.[51] Morrison didn't budge, and Beijing carried out its trade threat by reducing imports of beef, agricultural products, and wine. From an economic perspective, though China accounts for about 40 percent of Australian exports, these moves had mixed results, hurting Australia's agriculture while not touching its iron ore exports to China and actually incentivizing Australia to find new markets for its coal.

The real impact on trade and investment ties stems from the new way Australia now treats commercial relations with China—from a national security standpoint—though Morrison took some heat for exploiting fears of China for political gain.[52] The Huawei network, China's long-term lease of the port of Darwin, a proposed natural gas infrastructure investment by a Hong Kong consortium, the state of Victoria's signup for participation in the BRI—these and other Chinese projects have all been scrapped by the Australian government on national security grounds. Moreover, Australians must now register as lobbyists if they are working for a foreign government—*any* government, though clearly with China foremost in mind.

If there was any doubt about Australia's course correction, the joint announcement by Britain, the United States, and Australia in September 2021 that the United States would provide Australia with nuclear-power submarines clinched it. Though Biden was careful not to mention deterring China as the main motivation, commentators in Australia and elsewhere were quick to call it a watershed moment in that country's strategic thinking, since the agreement establishes a new security group: AUKUS, linking Australia, the United Kingdom, and the United States. The submarines most likely will patrol in disputed South China Sea waters, though it will be several years before they can be deployed. The impact on nuclear nonproliferation may also be important, since the United States had only once before—with Britain in 1958—shared nuclear technology with an ally.[53] In April 2022 Biden announced an expanded mission for AUKUS, to include joint work on hypersonic missiles and counter-missiles, further evidence of both Australia's deepening concern about China as a strategic threat and the evolving counter-China security arrangements. Australia is also putting more money into missile capability and production.[54]

China's reaction to AUKUS was predictably angry, pointing to the destabilizing effects of a new Cold War in which the three countries "ganged up to form an Anglo-Saxon clique."[55] As a countermeasure, in November 2021 Xi Jinping announced that China would sign a Southeast Asia Nuclear-Weapon Free Zone treaty—the first nuclear-weapon state to do so. China presumably sees the treaty, which is backed by the ten-member Association of Southeast Asian Nations (ASEAN), as a way to undercut any US or Australian plan to acquire or transport nuclear weapons in that region, which the treaty prohibits.[56] The following spring, China signed a security agreement with the Solomon Islands (see below), which had switched diplomatic recognition from Taiwan to China in 2019. The agreement is clearly payback to Australia over AUKUS, but it is also a signal that China has entered the strategic competition in a part of the Pacific long dominated by the US alliance system.

Australia's realignment of its China policy may please Washington, but it isn't necessarily in Australia's best interests. A report by the Australian Strategic Policy Institute in 2022 looked systematically at relations with China at the subnational level, that is, the states and territories, asking whether the China connection is worth it given the "astonishing" scope of China's involvement with Australian civil society. Though the report criticized "overoptimistic assumptions" about China and found Australia "hostage to [China's] trade," it recommended raising awareness of the risks of Chinese interference and espionage rather than severing ties.[57] Identifying cooperative projects, such as in trade, might be a way around the risks. Both China and Australia are among the more than one hundred members of the Asian Infrastructure Investment Bank (AIIB), a multilateral development bank founded in 2015 and headquartered in Beijing; and the Regional Comprehensive Economic Partnership (RCEP), launched in 2022 with thirteen other Asian members. China is petitioning to join the eleven-member CPTPP, but with Australia standing opposed. The United States is not a member of any of these groups, providing Australia with an opportunity to stake out its own position and deal with Chinese tariffs in a multilateral setting.[58] The election of Anthony Albanese and his Labor Party in 2022 could lead to a reset of relations with China, though those relations were not an election issue and Albanese seems deeply committed to AUKUS and other elements of security partnership with the United States.

New Zealand, though reliant on China for perhaps a third of its exports, has played a cagier game than Australia. The government has criticized China on a number of occasions yet has not gone so far as to alienate Beijing. New Zealand's parliament expressed concern about China's attempts to influence local Chinese-language social media and media organizations. A parliamentary committee said it had "concerns about the freedom of the press and the freedom of speech" in the country's Chinese communities.[59] One New Zealand China scholar suggested that Beijing resisted punishing New Zealand to gain leverage over Australia and be in position to intimidate New Zealand down the road.[60]

Canada's parliament took a more aggressive stance than New Zealand's, specifically citing genocide in Xinjiang. Although Prime Minister Justin Trudeau did not endorse that view, China's ambassador Li Yang ignored protocol in a vicious tweet that addressed Trudeau as "boy" and said: "your greatest achievement is to have ruined the relations between China and Canada, and to have turned Canada into a running dog of the US."[61] "Running dog"? Wolf warriors were reviving Mao-era rhetoric. Turns out the rhetoric hides Chinese interference in Canadian media. Canada's intelligence agency was reported to have warned Trudeau early in 2021 that "PRC media influence activities in Canada have become normalized. Chinese-language media outlets operating in Canada and members of the Chinese-Canadian community are primary targets of PRC-directed foreign influenced activities." Though vigorously denied by China's ambassador, it seems that China's embassy targets politicians, journalists, and local Chinese-language media to promote Beijing's viewpoint.[62]

Taken together, Chinese diplomacy has encountered significant pushback in US-allied countries. Beijing may now realize that money does not speak as loudly as it once did in promoting Chinese influence, even in business circles. Nor are China's foreign affairs officials responding very effectively to the pushback, choosing to use thinly veiled threats and influence peddling by local Chinese communities rather than show sensitivity in public diplomacy. In the next section I focus on the wolf-warrior phenomenon in China's diplomatic corps. It reflects the new, often belligerent assertiveness that could provide opportunities for US, EU, and other officials to offer a contrast, by demonstrating better ways to promote their countries' values and interests.

Wolf Warriors and China Critics

China's wolf-warrior diplomacy aggressively promotes Beijing's official position in response to the trade war with the United States, charges concerning the origins of the COVID-19 pandemic, and criticisms of China's violations of human rights aggressively promotes Beijing's official position and seeks to neutralize the blowback from it. Beijing's ambassadors in several countries have sometimes (as in Canada and Germany) openly threatened counteractions if criticisms of China were not muted. No matter the object of criticism, turning against China is routinely portrayed by Chinese media and authorities as part of a US-led anti-China campaign, one that might eventuate in a US-China war.[63] The wolf warriors have responded to criticism with an avalanche of social media trolling and disinformation, focused on all of America's problems: violence against Asians, democracy's decline, double standards on human rights, and disputes over the 2020 election outcome.[64]

How Chinese pressure tactics operate may be seen in relations with Australia, where Chinese diplomats and exchange students have mustered in response to criticisms of Beijing. China retaliated by jailing two Australian journalists of Chinese ethnicity on charges of divulging state secrets—and two others narrowly escaped detention. On Australian university campuses, such as the University of Queensland, nationalistic Chinese students backed by the CCP and the local Chinese consulate aggressively sought to muzzle opposing viewpoints. Pro-democracy Chinese students who in any way supported

Hong Kong's autonomy or criticized other Chinese policies faced physical danger. Fearful of retaliation on campus or back home if they reported threats to their safety, they practiced self-censorship. These students claimed little support from their Australian schools, where revenue from the huge number of Chinese students—about 160,000 in 2020, or around 10 percent of all Australian university students—gives Beijing considerable leverage.[65]

Actions deemed by Beijing to offend China's sovereign interests go well beyond governments and academia. Foreign businesses in China whose products or personnel touch on sensitive political subjects such as Hong Kong, Xinjiang, or Tibet face boycotts, demands for an apology, or termination of operations. Kowtowing to China is a modern-day version of the early Western missions to China's imperial court—or, in the case of individual China critics, the kind of self-censorship that Chinese intellectuals have long practiced.[66] Gap, Marriott, United Airlines, the National Basketball Association (NBA), Givenchy, Tiffany, and Cathay Pacific Airways, just to mention a few, have all had to defer to Beijing by avoiding or withdrawing comments likely to offend China and hurt their business. Even the World Bank has been found to give in to China rather than face its wrath.[67] "Minefield" is the word often used to describe the fraught circumstances of those who do business with China: One never knows when a particular act will touch a Chinese nerve. Take the NBA, for instance: When a general manager of one team, the Houston Rockets, posted on Twitter, "Fight for freedom, stand with Hong Kong," China's foreign ministry spokesman said the NBA "knows clearly in its heart what to say and what to do." China shut down streaming of NBA games in 2019 as the NBA's commissioner struggled to keep its lucrative business in China alive while defending free speech. A few years later, an NBA player had the audacity to speak up for "Free Tibet" and call Xi a "brutal dictator," which immediately resulted in his team's games being removed from viewing in China.[68] The China-NBA relationship remains tenuous.[69]

China's retaliation strategy has other dimensions: sanctions, censorship, and intimidation operations. It responded to Trump-era sanctions of Chinese officials on human rights grounds by sanctioning the same number of Americans: eleven. They included several right-wing members of Congress as well as the heads of five NGOs, such as Human Rights Watch, and US social media companies not previously banned. Beijing also closed the US consulate in Wuhan following the US-ordered closure of China's consulate in Houston in mid-2020. US social media companies that have carried criticisms of China have had to answer to Beijing. Some companies, such as Zoom, have bowed to Chinese censors, terminating the accounts of users, mostly Chinese but also some Americans, who met online in remembrance of the June 1989 Tiananmen crackdown.[70] Publishing houses are being forced to decide how to handle Chinese pressure to censor journal articles regarded as anti-China, such as those concerning Taiwan. This export of China's internal censorship has produced both compliance and rejection abroad. Some of the largest publishers, such as Germany's Springer, were willing to block critical journal content in China while others, such as Oxford University Press, angrily resisted and accepted loss of revenue.[71] Finally, China reportedly conducts an overseas operation, dubbed Sky Net (*Tian Wang*), that harasses, threatens, and sometimes kidnaps Chinese who have moved abroad. Among these thousands of fugitives are social activists and businessmen who have incurred Beijing's displeasure.[72]

(Chinese sanctions and overseas operations are hardly unique. We should keep in mind that sanctions are the US weapon of choice—the highest in the world and increasing every year, with more than 9,400 imposed in 2021, including nearly 250 on Chinese entities and individuals.[73] China's Sky Net is reminiscent of agents of pro-US authoritarian regimes—I think of Chile, Taiwan, and the Philippines in the 1970s and 1980s—who threatened and killed those regimes' dissidents in the United States.)

Xi Jinping, surely anxious to promote a positive image of China abroad, has apparently taken note of the angry international reaction to wolf warriors. The official Xinhua news agency reported Xi saying: "It is necessary to make friends, unite and win over the majority, and constantly expand the circle of friends [when it comes to] international public opinion." China should be "open and confident, but also modest and humble" in its communication with the world.[74] The "kindlier and gentler" face may have concealed disappointment that the BRI had not always won over its beneficiaries. In any case, Xi was not alone. In a speech in Beijing understood to be directed at the wolf warriors, China's former ambassador to the United States, Cui Tiankai, warned against fighting "a war of anger and attrition" with the United States. "Every ounce of our peoples' gains has been hard-won, and we must not allow them to be plundered by anyone or suffer losses due to our own carelessness, laziness and incompetence." If there was any doubt about his target, Cui added: "In the face of complex situations, we must always have the country at large in mind, and not always think about being an internet celebrity."[75]

Criticisms have not stopped Zhao Lijian, foreign ministry spokesman and wolf-warrior-in-chief, from continuing with his brusque style. Indeed, far from being consistently kindly and gentle, we have seen that China's face to the world often is defensive and hostile. Criticism, no matter how well intentioned, is met with testiness, and sometimes retaliation against the critic. Reporting on China's problems is taken as evidence of anti-China sentiment, and not just on human rights. A stubborn, edgy nationalism, which often extends to the blogosphere, leaves little room for dialogue and mutual understanding.

Beijing can take heart, however, from the support it essentially buys to continue repression in Xinjiang. Countries with Muslim majorities as well as others beholden to Chinese loans and trade generally refuse to criticize Beijing's conduct. Indonesia, with the world's largest Muslim population, has never uttered an official word in protest of China's treatment of Chinese Muslims. Nor have any of the other nine member-states in the ASEAN. Turkey's Erdogan government, which at one time was an outlier among Muslim countries in not publicly supporting the Xinjiang repression, signed an extradition treaty with China in December 2020, posing a threat to the Uyghur population of about 40,000. (Other Middle East countries, as well as Myanmar, have also extradited Uyghurs at China's request.[76]) Only Erdogan's political opposition criticized China's history of repression of Uyghurs, leading China's ambassador to "condemn . . . any person of power" who challenges China's "sovereignty and territorial integrity."[77] Still, as two writers note, "at the U.N. Human Rights Council, China rallied 37 countries to praise its genocidal policies in Xinjiang as advancing the 'international human rights cause' and then 54 nations to categorize the policies as 'remarkable achievements in the field of human rights.' China then secured reelection to the Human Rights Council with 139 votes."[78] The same writers also reported that sixty-three countries, many involved with China's BRI, are recipients of China's infamous surveillance technology that is so prevalent throughout the PRC.

RUSSIA AND THE UKRAINE CRISIS

When it comes to support of China on international issues, from human rights to Taiwan, Beijing could always count on Vladimir Putin. And the reverse has generally been true. In nearly forty meetings since Xi and Putin became top leaders, the China-Russia relationship has consistently been described in the most exalted terms. They're "dear friends," their relations "the best in history and "a model of interstate cooperation in the 21st century." China-Russia trade has risen substantially in recent years, though while China is one of Russia's most important trade partners—the EU is first—Russia's share of China's total trade is tiny.[79] Russia participates in the BRI. Joint military maneuvers have become a regular event, and the weapons trade between the two countries continues to flourish.[80] Symbolizing their closeness, Putin attended the Beijing Winter Olympics in 2022 at a time when US and other countries' diplomats stayed away. That meeting became historic as Putin ordered a full-scale invasion of Ukraine immediately after the games. The timing may have been at Xi's request.[81]

China and Russia are aligned with each other in viewing the United States as their principal opponent and chief obstacle to the achievement of their respective aims in Asia and Europe. But theirs is a marriage of convenience, not a security alliance.[82] They are divided by many issues, including a history of conflicting national interests and ideological differences, unresolved territorial claims, competition for influence in Central Asia, and the large gap between them in economy and technology. While US analyses typically lump China and Russia together as threats to US national security, they are actually far apart in their international status and conduct. Unlike Russia, China has taken full advantage of globalization—in everything from contributions to UN peacekeeping and tourism to scholarly and scientific exchanges and overseas investments.[83] Thomas Christensen reports on "a former Chinese diplomat stationed in Russia, Shi Ze, who summed up the difference between Moscow and Beijing this way: . . . 'Russia thinks it is the victim of the current international system, in which its economy and its society do not develop. But China benefits from the current international system. We want to improve and modify it, not to break it.'"[84] Another major difference is that while Russia has intervened with force in several countries near and far in the Putin era—the South Ossetia and Abkhazia regions in Georgia, Syria, Libya, Kazakhstan, Belarus, and Ukraine before 2022, when it seized Crimea in 2014—China has used force sparingly under Xi and has found greater influence by taking the lead in multilateral economic organizations and by exercising soft power, such as BRI loans, trade and investment, Confucius Institutes, and media.

As for relations with the United States, a few examples illustrate the depth and breadth of US-China relations in comparison with Russia. US trade with China is roughly twenty times its trade with Russia, and China's trade with the United States is about four times its trade with Russia. Hundreds of thousands of Chinese students and scholars attend US universities, a huge plus for the talent and commitment they bring. US-China people-to-people exchange programs far surpass any that the United States has with Russia or had with the former Soviet Union. China, like Russia, has a highly sophisticated data hacking network to pry into US corporations in search of trade and technology secrets.[85] But China has not meddled in US elections, such as Russia did in the Trump years by secretly working alongside a particular candidate's campaign and using social media to move public opinion. According to the US intelligence community's assessment in 2021, "China sought stability in its relationship with the United States, did not view either election outcome as being advantageous enough for China to risk getting caught meddling, and assessed its traditional influence tools—primarily targeted economic measures and lobbying—would be sufficient to meet its goal of shaping U.S.-China policy regardless of the winner."[86] Nor does China have the strategic threat capability that Russia has, or the USSR once had.

All these historical and contemporary differences played out in China's carefully calibrated approach to the Russian invasion of Ukraine. The distinction between Ukraine and Taiwan in Russian and Chinese policy is relevant here, since many commentators speculated that China might view Putin's invasion as motivation to attack Taiwan. Putin and Xi commonly believe those territories cannot be considered independent states, histori- cally and culturally belong to the mother country, and are only prevented from being absorbed by foreign interference. Yet they see the recovery of Ukraine and Taiwan as fitting testimony to their legacy as a great leader. But there the similarities end. Putin insists Ukraine is a security threat because of NATO's eastward expansion. But judging from his speeches, his objective in waging war against Ukraine suggested a different rationale: to shake up the European security order by disrupting the NATO alliance and reestablishing pro-Russian regimes around Russia's periphery. Just prior to the invasion, in February, Russia "recognized" the two separatist enclaves of eastern Ukraine as "people's republics." As we will see in the discussion of the Taiwan issue in chapter 5, Xi has so far abided by the goal of peaceful unification of Taiwan. Taiwan and the China mainland have strong interdependencies, marked by substantial cross-Strait trade and investment, tourism, and traffic involving hundreds of thousands of Taiwanese who live and work in China. China has displayed its military capabilities in the Taiwan area, but China has not threatened Taiwan with attack or asserted that Taiwan poses a threat to the mainland. Nor has China sought to arouse a pro-China force inside Taiwan or demanded that the US alliance system in Asia be dismantled. Thus, Chinese officials denounced any connection between Russia's war in Ukraine and Beijing's Taiwan policy.[87]

China's hedging and fence-sitting on Ukraine began before Putin's visit to Beijing. Foreign Minister Wang Yi urged the United States to take a "bal- anced" approach on Ukraine that would respect Russia's "reasonable security concerns."[88] Yet, on the brink of Russia's invasion, Wang also said that the "sovereignty, independence and territorial integrity of any country should be respected and safeguarded," adding, "Ukraine is no exception."[89] The final Putin-Xi text on their talks got worldwide attention for its reference to "no limits" on Russia-China ties, with some specialists arguing that it came close to promising a military alliance and fulsome Chinese support of Russia's cause in Ukraine.[90] But that proved to be a serious misreading: The lengthy joint statement did not even mention Ukraine, merely saying: "The two sides oppose continual expansion of NATO, and call for NATO to reject the ideol- ogy of the Cold War, respect other countries' sovereignty, security, interests, and multicultural diversity."[91] Most of the statement discussed cooperation on other matters, such as the pandemic, foreign aid, arms control, even human rights, as well as identified common threats from the West such as its support of color revolutions. Once the Russian invasion was in full swing, "no limits" actually meant "with limits."

A week after the war started, Wang Yi told Ukraine's foreign minister: "the top priority is to ease the situation to prevent the conflict from escalating or even getting out of control." Wang added: "One country's security cannot be at the price of harming another's; regional peace cannot be realized by expanding military blocs."[92] According to China's ambassador to the United States, Xi called Putin right away to urge peace talks, claiming Xi "received a positive response."[93] Comments like those might have led to a more neutral stance on the war, but while Beijing did not endorse Putin's invasion, neither did it criticize it. Clearly, Xi had decided that not only did partnership with Russia dilute US global leadership; it also might distract the United States from its strategic preoccupation with China.

Still, there were limits to China's war policy. Worth recalling is that although China did support Russian intervention in Belarus in 2020 and Kazakhstan in January 2022 to quell potential color revolutions, an event Beijing fears might happen in China, it did not support Russia's seizure of Crimea in 2014. When Putin recognized the two "people's republics" in eastern Ukraine, China did not go along, consistent with its stance on separatism when it comes to Xinjiang, Tibet, and Taiwan. China abstained from voting on two UN resolutions that condemned Russia's invasion, one in the UN Security Council and another in the General Assembly that also called for Russia's withdrawal from Ukraine and urged a negotiated end to the war.

The chief limitations on China's support of Russia are economic, starting with the war's impact on China's economy. Every sign out of China as of mid-2022 was that Beijing officials were determined to steady the economy and not run afoul of US regulators on sanctions imposed on Russia.[94] First, as Xi acknowledged, the war was causing major disruptions in "the global economy," meaning China's economy in particular.[95] Second, China's capacity to buy Russian goods is not unlimited and cannot replace the Russia-EU trade.[96] Third, even though China began purchasing Russian wheat and increased imports of Russian gas, two of its main banks abided by US sanctions in refusing to issue dollar-denominated letters of credit for purchases of Russian goods.[97] Initially, the principal Chinese state oil companies did not buy excess Russian oil—that is, oil beyond what has been contracted for—for refining,[98] though once cheap oil became available as Russia shifted to the Asia market, China took advantage. Chinese businesses were leery of dealing with rubles, whose value was suspect. Allowing Russia to convert its major holdings in Chinese yuan to dollars or euros would have helped Moscow, but Beijing evidently rejected that idea because it would breach the sanctions.[99] Fourth, China has a lucrative economic relationship with Ukraine: Its weapons factories are highly regarded in China, and China is Ukraine's most important export market.[100]

The strength of official Chinese statements of support for Russia seemed to vary depending on the course of the war. By early March 2022 it was obvious to Beijing that Putin had badly miscalculated and faced a lengthy and costly war brought on by Ukrainian resistance and an unprecedented array of sanctions on Russian trade, banking, and overseas investments. Not only were China's economy and trade being affected; the leadership surely was as unnerved as Western leaders when Putin raised the possibility of using nuclear weapons. And Chinese leaders had to take note of how European governments that traditionally did not provide arms to war zones (such as Germany) or were not NATO members (Finland, Sweden, and Switzerland) or previously were friendly to Russia (Turkey and Hungary) now were united in defense of Ukraine. The Putin-Xi ambition to break up the Western alliance had boomeranged. This was not what China had signed up for. At that point, China's emphasis shifted to promoting a diplomatic resolution over Ukraine, urging the parties to "seek reasonable solutions."

Yet Beijing balked at playing a peacemaker's role, evidently anxious not to offend Putin. In a word, *China failed the leadership test.* Far from being a "responsible great power," it chose to straddle the fence at a defining moment in European and perhaps global security. To be sure, Beijing may have been caught flatfooted by the scope of Putin's ambitions. But it had plenty of time to recover. Instead, China offered platitudes and belated offers to mediate—such as Chen Yi's and Xi's expressions of a willingness to "play a constructive role" in peace talks and work together with "the international community."[101] Pure self-interest—removal of sanctions, which might one day be imposed on China if it were ever to attack Taiwan—was the main factor in China's position on Ukraine, yet that factor was not enough to spur a serious Chinese effort to stop the war and elevate China's international standing, such as organizing a peace conference of the major players, calling for a cease-fire, or sending substantial aid to Ukraine.

China could have used its economic leverage with Russia to try to force Putin to accept a settlement short of victory, but it didn't. In international fora, Chinese representatives shied away from criticizing Russia. The Chinese judge on the International Court of Justice joined her Russian colleague in dissenting on the court's decision to condemn Russia's invasion of Ukraine. China rejected putting the war on the G20's agenda. Beijing's media kept asserting Russia's right to protect its security, repeated Putin's disinformation campaign on Ukraine, and harped on China's many foreign policy differences with the United States. Chinese state media became the mouthpiece for Russian propaganda that has been banned on Western social media.[102] Ultra-nationalists in China pointed to the advantages of close ties with Russia.[103] Few authoritative voices were raised against the war.[104]

Evidently, the Xi government saw more positives than negatives in staying aligned—but not too tightly—with Russia. That conclusion became firmer when, in mid-March, Putin put Xi on the spot by requesting military and economic aid for the war. How Xi responded would be a telling sign of where China stood on a war against an independent country *and* on relations with the United States, since at that very moment Jake Sullivan was arriving in Rome for talks with Yang Jiechi.[105] Sullivan told Yang that there would "absolutely be consequences" if China provided "large-scale" aid.[106] Biden reiterated that warning in a phone conversation with Xi on March 18. Xi might finesse the issue, and evade secondary US sanctions, by supplying Russia with nonlethal, "small-scale" aid. But he did not send Russia significant weapons aid. Still, missing from the US approach was *incentives* to gain China's compliance—incentives that would not only move China away from Russia but also improve relations with the United States and help bring the Ukraine war to an end. That would be a second instance in which the administration tried but failed to enlist China's help in deterring Russia.[107]

Engaging China would have enabled Washington to practice a new strategic triangle diplomacy designed, as in the Nixon-Kissinger days, to weaken the China-Russia connection.[108] Granted, China's encounter with NATO in the Belgrade embassy bombing in 1999 and NATO's adoption in June 2021 of the US request that it classify China as a security concern were probably fresh in Xi's thinking.[109] Still, with proper incentives, such as on military aid to Taiwan, technology sharing, or COVID vaccines to supplement China's less effective ones, a US engagement policy might have produced a different reaction from China. As Yun Sun writes, "strong voices in China advocate against abandoning Russia because the U.S. offers no 'rewards' for doing so and they fear China 'will be the next on the list after Russia.'"[110] It seems that Biden provided no such incentives.

The Biden administration should have learned two things from dealing with China during the Ukraine war. First, it should stop conflating China with Russia, since their mutual admiration conceals more than it reveals. China acts out of pure self-interest, and neither tight alignment with Russia nor adherence to UN norms about nonaggression are among China's actual national interests. Second, engaging China is of the utmost importance to US foreign policy, especially at a time of Russian adventurism. But as Xi Jinping conveyed to Biden in their March 18, 2022, conversation, any change in China's foreign policy is only conceivable if US policy on China changes.[111]

SEEKING PREDOMINANCE IN ASIA,
WITH MIXED RESULTS

"Hegemony" used to be China's principal way of characterizing US foreign policy, especially in Asia. Now that both countries are Pacific powers, the discourse has changed. China's checkbook diplomacy and expanding military power challenge traditional US predominance, which has always rested on formal and informal allies that provide naval and air bases and military access points. China has always lacked those assets, but in recent years it has outdone the United States when it comes to commerce, finance, and aid, leading to vigorous Chinese assertions of superior overall strength.[112] The results have been mixed: China's opportunistic diplomacy has won new partnerships, its trade and investment have survived Trump's pressure tactics, and US-led criticisms of China's human rights violations have not galvanized a coordinated international outcry. But China has also suffered setbacks in diplomacy and international opinion, and it has not made inroads into the traditional US alliance network in Asia or Europe. At least among the advanced economies, opinion on China's political system, human rights in particular, is strongly negative.[113] Reputation and security interests matter to other countries besides China. Following are some examples of both Chinese successes and failures around Asia.

In Japan, the US-China tussle, once mainly over rival Japanese and Chinese claims to the Senkaku-Diaoyutai islands in the East China Sea, has shifted to Taiwan. Tokyo has expressed more than the usual unease over China's foreign policy assertiveness. In its 2021 white paper, released in July, Japan's defense ministry expressed a "sense of crisis" over the tense situation in the Taiwan Strait. "The overall military balance between China and Taiwan is tilting to China's favor, and the gap appears to be growing year by year," the paper said. The ministry slightly toughened language previously used in these papers, saying that "stabilizing the situation surrounding Taiwan is important for Japan's security and the stability of the international community."[114] Japan's deputy prime minister at that time, Aso Taro, went further—perhaps further than his superiors would have liked—when he said in a speech that Japan should help the United States in a US-China clash over Taiwan. "If a major incident happened," Aso said, "it's safe to say it would be related to a situation threatening the survival [of Japan]. If that is the case, Japan and the U.S. must defend Taiwan together." Zhao Lijian was quick to pounce on these statements as evidence of Japanese interference with China's internal affairs. "Extremely wrong and dangerous," he said.[115]

Aso's statement may indeed have gone beyond what either his boss, Prime Minister Suga Yoshihide, or his successor in October 2021, Kishida Fumio, were prepared to commit to in defense of Taiwan. Strategic ambiguity is as central to Japan's stance on Taiwan as it is to the US stance. Exactly what Japan might or might not do should China attack or threaten to attack Taiwan, such as allowing US use of its bases in Japan to counter China, is unclear. Though conservatives such as Aso Taro prefer a clear Japanese commitment to Taiwan's defense if under Chinese attack, Tokyo may prefer to avoid taking that highly risky step—especially because policy since 1972 has been to recognize Taiwan as a part of China and not a separate state.[116] Japan's new leadership is strengthening deterrence of China, significantly increasing the defense budget and acquiring a range of weapons dedicated to air and naval surveillance.[117] This view coincides with Japan's continuing commitment to the notions of a "free and open Indo-Pacific" and a "rules-based order," both code for close security ties with the United States that now go beyond their bilateral security treaty to include the Quadrilateral Security Dialogue, or Quad (US, Japan, Australia, India).

India has moved in Japan's direction: While it cannot escape the reality of deep economic ties with China, like Japan, and a long common border, India has become a quasi-security partner of the United States. Since the Obama administration, Washington has sought ways to cultivate ties that would take advantage of India-China border tensions. The relationship tended to emphasize military cooperation, such as joint naval exercises that later included Japan. With the revival of the Quad arrangement in 2017, the Asia-Pacific became the Indo-Pacific. The United States, Japan, India, and eventually Australia in 2020 began having regular military contact and exchanges, leading some observers to conclude that the Quad was "acquiring the contours of a military bloc."[118] That may well be, since in 2022 the parties agreed to share satellite maritime intelligence that would, among other things, track China's fishing fleet, which sometimes fronts for military activities.

That development came as the always tense and uncertain border with China in the Ladakh region again erupted in clashes in 2020, with India losing twenty soldiers. One thoughtful analysis of Chinese motives suggests the conflict was "the result of China reacting to the perception that India was stabbing it in the back by its move into territories China sees as off-limits to India. The unique timing of COVID-19, the context of the U.S.-Chinese strategic rivalry and China's self-perceived vulnerability all contributed to a sense of insecurity amongst officials in Beijing."[119]

India's prime minister Narendra Modi may come under US pressure to permit US access to Indian naval facilities, at the risk of antagonizing Beijing. In the meantime, the United States has tied India ever more closely to military partnership, including arms sales and access to sensitive US military technology.[120] The unresolved border issue stands in the way of a rapprochement, notwithstanding agreement between New Delhi and Beijing on the war in Ukraine—namely, unwillingness to condemn Russia, as well as India's ongoing arms and oil purchases from Russia. Thus, Wang Yi's appeal for a common voice on visiting India in March 2022 may not have changed Indian views not only on the border but also not on Quad membership.[121]

Other developments besides the border clashes hastened the India-China disengagement. Much to China's chagrin, the Modi government rejected the BRI and China's 5G network, choosing instead to expand road, rail, and tunnel networks along the border with China—a militarization of the border area that China has matched and perhaps precipitated. Modi took advantage of Trump's anti-China tariffs to become an important customer for US arms and to accept intelligence sharing. Under Biden, that trend is continuing via the Quad as well as bilaterally, fueled by China's hardline policies on Hong Kong and Taiwan. As an Indian analyst observes, even as border talks to reduce tensions go on, "the trust deficit and the security dilemma [occasioned by the border clash] have dented the relationship between [India and China] as never before."[122] Even India's presumed sphere of influence in the nearby Indian Ocean nations of Comoros, Maldives, and Sri Lanka has become a competitive arena, with both China and India dangling economic and military assistance before opposing political leaders.[123]

Competition for the affection of small island nations in fact is playing out all around the Pacific, as recent developments in the *Solomon Islands* demonstrate. A once-secret security arrangement with China, signed in April 2022, allows the prime minister of the Solomon Islands, whose population is only about 700,000, to invite Chinese police and military forces to intervene "to assist in maintaining social order, protecting people's lives and property."[124] Australia and New Zealand had evidently made a strategic error in 2021 when they responded to rioting in the Solomons by sending in troops. Its pro-China prime minister was able to defeat a no-confidence vote in parliament, greatly helped by Chinese bribes to its members of more than $2.2 million. Now, Australia and New Zealand worry about a Chinese base in the Solomons and the possibility that China might one day obstruct traffic into the Indian Ocean.[125] The shock was felt equally in Washington, where various commentators reacted as though US defense of Northeast Asia and even Hawaii was now in doubt.

This diplomatic coup for China took advantage of Australian neglect to take the island nation and its problems, climate change in particular, seriously. The Solomons pact, writes Anne-Marie Brady, builds on Chinese military activity that includes providing "weapons, military vehicles and vessels, uniforms, training and military buildings to the military forces of Fiji, PNG [Papua New Guinea] and Tonga, and to the police forces of Vanuatu and now the Solomons."[126] Building on those arrangements, Foreign Minister Wang Yi visited eight Pacific Island nations in May 2022, with a sweeping proposal for trade, security training, humanitarian relief, and other benefits applicable to all of them. The mission failed to gain their collective approval, but Wang promised a position paper and further discussions, saying "Don't be too anxious and don't be too nervous"—a clear indication of these nations' unease over too-close ties with China, especially on security matters such as police training and maritime mapping.[127]

Chinese opportunism stands against the long-standing US strategic presence in the western Pacific. Aside from close military and political ties with Australia and New Zealand, the United States has crucial shipping and military access to several Pacific Island states, including the Federated States of Micronesia and US territories such as Guam. US missile and space programs are also based in the region. Nevertheless, US military predominance has made it complacent, alarmed by the sudden Chinese "intrusion" and out of touch with China's actual challenge, which is economic access via the BRI, trade, and investment. The United States hasn't had an embassy in the Solomon Islands for many years and only in 2022 announced its intention to appoint ambassadors there and to all the other Pacific Island states. Those states, not wanting to get caught up in the US-China competition and needing help on trade and basic environmental problems such as rising sea levels and illegal fishing, face difficult choices. One way they can be assisted is by identifying with the regional fora these states have created to maintain policy-making independence and promote common priorities, such as on climate change protection.[128]

A Solomon Islands journalist offered Americans some thoughtful advice. While expressing concern about Chinese intentions, she wrote that what the United States should learn from China's initiatives in the South Pacific is this: "You have got to show up. And the United States has not." Unless it does, "China will pick us off one by one with its promises of business projects and development aid."[129]

North Korea reveals a different face of Chinese diplomacy. Through various crises over the North's intentions regarding nuclear weapons and missiles, Chinese policy has remained consistent: ensure the Kim dynasty's survival with food and fuel aid (which amounts to keeping Korea divided); prevent another war on the Korean peninsula; and seek denuclearization of the peninsula.[130] Yet US policy makers since the George W. Bush administration have been equally persistent in believing that China holds the key to forcing North Korea to denuclearize. The history of China's Korea policy suggests otherwise: first, because the North's leaders are militantly nationalistic and cannot be forced by any foreign power to give up nuclear weapons, their main bargaining chips; second, because with US-China relations tense and confrontational, Beijing is especially unlikely to help Washington out. Adding to the obstacles to denuclearization is that under Trump, promising developments in inter-Korean diplomacy were obstructed, evidently convincing Pyongyang that the South Koreans are not independent of the United States in negotiations.[131]

Early on in the Biden administration, his new foreign policy team proposed talks with North Korea "without preconditions." It got no response. It probably should not have expected one for two reasons: Biden offered no sanctions relief, despite knowing that North Korea's economy and health care system are in a shambles; and the United States resumed joint military exercises with South Korea. Those actions prompted Kim Jong-un's sister, Kim Yo-jong, to warn Washington not to "cause a stink at its first step." But the exercises went ahead, and North Korea responded. The Kim regime has invested heavily in missiles, carrying out more than 150 tests since 1984, roughly 80 percent of them since Kim Jong-un succeeded his father in 2010. Some of the tests in 2021 and 2022 show that North Korea is working on new long-range weapon systems—submarine-launched and hypersonic delivery systems that could serve either as an attack force or, more likely, as a deterrent against US attack. Most of the missile tests, however, are within range of South Korea and Japan.

China is effectively burning both ends of the candle. It reaffirmed its close ties to North Korea in 2021 and continued to violate UN sanctions on oil and other nonhumanitarian commodities that are vital in keeping the Pyongyang regime afloat. North Korea may chafe at its dependence on China for food and fuel, possibly providing an opening for US diplomacy. But that possibility has never been explored. Meantime, in 2022 China and South Korea are celebrating thirty years of diplomatic relations that have included substantial trade (China is South Korea's top trade partner), tourism, and military exchanges. On North Korea, Beijing and Seoul see eye to eye more than do Seoul and Washington, since PRC and South Korean officials support high-level multilateral dialogue on Korean peninsula issues, a treaty to end the Korean War, and synchronized actions to reduce the threat of war and promote denuclearization.[132] They are upholding the principle of "commitment for commitment, action for action," which was adopted by all six parties (including the two Koreas, the United States, Russia, China, and Japan) to a September 2005 agreement. If there is any chance to restore a North Korean moratorium on missile tests, it most likely would have to be linked to gradual removal of sanctions—that is, "action for action."

In the *Philippines*, Chinese assertiveness in the South China Sea has backfired, and the enticements of the BRI proved insufficient to move the Rodrigo Duterte government into China's column. Chinese pressure tactics to reinforce its claims in the South China Sea, notably deployment of armed coast guard vessels under a new coast guard law, no doubt upset Duterte, who had hoped for more cooperative Chinese behavior on the disputed islands.[133]

Where once he had seemed to cast off alignment with Washington, Duterte changed course:

> Manila has moved to fully reinstate security ties and rebuild trust with Washington in a vigorous attempt to deter Beijing. Steps include a series of high-level visits; the restoration of wide-ranging defense agreements; Manila's full endorsement of the AUKUS security pact joining Australia, Britain, and the United States; the reestablishment of the Philippines–United States Bilateral Strategic Dialogue; and expanded joint military exercises next year.[134]

By the end of 2021, China and the Philippines were at a diplomatic and maritime standoff, disputing sovereignty over particular shoals and reefs in the South China Sea.[135] Beijing has overwhelming military superiority in the area, but it also has to weigh the May 2022 presidential election in the Philippines, which might result in a more pro-American administration. But that may depend on how Washington reacts to the new government that looks very much like the old one, headed by the children of two former Philippines presidents: Ferdinand Marcos Jr. and Sara Duterte. They promise more illiberal politics and cronyism, characteristics that might raise cautions in Washington but certainly not in Beijing.

Myanmar's military coup on February 1, 2021, gave insight to China's approach to human rights. China clearly sided with the military as it proceeded to crack down on peaceful protesters. There was no way the UN Security Council would come together to condemn either the coup or the bloodbath that followed. The Chinese press was silent on events in Myanmar, and the only comment of significance came from Zhao Lijian, who tweeted on March 15: "The burning & looting of co[mpanie]s is abhorrent. We hope the #Myanmar side will take concrete measures to protect the safety of citizens in #Myanmar." China's embassy in Myanmar called on the government to "stop all terrorism activities."[136] These messages seemed mainly directed at saving *Chinese* companies that were being set afire, apparently by the protesters in retaliation for China's support of the Tatmadaw, the military leadership. China's foreign ministry had nothing to say about the military's killings, torture, and rounding up of ordinary citizens. Myanmar descended into civil war as the Tatmadaw opposition organized a shadow coalition government and military force. As of early 2022, the opposition has not been able to present a united front under the National Unity Government (NUG). China has ignored the NUG in favor of the coup regime, but with a civil war raging, Beijing, though better positioned than the United States to influence events, may find itself on the outside looking in.[137]

The other human rights tragedy in Myanmar is the regime's persecution of its mostly Muslim Rohingya population.[138] Here again, China is on the wrong side. Roughly 1.5 million Rohingya are now displaced, about half in refugee camps in neighboring Bangladesh and the other half inside Myanmar. The military junta has variously been charged by UN agencies (including the UN High Commissioner for Human Rights in 2018) and governments with ethnic cleansing, crimes against humanity, and genocide. In January 2020, the International Court of Justice agreed that Myanmar had breached the Genocide Convention. It ordered the government and military to prevent genocidal violence against its Rohingya minority and preserve evidence of past attacks.[139] The court's decision is binding, but violence against the Rohingya continues, finally leading in 2022 to the US designation of the repression as a genocide—a decision the Trump administration had been unwilling to make.[140] China, expectedly, has had nothing to say on behalf of the Rohingya.

China's competitiveness around Asia has been matched by a US rush to get back into the influence game. One may, however, question the US approach, which is to remind Asian governments that the United States has their back when it comes to resisting Chinese advances. In the summer of 2021, for instance, the US defense secretary visited Hanoi, Vice President Kamala Harris visited Vietnam and Singapore, and the secretary of state took part in an ASEAN defense forum. All the US officials reportedly challenged Chinese policies in the South China Sea controversy. Emblematic of the Southeast Asian reaction, however, were comments by Singapore's prime minister. On one hand he welcomed the revival of US involvement in the region. But on the other he lamented the drift in US-China relations "because many U.S. friends and allies wish to preserve their extensive ties with both powers."[141] The message was clear, sensible, and in keeping with Southeast Asian tradition: When elephants clash, the grass gets trampled, so the best course is to urge compromise and not take sides with either elephant. Joint US and PRC membership in the CPTPP would surely be welcome in Southeast Asia, easing concerns there about being caught in the middle of US-China tensions.

SEIZING OPPORTUNITIES IN THE MIDDLE EAST

After the Trump administration overturned Obama's signature diplomatic triumph with *Iran* in 2015—the nuclear deal, formally known as the Joint Comprehensive Plan of Action (JCPOA)—and began exerting "maximum pressure" in hopes of regime change, Iran defiantly entered on a path of nuclear breakout. Biden came into office with a promise to return to the JCPOA, but with stricter requirements on Iran in exchange for lifting of sanctions.[142] China, though a party to the nuclear agreement, also saw an opportunity for itself, and in early 2021 it wrapped up a twenty-five-year investment-for-oil deal with Iran that was premised on Iran's participation in the BRI and relief from US sanctions. To some Iranians, the price was too high: It hinted at military cooperation as well as promising Chinese investments in ports, banking, railways, and telecommunications. China would also get heavily discounted oil. The deal evoked memories of Iran's territorial dismemberment in the nineteenth century—and it was consummated by Iran's government without going through parliament or publishing the text.[143] What actually comes of the deal remains to be seen: The optics—Iran's thumbing its nose at the West and China again showing its diplomatic opportunism—may be more important than any concrete economic or military projects.[144]

In *Afghanistan*, the Biden administration's decision to withdraw ground forces by September 2021 was roundly criticized by China. When Blinken spoke with Foreign Minister Wang Yi in mid-August, apparently about their common concern over a Taliban takeover, Wang agreed on the need to arrange for a "soft landing of the Afghan issue and avoid a new civil war or humanitarian disaster . . . and not let [Afghanistan] become a breeding ground and shelter for terrorism once again." But Wang reminded Blinken that the price for cooperation is that the United States stop attacking "China's legitimate rights and interests."[145] In fact, China had already moved on, making its own peace with the Taliban and criticizing the United States for withdrawing from Afghanistan "in a completely irresponsible way."[146] A Taliban delegation visited China in July, where it was hailed by Wang for its "pivotal" role in peace and national reconstruction. Beijing followed up with a small humanitarian aid donation. A Taliban government spokesperson made the astonishing claim, given China's repression of Muslims: "China is our most important partner and represents a fundamental and extraordinary opportunity for us, because it is ready to invest and rebuild our country." Citing China's New Silk Road concept, the spokesperson also said that Afghanistan's "rich copper mines in the country . . . thanks to the Chinese, can be put back into operation and modernised. In addition, China is our pass to markets all over the world."[147]

China is calling for political stability in Afghanistan, for at least two reasons: border security and economic benefit. Keeping radical Islam from either leeching into China or becoming a haven for so-called Uyghur separatists is a priority, since one Afghan province borders Xinjiang. Beijing may have exacted a promise from the Taliban not to interfere in China and, as happened in the past, lend support to a separate "East Turkestan" state. The other Chinese concern is to protect its economic projects in Afghanistan, chiefly minerals extraction, that had benefited from the US military presence. The minerals, including copper and rare earth, are said to be vast and of high value, but mining them may take several years.[148] Beijing surely wants to ensure safe access to its investments as well as an "economic corridor" to

Middle East oil.[149] All of these benefits for China require a degree of stability that seems highly unlikely, for Afghanistan today is in economically and financially desperate circumstances, with the United States and other countries unwilling to lift sanctions. That may leave China holding the bag.

Chapter 5

Managing Conflict in
US-China Relations

TWO MIND-SETS

In chapter 1 I quoted the influential scholar Wang Jisi's description of the different mind-sets of Chinese and Americans when it comes to resolving tensions. The Chinese insistence on putting principles first and the American insistence on dealing with specific issues first certainly presents a significant roadblock to problem solving. But the Americans have their principles too. Take as an example the controversy over the Chinese military buildup in the South China Sea. For Beijing, Chinese sovereignty over the islands is nonnegotiable and the principle of noninterference by other countries is controlling. The United States, in Beijing's view, has no role to play in the drama. For Washington, prevailing laws and customs should apply, such as freedom of navigation, but also the principles of a rules-based order and international law. Its view is that China is being the bully, violating both practice and principle, as well as the interests of the five other claimants to the islands: Vietnam, Philippines, Taiwan, Malaysia, and Brunei. Neither the PRC nor the United States believes it can accept the other's framework for discussion without disadvantaging its economic and military interests. Thus, the only way to avoid a violent confrontation over the islands is to find a way to *manage* it.

Conflict management is not conflict resolution. US-China disputes discussed in this chapter over Taiwan, human rights, and technology, like the South China Sea controversy, are highly unlikely to be resolved by one side's acceptance of the other's position. But they can be managed in the common interest of preventing disputes from spilling over into actual conflict. How to do so is the challenge. In the Obama era, the answer was numerous US-China dialogue groups focused on specific issues. Under Trump, these were largely abandoned, without sustained diplomacy to replace them. Instead, Trump played the blame game on COVID and trade while making China the United States' number-one enemy. Biden has neither restored the dialogue groups nor erected a new scaffolding for repairing relations with China. His national security team, as I have indicated, is made up of people who believe that engagement with China has not produced many results and therefore should not be restarted. Consequently, we don't have a structured way to address not only old problems with China that are intensifying, but also new problems, such as reducing nuclear weapons and preventing confrontations at sea. When the two presidents met virtually in November 2021, Biden urged establishing "commonsense guardrails," and Xi said that friction in their relations should not be allowed to spiral out of control. But their meeting did not resolve the issue of structure.

In this chapter I examine some of the key issues that are causing serious friction in US-China relations. I start with the initial meeting of Biden's foreign policy team with its Chinese counterparts, a meeting that illustrates Wang Jisi's clash of mind-sets but also reveals an even deeper clash over global prerogatives. I then discuss four issues that divide the United States and China: Taiwan, human rights in Hong Kong, Xinjiang, and Tibet, the technology competition, and educational and scientific exchanges. I argue that the United States and China have a shared interest in cooperation and tension reduction in all those issues except human rights, where their differences are stark and profound.

A Rules-Based Order?

Antony Blinken said he knew, going into his first face-to-face meetings with China's top two foreign affairs officials in Alaska on March 17, 2021, that "we are fundamentally at odds." Bad omen. The opening session was evidently just below a shouting match, lacking both mutual respect and a commitment to seek the positives. "This really is a one-off meeting," one US official said. "This is not the resumption of a particular dialogue mechanism or the beginning of a dialogue process." One wonders, why not? Starting a dialogue process after four years of Trumpian neglect surely was called for.

Blinken and his partner, Jake Sullivan, the national security adviser, seemed to think they had home field advantage. But they were sitting opposite two seasoned diplomats, Yang Jiechi, a communist party politburo member and former foreign minister, and the current foreign minister, Wang Yi. These guys have been around the block, so to speak, and were not about to be lectured to or put on the defensive, least of all when the Biden administration had just placed sanctions on Chinese officials in Hong Kong. The setting promised confrontation, not cooperation.

The most difficult issue seemed to be the US insistence that China respect a "rules-based order," which to Blinken and Sullivan meant that China should stop repression and end pressure tactics against Taiwan and the South China Sea islands. Those activities, said Blinken, are "not merely [Chinese] internal matters." But to the Chinese a "rules-based order" means rules made in the United States; they are totally inapplicable to China's internal affairs. Thus, emphasizing such rules is a nonstarter in talks between equals. So when Blinken insisted that a rules-based order was good for everyone—"It helps countries resolve differences peacefully, coordinate multilateral efforts effectively and participate in global commerce"—and protected people from "a world in which might makes right and winners take all," the Chinese scoffed.

Yang Jiechi replied by challenging the US claims to global leadership, saying that "the US does not represent the world, it only represents the government of the United States."

Yang was kind enough not to recite the long list of ways that Washington has broken the rules on might making right, such as unilateral military interventions abroad, sanctions, attempts at regime change, and tariff wars. Instead, he pushed back vigorously, saying—to great applause in China's social media—that "the US has no qualification to say you speak to China from a position of strength." He went on to remind the Americans that they too have "internal problems," adding that "it is important for the United States to change its own image, and to stop advancing its own democracy in the rest of the world."

The Alaska encounter spurred a number of harsh Chinese commentaries on the United States. One televised chart, titled "The Eight 'Firsts in the World' that the US Unapologetically Stands For," included items such as fake news, defeat in the fight against the pandemic, and support of terrorism. Another example is a *China Daily* opinion piece on "The Seven Deadly Sins of the US Alliance System."[1] Thievery, violence, aggression—a lengthy critique of American adventurism in company with the alliance partners that Biden was then trying to bring into his anti-China coalition. Comments such as these, coming after Yang Jiechi's tough riposte to the US representatives, reflect Beijing's conviction that we're in a new ball game. China is now going to contest a "rules-based order" and every other sacred American principle.

TAIWAN AND "STRATEGIC AMBIGUITY"

Taiwan has always been the most contentious issue in US-China relations. That is even more true today. Rival positions—the US view of the island's autonomy versus China's claim of sovereignty—are no longer merely being debated. Heightened tension between China and the United States has raised the possibility of a direct confrontation for the first time since Chinese missile tests near Taiwan in 1996. The new round of tensions can be traced to the Trump administration's upgrading of support of Taiwan—additional arms sales, which Trump immediately authorized; an official visit to Taiwan by the US secretary for health and human services, the highest-level visit by a US official since 1979;[2] and strong official statements backing Taiwan's separateness from China. Early on in the Biden administration, the Chinese responded with pressure of their own: repeated violations of Taiwan's self-defined air defense zone by PLA aircraft and regular coastal patrolling by China's coast guard and naval vessels. These activities were officially justified as reactions to US naval maneuvers near Taiwan, increased US military aid to Taiwan (including an undisclosed number of Marine and Special Forces trainers, continuing a deployment that Trump started), and visits to Taiwan by US legislators.

The bedrock principles of China's Taiwan policy are that Taiwan is a part of China and is a Chinese internal affair; Taiwan's independence and outside interference in Taiwan's affairs will never be accepted. US policy since the Nixon visit to China in 1972 has rested on support of "one China," coupled with military and political support of Taiwan and "strategic ambiguity" about what the United States might do if China were to attack Taiwan. Those clearly contradictory policies have always rankled Beijing, all the more so as US policy on Taiwan has become even more ambiguous under Biden. Some US officials argue for a stronger verbal commitment to Taiwan's defense, others for directly warning Beijing not to attack Taiwan, still others for increasing military aid or the number of official US visits to Taiwan. A major congressional report urged an immediate step-up of military aid to Taiwan and deployment of additional US deterrent forces to Asia.[3] Biden himself added to the confusion—or the policy ambiguity. He more than once compared the US "commitment" to defend Taiwan with its defense obligations to Japan and South Korea. That is not true. He said he told Xi at their virtual summit meeting in November 2021 that the United States is "not encouraging [Taiwan's] independence," but also said Taiwan may act "independently" as it sees fit. After that meeting, Biden said the United States still upholds the Taiwan Relations Act, passed by Congress in 1979, but (again, incorrectly) suggested that the act committed the United States to Taiwan's defense if Taiwan's government so desired.[4] Then, during his first Asia tour in 2022, Biden for a third time expressed a commitment to defend the island from a Chinese attack. As before, the statement was walked back—including by Biden himself. He also said he supported the one-China principle but likened a Chinese attack on Taiwan to Russia's invasion of Ukraine.

China reacted to these statements by applauding the US acceptance of one China but warning that talk of Taiwan's independence was "playing with fire." The State Department has had to "clarify" Biden's remarks by reaffirming US strategic ambiguity. For example, at a news briefing, a State Department spokesman said that under the Taiwan Relations Act, "the United States maintains the capacity to resist any resort to force or other forms of coercion that would jeopardize the security or the social or economic system of the people on Taiwan."[5] Blinken followed up with this statement on April 11, 2021: "All I can tell you is we have a serious commitment to Taiwan being able to defend itself. . . . it would be a serious mistake for anyone to try to change that status quo by force."[6]

The Chinese have their own version of strategic ambiguity. Xi Jinping adheres to the long-standing PRC view that reunification with Taiwan is a sacred responsibility. That position has never ruled out the use of force, particularly if Taiwan should prepare for or outright declare its independence. Xi, however, has not threatened to use force and in fact has repeatedly emphasized reunification by peaceful means. Nor has he or any other authoritative Chinese source ever put a deadline on reunification.[7] For instance, in a speech on the hundredth anniversary of the CCP's founding, Xi attacked the notion of Taiwan independence as usual but vowed to "uphold the one-China principle and the 1992 Consensus, and advance peaceful national reunification."[8] Not long after, in another speech, Xi elaborated, denouncing Taiwan "separatism" and underscoring the urgency of fulfilling the mission of regaining Taiwan.[9] The speech came as Chinese flights near and into Taiwan's air defense zone (but not its airspace) greatly increased, a sharp contrast with what Xi said:

> Using peaceful methods to achieve unification of the motherland most fits with the overall interests of the Chinese people, including our Taiwan compatriots. We firmly support the basic direction of "peaceful unification and one-country one-system," and firmly support the One China principle and the "1992 Consensus," in promoting peaceful development on both sides of the Taiwan Strait. Compatriots on both sides want to stand on the correct side of history and the glorious undertaking of together completing the unity of the motherland and the great revival of the people. . . . No one should underestimate the strong resolve of the Chinese people to defend national sovereignty and territorial integrity, the firm will, and the great strength. The historical task of completing the unity of the motherland will certainly be realized, and certainly can be realized.

According to the Chinese recounting of Xi's conversation with Biden in November 2021, Xi reiterated both China's resolve on reunification and the hope it would be peacefully accomplished. He blamed the "Taiwan authorities" and certain Americans who support "using Taiwan to control China" for the latest tension. China will be patient about Taiwan, Xi said, but "if the 'Taiwan independence' splittist forces are provocative and forceful, to the point of breaking the red line, we will have to take drastic measures."[10] Contrary to prevailing media and academic discussion of the Taiwan issue, Xi's statement does not portend imminent attack or his determination to absorb Taiwan while he is at the height of his power and America is divided. "The US side has misread and misjudged China's strategic intentions," Xi told Biden in their March 18, 2022, conversation, possibly referring to speculation about China using the Ukraine crisis as an opportunity to attack Taiwan.[11] China's red line on Taiwan is clear, and the military activities nearby Taiwan reinforce it; but so long as the United States and Taiwan maintain the status quo—no movement toward independence on Taiwan and no formal US commitment to Taiwan's defense—that red line is unlikely to be crossed.

The central issue regarding Taiwan should be self-determination: Do the people of Taiwan want to remain politically separate from the mainland or become a Chinese province? Separation has long been the preferred choice, growing stronger by the year as the Taiwan-born population increases. As polls consistently show, people on Taiwan overwhelmingly identify as Taiwanese; those identifying as Chinese barely register. Recognizing the risks associated with declaring independence, however, Taiwanese prefer maintaining the status quo, as does President Tsai Ing-wen.[12] China's crackdown on dissent in Hong Kong only strengthens separation sentiment on Taiwan. On the mainland, the determination is of a different order: The PRC leadership's patience to achieve reunification with Taiwan may be running low, Xi Jinping's desire to be the leader who achieves reunification is probably very strong, and China's capability to achieve reunification by force is greater than ever.

Thus, the risks of a US-China collision remain if only because of the persistence of tensions, careless language, provocative actions by both countries, and the absence of structured dialogue.[13] Amid tensions, misperceptions, which have regularly plagued US-China relations since the Korean War, heighten the chances of overt conflict. Each side's aim to deter the other, as in the current situation, is easily confused with offensive intent. A previous crisis over Taiwan in 1958 serves as a warning: It might have escalated to the nuclear level had not President Dwight D. Eisenhower ruled that option out.[14]

Today, despite alarm bells being sounded in Taiwan and among some US China watchers, war is not imminent. General Mark A. Milley, chairman of the Joint Chiefs of Staff, offered the assessment late in 2021 that a Chinese takeover was unlikely over the next two years, though he added that China has the military capability to attempt it.[15] Beijing does have options besides an invasion: blockade, cyberwar, or attacks on US planes and ships that might try to defend Taiwan are often mentioned.[16] Still, the risks of use of force cannot be ignored. So long as tensions with the United States persist, the possibility grows of a disastrous miscalculation by one or the other side—a miscalculation that could escalate to use of nuclear weapons. A RAND Corporation study concludes: "China may opt to delay the resolution of Taiwan's status and that of other disputed regions until it has prevailed in its competition with the United States."[17]

Though Washington and Beijing probably will never agree on Taiwan, their common objective must be to avoid a deadly confrontation over the island's status. Both sides, and Taiwan as well, need to accept responsibility for the ratcheting up of tensions in recent years. Defusing the dangerous current situation is, however, entirely possible; after all, the long-standing US position on a "peaceful resolution" of the Taiwan question is not so far removed from China's stated interest in "peaceful reunification." US policy should be to reduce overall military aid to Taiwan, maintain Taiwan's capability to deter attack, and stop actions that give the impression of supporting Taiwan's independence. Xi expressed appreciation for Biden's reassurances on US support of the one-China principle in their March 18, 2022, conversation. China should support ways to engage Taiwan at both the official and nongovernmental levels without provoking a security crisis through continued military intimidation. And for all the parties, reducing tensions means maintaining the strategic ambiguity that has served well in preventing war.

HUMAN RIGHTS OR SOVEREIGN RIGHTS?

Authoritarian rule is by nature incapable of tolerating dissent, the rule of law, freedom of press and speech, and organized political opposition. Institutions erected to support representative government become mere shells, operating to cloak predetermined policies and give the pretense of legitimate authority. The Hong Kong Special Administrative Region and the Xinjiang Uyghur Autonomous Region are anything but special and autonomous. The local Chinese authorities there, like their bosses in Beijing, are ruthlessly efficient when it comes to curtailing or simply extinguishing democracy and basic human rights. They force the closure of independent media and other elements of civil society, arrest protest leaders and other outspoken critics, and track and threaten critics who have managed to go abroad. In the extreme, as in Xinjiang, the authorities will systematically destroy a culture and replace it with a more pliant one. In both territories and throughout much of the country, China operates perhaps the world's most formidable surveillance system for personal identification and data gathering. Yet, using Orwellian language, the Chinese party-state insists it is promoting real democracy, respecting human rights, securing a better life for the very populations under assault, and only arresting people who "make trouble" and engage in "subversion."

Hong Kong: One Country, One System

On July 1, 1997, the United Kingdom formally handed Hong Kong over to China under an agreement that was supposed to give Hong Kong fifty years of autonomy. That same year, students and professors at the University of Hong Kong erected a statue, called *Pillar of Shame*, to commemorate the 1989 Tiananmen massacre. The tall sculptor by a Danish artist lasted until the end of 2021 when, in the dead of night, it was carved in half and removed. Two other sculptures of the same event at two other Hong Kong universities were also removed. The ongoing eclipse of civil society by the PRC authorities could not have been more starkly demonstrated.

In Deng Xiaoping's time, China's promise to Hong Kong was "one country, two systems," which was commonly understood to mean that Hong Kong could go on as a special zone of free enterprise and democratic governance for another half century. It took less than half that time for China unilaterally to scrap the arrangement and turn Hong Kong into another piece of the people's republic, its economy intact but its politics and society under tight control from Beijing.

Many observers as well as people in Hong Kong took the attitude of "It can't happen here," believing that Beijing would never crack down on a financial and trade "golden goose." Moreover, the extraordinary Hong Kong protests in 2019 and 2020, which started over an extradition bill and broadened to demands for greater autonomy, seemed to have the support of a clear majority of the city's 7.4 million people. The lopsided victory of pro-democracy candidates in district council elections on November 24, 2019, strengthened that conclusion. Optimists thought Beijing wouldn't crack down on a highly visible and defiant uprising in an international trade and financial hub—in other words, that it would prefer, as with Taiwan, to avoid use of force against a major part of Greater China. The protesters, however, had no central leadership and no game plan, an advantage while in resistance but a disadvantage if the aim was a settlement. Nor did they have substantive external support. Beijing had no interest in a settlement, which it saw as legitimizing the protests and weakening its rule. What Beijing did have was control of the police, the courts, and, if necessary, the PLA bivouacked on the edge of the city. The crackdown effectively terminated Hong Kong's rule of law, governing model, and the right to protest.

Although the Hong Kong demonstrations raised clear issues of constitutional order and democratic governance, the United States did not challenge China's violations of its commitments. But Donald Trump kept *his* promise, reportedly made to Xi Jinping in June 2019, that Washington would "tone down" its comments on the spiraling protests. "Very tough situation," Trump tweeted on August 12, 2019, "hope it works out for everybody, including China." Legislation such as the US Senate's Hong Kong Human Rights and Democracy Act[18] appropriately sanctioned Chinese and Hong Kong officials but also reeked of political posturing about American values and bipartisanship. Once again Trump was inconsistent. He quietly signed the act but indicated he would not honor all its provisions. He said, in another tweet two days later: "Of course China wants to make a deal. Let them work humanely with Hong Kong first!" But that was disingenuous; it didn't keep Trump from reaching an interim trade deal at year's end that was at least as advantageous to China as it was to the United States.

Step by step, political repression and surveillance became the order of the day in Hong Kong. To stymie the pro-democracy demonstrations, the Hong Kong authorities arrested dozens of activists and journalists. Beijing proclaimed the right to "supervise" Hong Kong's internal affairs, in violation of the Basic Law that was supposed to protect Hong Kong's autonomy. China's legislature sealed the demise of the one-country, two-systems principle by passing a new national security law and suspending legislative council elections in Hong Kong for a year. The new law bypasses approval by the Hong Kong authorities under Article 23 of the Basic Law and gives the authorities extraordinary leeway to arrest protesters, who can be guilty of any number of acts that entail "subversion of state power," a category long used to justify repression. The national security law is now incorporated in school curricula, even at primary level. Beijing now has its own security officials in Hong Kong to adjudicate cases and make decisions that may override local law.[19]

In early 2021, what little remained of democratic governance in Hong Kong was obliterated by imposition of a loyalty oath that candidates for district councils would have to take. The oath, to China and the CCP, was announced as a test of patriotism and evidence of "political reform." In practical terms, this new requirement will squelch pro-democracy voices at the local level.[20] At the individual level, a roundup of pro-democracy activists in 2021 on the charge of "conspiracy to commit subversion" left only those in exile.[21] As all vestiges of democratic rule were eliminated during the remainder of 2021, one commentator at the scene reported that China's crackdown "has absolutely worked. There are no more street protests. There's extensive self-censorship. Virtually every prominent pro-democracy activist is in exile, in jail, awaiting trial or has disappeared from public life."[22] Hong Kongers who organized annual vigils since 1989 to mark the Tiananmen crackdown were jailed, with the police using the pretext of investigating foreign support under the national security law.[23] Hong Kong legislative elections in December 2021 under Beijing's new rules yielded predictable results.

Turnout was a record low and only "patriots" were allowed to run. Pro-China candidates won all but one seat, including all the directly elected seats that normally would have been won by opposition forces.[24] Beijing capped off its full control in May 2022 with the "election" of John Lee, a proven loyalist, as Hong Kong's chief executive. He was the only candidate.

Virtually all elements of civil society, such as labor and student unions and NGOs, have been disbanded. Independent news sources have one by one disappeared, culminating in the arrest of the editors of the independent newspaper *Apple Daily*, followed by its closure. Apparently under orders from Beijing, the Alibaba Group was ordered in 2021 to divest certain media holdings, most prominently the *South China Morning Post* (*SCMP*), an independent Hong Kong newspaper for more than a hundred years. The group's founder, Jack Ma, is an occasional critic of Beijing's economic policies. *SCMP* was not especially critical, but it could be counted on for reliable reporting on China. That day may soon be over.

As in 1989, the twists and turns in Hong Kong's politics reverberate in Taiwan, cementing Taiwan's determination to maintain its own system. The landslide reelection of Tsai Ing-wen as president in January, despite Beijing's disinformation campaign against her, showed that. (Immediately after the vote, Tsai said the election was a victory for "democracy and sovereignty.") Some Hong Kongers traveled to Taiwan for a four-day election tour, to see how a real democracy operates, while student protesters marked for arrest in Hong Kong fled to Taiwan, in essence voting with their feet. These dramatic changes are meant literally to alter Hong Kongers' political identity, but tens of thousands of them see no future and are leaving.[25] For Taiwan, "one country, two systems" is a dead letter for many years to come.

Hong Kong is not going to become another Xinjiang, but neither will it be just another Chinese province. Hong Kong is a highly visible enclave, a dynamic center of international business with a well-educated Cantonese-speaking population that has its own diaspora. It has voluble supporters in the US Congress, in Australia, and in Canada. The Biden administration and members of Congress have responded to China's policies in Hong Kong with vociferous criticism and sanctions. But to little effect: Not only has Beijing shrugged off the criticism, it has refocused Hong Kong's economy on those international investors and banks that don't make an issue of political repression. Instead of experiencing capital flight, Hong Kong has seen a higher inflow of capital as the national security law took effect. Western sanctions, in short, are proving to be insufficient to derail Xi Jinping's aims, and China's apparent reluctance to impose harsh rules on companies and banks that remain in Hong Kong may be helping its cause. As one observer noted, "The way things are playing out in Hong Kong demonstrates just how hard it will be for Washington and its partners to carry out a comprehensive 'strategic competition' with China."[26]

Genocide in Xinjiang

The assault on Chinese Muslims in Xinjiang has reached staggering proportions: One expert, Dr. Adrian Zenz, estimates the number of incarcerated persons at 1.8 million.[27] Other estimates range from just under 1 million to 1.5 million. The crackdown, apparently initiated following an attack by Uyghurs on ethnic Han people in 2014, seems to have been based on Xi's personal orders.[28] A top-secret speech by Xi on "investigative work in Xinjiang" in 2014 anticipated Beijing's later plans for suppressing Muslims and destroying their culture.[29] High-level Chinese documents reveal Xi's mounting concern over instability in Xinjiang, which he believed could have nationwide consequences. Xi became riveted on extirpating "religious extremism" from Xinjiang by "transformation through labor," meaning internment for reeducation and labor transfers from rural to urban employment. Xinjiang's Communist Party secretary, Chen Quanguo, personally commanded officials in 2018 to "round up all who should be rounded up," echoing Xi's similar call four years earlier. The order went out that party officials should show "absolutely no mercy" toward its "enemies." Other coercive policies followed, such as changing the ethnic makeup of Xinjiang through suppression of Uyghur births and resettlement of Han Chinese from eastern China, a practice of diluting troublesome populations that has a long history.[30]

Arguing that Xinjiang's Muslims are potential terrorists, separatists, and extremists—the catchall phrase for ethnic and other threats to social stability—Beijing actually aims to impose a new identity on Chinese Muslims and break up any sense of Uyghur community. Its methods include long-term confinement, intense psychological pressure ("reeducation"), birth prevention to reduce the Muslim birthrate,[31] deployment of Uyghur labor outside Xinjiang,[32] forbidding of common cultural practices, compelled learning of Han Chinese, and destruction of mosques, cemeteries, and cultural sites.[33] History is likely to regard these policies as being on a par with anti-Jewish pogroms in Europe before the Holocaust, Stalin's Great Purge, and China's own Cultural Revolution—another systematic attempt to terrorize and culturally destroy "enemies of the people."

A mountain of evidence has been collected to document Chinese policy in Xinjiang. Satellite photos, personal testimonials, human rights groups, journalists with hidden cameras, and reports from the Uyghur exile community underpin the description offered by Amnesty International's secretary general: a "dystopian hellscape on a staggering scale."[34] Much of the evidence was presented at the Uyghur Tribunal in 2021. In December, the tribunal found China guilty of torture, crimes against humanity, and (with specific respect to preventing births) genocide.[35] Subsequently, computer hacking of internal police networks in Xinjiang revealed the prison-like nature of reeducation camps and top Chinese leaders' direct involvement in the mass internment campaign.[36]

As the Uyghur Tribunal discussed, China's policy in the Xinjiang Uygur Autonomous Region (XUAR) is sometimes called a cultural genocide, other times a crime against humanity. The Chinese authorities have traumatized rather than slaughtered the Muslim population, which includes Kazakhs and other ethnic groups besides Uyghurs. But when the tribunal examined all the elements of Chinese policy—including the separation of families and forced labor (assignment of Uyghurs to other provinces once they have completed reeducation along with the other charges mentioned—it concluded that China was systematically seeking to eradicate a people's identity.[37] Like the tribunal, I call the policy *genocide* in accordance with the definition in three parts of the 1948 Convention on the Prevention and Punishment of the Crime of Genocide, to which China is a party: "(b) Causing serious bodily or mental harm to members of the group; (c) Deliberately inflicting on the group conditions of life calculated to bring about its physical destruction in whole or in part; (d) Imposing measures intended to prevent births within the group."

The internment camps are in every respect totalitarian in design and operation.[38] They are of a piece with China's deployment of advanced surveillance technology and collection of blood samples that can be used to identify not just Muslims but potentially any minority group or individual through DNA analysis.[39] China's ministry of public security has announced plans to obtain the DNA via blood samples of tens of millions of male adults and children, a database sufficient to cover virtually the entire population and give police additional capacity to pressure the families of criminals, real and political.[40]

China's defense of its policies and practices in Xinjiang is exceptionally weak, resting on two foundational principles: national security and state sovereignty. Xinjiang is Chinese territory and the central government can do what it wishes, without foreign interference. Foreign reporting on Xinjiang is biased and outlandish. Many Uyghurs are part of a terrorist organization; even the United States agreed.[41] The United States should not engage in "lie diplomacy," especially in view of its own human rights problems.[42] Least credible is China's insistence that its policies are in the best interests of Xinjiang's people. A statement from the PRC embassy in Washington, posted on Twitter January 8, 2021, says: "Study shows that in the process of eradicating extremism, the minds of Uygur women in Xinjiang were emancipated and gender equality and reproductive health were promoted, making them no longer baby-making machines. They are more confident and independent." No study is cited. Other official statements, equally divorced from reality, insist that the "reeducation" of Uyghurs would make them better and happier workers, that forced labor sent to distant factories is actually intended to reduce rural employment, and that Uyghur women who testified to abuse are bad characters.[43] Pulling out all the stops, Chinese hackers evidently created false UN Human Rights Council documents to lure Uyghurs inside and outside the country to respond and gain entry to their computers.[44]

Chinese officials relentlessly push the official narrative, applying intense pressure on foreign journalists and professors, social media outlets, multinational companies, academic institutions, and international organizations to avoid criticizing China's repression of human rights and even indirectly support it. A number of journalists have been forced to leave China; social media such as YouTube, Twitter, and Facebook have been blocked; and the BBC was among news companies that were attacked for being "anti-China" and having links to intelligence agencies.[45] Microsoft is among the companies that are complying with Chinese censorship, allowing China's regulators to filter its search engine (Bing) for undesirable references.[46] Companies such as Intel and Adidas that express solidarity with the Uyghurs in Xinjiang, either in public statements or termination of business ties, risk a nationalist backlash and a boycott of their products.[47] The World Bank may also be complicit. A report by British and American researchers says that the International Finance Corporation, a World Bank lending unit, provided $486 million in financing to four Chinese companies that recruited labor from Xinjiang under "labor-transfer" and "poverty alleviation" programs.[48]

What can the international community do to mitigate the human rights violations taking place in the XUAR? Naming and shaming can sometimes help. Bringing the Uyghur repression before the UN High Commissioner for Human Rights produced a joint statement of twenty-two countries, in July 2019, condemning "large-scale arbitrary detention" and other violations.[49] The statement called on China to allow UN and independent access to the so-called retraining camps. But all the UN commission could get from China was agreement to an "exchange," not an investigation.[50] There the matter has sat for three years, with the UN commissioner, Michelle Bachelet, herself once a victim of torture in Chile, withholding a report on Xinjiang that is probably highly critical of China.[51] Instead, she made an ill-advised trip to China in May 2022 that included two days in Xinjiang. It became a propaganda coup for Beijing. She reported she was "unable to assess the full scale" of the so-called vocational education centers but was "assured" they had been "dismantled." People with whom she spoke, none of them Uyghur prisoners, were clearly handpicked by Beijing. In all, the visit amounted to a Potemkin village experience.[52]

Britain separately urged China to "allow UN observers immediate and unfettered access to the region." China's belated response to that idea was that "the door to Xinjiang is always open," but—just as happened with the UN commission—an investigation should "aim . . . to provide exchanges and cooperation" rather than engage in "politicization."[53] Besides Canada's parliament, the European Union has also criticized China's conduct in Xinjiang, but only two EU parliaments—Netherlands in 2021 and France in 2022—have directly condemned China for "genocide."

The United States has gradually moved to the forefront of countries that have given Xinjiang prominence in their China policies. Under Trump, however, as John Bolton (a top foreign policy adviser) writes in his memoir, Xi privately got a pass on Xinjiang just as he did on Chinese repression in Hong Kong. At a meeting in Osaka in 2019, according to Bolton, Trump said that Xi should go ahead with building camps for the Uyghurs—"exactly the right thing to do." But as Bolton reports, these comments were really all about Trump's reelection hopes, "alluding to China's economic capability to affect the ongoing campaigns, pleading with Xi to ensure he'd win."[54] Knowing Trump's real priorities, and reading reports that major US corporations worry about their supply chains if legislation on forced labor passes,[55] Chinese leaders had reason to scoff at American protestations on behalf of China's human rights victims. Late in the game, the Trump administration did use *genocide* to characterize China's actions. Biden followed suit soon after taking office.[56] Since then, US and British officials have reacted angrily to reports of systematic rape and humiliation of Uyghur women in Chinese internment camps.[57] Both the United States and the EU imposed financial and travel sanctions on various Xinjiang officials believed to be directly responsible for the genocide, and in 2022 the Biden administration banned nearly all imports of goods made in Xinjiang.

Representative of China's fierce reaction to these criticisms, China's foreign minister Wang Yi said in February 2021: "Places inhabited by ethnic minorities, such as Xinjiang and Tibet, have stood out as shining examples of China's human rights progress." Likewise, the Chinese embassy in The Hague said of Holland's resolution that it "deliberately smeared China and grossly interfered in China's internal affairs." When Lithuania sharply criticized the "genocide" and withdrew from the China–Central and Eastern European Countries Cooperation Forum in May 2021, China's foreign ministry and nationalist press were livid. Their view: Small countries have no right to interfere in the affairs of great powers or curry favor with the United States.[58] Every restriction imposed by the West has been greeted with denials, counter-sanctions, and insistence that other states practice noninterference in China's affairs.

Naming and shaming, however, rarely works by itself. It takes international solidarity, strict legal guidelines, and targeted sanctions. Many countries, including Muslim-majority ones, are reluctant to criticize China while being dependent on its BRI or other financial sources. To the contrary, their governments have openly defended Chinese policies in Xinjiang and, as mentioned earlier, at least three Middle East countries have deported Uyghurs at China's request.[59] Developing countries, notably those with strong-arm governments, do not accept Western notions of universal human rights, as became evident in an October 2020 UN General Assembly vote not to condemn China over Xinjiang or Hong Kong. Or consider the International Criminal Court's (ICC) decision at the end of 2020 not to consider the complaint of two Uyghur groups that China is guilty of genocide and crimes against humanity in the XUAR. The court's reasoning was limited: The allegations involve Chinese citizens within China, which is not a party to the treaty that established the ICC. No country has appealed to the International Court of Justice to take on the genocide accusation, a requirement for starting an inquiry. Nor, finally, do the Uyghurs have what other mass victims of human rights violations have: an organization and a leader with an international profile. The Chinese authorities have done their part, limiting foreign access to Xinjiang and preventing most people with firsthand information from getting out.

On the corporate side, a statement issued by a gathering of leading globalists, including Henry Kissinger and Condoleezza Rice, seemed to support taking China to task over Xinjiang. "The best outcome for U.S.-China relations," the statement reads, "is likely managed competition—an accommodation that avoids military conflict while allowing for limited cooperation." But when it came to corporations pulling out of Xinjiang, these leaders demurred: "It is impractical to think that supply chains and manufacturing can be moved simply, affordably or comprehensively out of China."[60] Companies such as Apple and Nike, which acknowledged having used forced labor from Xinjiang in their factories, were leery of supporting sanctions.[61] Others, such as Intel, which has a large labor force in China and whose computer chips are used in surveillance of Muslims, backtracked immediately when confronted by Chinese authorities over the company's seeming support of human rights.[62]

NGOs naturally have a very different view of corporate responsibility. Human Rights Watch cautioned: "Any firm that cannot show it has assessed the human rights impact of its commercial activities and mitigated harm in what United Nations experts have labeled a 'no rights zone' should do so now."[63] Boycotting Xinjiang was in order, and in at least three instances, boycotts produced results. In two cases the target was China's use of forced labor, either in Xinjiang's factories and fields or in the factories of distant provinces. One boycott, reportedly with pledges of support from Chinese companies, involved a specific chemical ingredient made with forced labor in Xinjiang.[64] The second came from the Fair Labor Association (FLA), whose members include more than a hundred major clothing companies such as Nike, Patagonia, and Adidas. The FLA issued its first-ever ban, covering all

parts of the supply chain coming out of Xinjiang, from raw materials to fin-
ished goods.[65] The third is against the Xinjiang Production and Construction
Corps (XPCC), described as a paramilitary organization that accounts for
a significant share of the province's cotton and tomato production and is a
major employer of mostly non-Han workers.

Sanctioning XPCC, and then banning all cotton and tomato exports originating in Xinjiang, came about near the end of the Trump administration.
Since a large percentage of the world's cotton originates in Xinjiang, the
ban surely put a crimp in its economy.[66] Biden extended that ban, as noted.
Companies were upset; they have to prove that a product is not made with
forced labor in order to import it. In 2021 US imports of Chinese textiles
dropped by 23 percent; but the shortfall was picked up by China's neighbors.[67]

Finally, China's use of DNA samples to abet its surveillance can be
addressed by the global scientific community. Articles by Chinese scientists
that rely on information from surveillance agencies or that have been prepared without the informed consent of the people studied should not be published. The 10,000-member American Anthropological Association (AAA)
has condemned the "eradication of [Uyghur and Kazakh] indigenous identi-
ties."[68] The overwhelming number of Chinese scientific papers in the field
of forensic genetics have been of Uyghurs and Tibetans, often with a police
or military co-author.[69] (Two such studies, published in 2019, were retracted
in 2021 after questions were raised about Uyghur consent for use of DNA
samples.[70]) Scientists in the West have, knowingly or otherwise, contributed
to China's abuses of this kind of genetics research. One genetics journal published papers on use of DNA for ethnic profiling that may have been applied
in Xinjiang. Several members of the journal's board resigned in protest.[71]

Tibet

Thanks to effective lobbying by the Tibetan community and its US supporters, presidents and Congress members have consistently lent rhetorical
backing to the cause of free Tibet and an end to China's well-known human
rights violations there. The legislation includes the Tibetan Policy Act in
2002, the 2018 Reciprocal Access to Tibet Act, and, at the end of Trump's
tenure in December 2020, the Tibetan Policy and Support Act. All these laws
are guaranteed to antagonize the Chinese leadership. They support Tibetans,
not the PRC authorities, on deciding the Dalai Lama's successor. They urge
stronger US diplomatic efforts to gain negotiations between Beijing and the
Dalai Lama's representatives. They fund humanitarian projects for Tibetans
inside and outside Tibet. And they prevent China from establishing another
US consulate until a US consulate is allowed in Lhasa.[72]

Sanctioning Technology

The trade war that started under Trump came to embrace China's access to US technology. The prevailing notion in Washington seemed to be that denying access to military-sensitive technology, and persuading allies to do the same, would hamper China's growth and force economic and political concessions. But technology is a globalized product; like so many other products—from public health devices to weapons—the market offers many sources.

Facial recognition and DNA technology make the point. US companies have been among those that supplied those technologies to Chinese public security officials to identify Uyghurs and other minorities.[73] But under Trump, sanctions were slapped on more than thirty Chinese entities, including Huawei, to prevent access to this technology.[74] He also signed off on a Uyghur human rights bill in June 2020. One of the US companies that supplied genetic sequencers to the Xinjiang police asserted it had stopped doing business there, as a matter of ethical concern. But it's unclear if that commitment extended to other Chinese police forces, to other DNA technology that could be used to control populations, and to several other countries where the company had customers.[75] Biden expanded Trump's restrictions, barring US investments in some sixty Chinese companies that deal in surveillance technology.

Unfortunately, according to one company that tracks surveillance technology, sanctioning foreign suppliers is undermined by Chinese producers of the same technology. The technology is said to be able to pick out Uyghurs and other non-Han people from crowds. Some of China's biggest technology firms, such as Huawei and Alibaba, the cloud computing giant, are among the producers, though they claim unawareness of use of their technology by client companies to target Uyghurs.[76] Like Huawei, Alibaba at one time offered facial recognition technology on its website with specific application to ethnic minorities, then denied such an intention.[77] Given the widespread publicity about the technology, the claim is not credible, especially since it is well known that Chinese firms have marketed it to a number of authoritarian governments.

Then there's the problem of US technology corporations in China operating in compliance with Chinese rules governing citizens' personal information. Apple, for example, is reported to "store the personal data of its Chinese customers on computer servers run by a state-owned Chinese firm." The data is stored at two giant facilities, one in southwestern China and the other in Inner Mongolia. The Chinese government, not Apple, is said to manage and hold the key to unlocking the data.[78] The notion that Apple, or any other foreign data collector in China, can protect the civil liberties of Chinese citizens is clearly not credible, particularly when the company (and Apple is just one) depends heavily on China for revenue and production.

Cyber Security or Cyber Sovereignty?

The United States and China are at loggerheads over several issues related to cyber space, including international standards, internet openness, personal privacy, and especially hacking for purposes of economic espionage and spying. In 2016 President Obama and President Xi reached an understanding on preventing hacking of commercial firms. It worked for a few years, until Trump's trade war and US actions against Chinese telecommunications firms that process data for the PRC government. Chinese hackers, at the time based in the PLA, seemed most interested in acquiring personal data and industrial secrets. In July 2021 the Biden administration formally charged China's ministry of state security with using criminal groups to hack Microsoft Corporation and demand ransom from corporations around the world.[79] Australia, Japan, and other US allies followed suit. The administration also warned oil and gas pipeline owners, in the wake of successful Russian hacking of Colonial Pipeline that forced it to shut down, that Chinese hackers had attacked US pipelines in earlier years, from 2011 to 2013. China has responded to the hacking charges with its own accusations of US cyberattacks.[80] In 2022, during the Ukraine crisis, China charged that cyberattacks originating in the United States were accessing Chinese computers in order to attack Russia and Belarus—a rather disingenuous charge inasmuch as Chinese state-sponsored hackers have reportedly pried into Russian defense computers.[81]

Just how dangerous cyberattacks can be became clear in 2021. President Biden warned President Putin that if Russia launched a cyberattack on any of sixteen areas of critical infrastructure, such as telecommunications and financial services, Putin could expect a devastating cyber counterattack. Chinese leaders and analysts surely paid that conversation due attention. In the wake of the Ukraine invasion, with the United States and NATO on alert for possible Russian cyberattacks on their economies, the issue assumes immediate relevance.

Agreements on cyber security are particularly difficult to craft and implement, but not impossible or worthless.[82] Differences over internet standards can be separated from national security concerns. China and the United States have a shared interest in avoiding an escalation of cyber activity and trading of veiled threats such as have consumed US-Russia relations. That interest extends beyond hacking of corporate or government data. The possibility, for instance, of a Chinese cyberattack on Taiwan has often been mentioned. Coming to a new understanding on trade might put an agreement on cyber activity back on track. As with so many other issues in US-PRC relations, progress on cyber security ultimately depends on the overall state of those relations and the domestic politics that underlie them.[83] It may also depend on getting Russia, the EU, and other countries behind a multilateral approach, though Russia's cyberattacks on Ukraine before the invasion would seem to eliminate Moscow for years to come.

Dragnet: Educational and Scientific Exchanges under Fire

Under Donald Trump and Mike Pompeo, disengaging from China led to taking aim at educational ties, arguing that any benefits (which it rarely acknowledged) had to be measured against numerous risks that included espionage and giveaways of information. Thus began an intense scrutiny of all elements of educational exchanges with China: visa applications, the activities of Chinese consulates, the conduct of students and research scholars, Confucius Institute (CI) programs, research collaboration, donations by Chinese entities to universities, and research contracts. All were targeted in a manner that called to mind McCarthyism tactics of the 1950s: No Chinese, including Chinese Americans, were above suspicion.

The Trump administration's restrictive measures did not affect only China—they were applied to Middle East countries among others, and to immigrants as well as students—but China clearly was tops on the US government's list. Approximately 370,000 students and scholars from China were in the United States as of 2020, nearly a third engaged in STEM (science, technology, engineering, mathematics) research. But as relations with China deteriorated, Democrats and Republicans alike came to view Chinese graduate students and researchers, especially those in science and technology, as potential spies or thieves, thus tempting targets for warrantless surveillance.[84] The objective apparently was to disrupt the academic "supply chain"—to decouple US-China scientific ties in a manner similar to decoupling trade relations.

Confucius Institutes, established on US campuses to promote Chinese language and cultural learning, particularly in communities that could not afford such programs, were caught up in the clampdown on Chinese visitors. Once numbering more than one hundred in the United States and only twenty-eight in 2022, the CIs came to be regarded by conservative and liberal legislators alike as not simply projecting China's soft power, which almost goes without saying. The institutes were also charged with using the teachers and textbooks supplied by China's education ministry to interfere with academic freedom, promote the CCP's political line on current events, and corrupt young Americans' minds. This thinking became law in 2019 when the National Defense Authorization Act was passed. It denied US Defense

Department funding to universities that hosted a CI. This was followed in 2020 by another law, with bipartisan cooperation (US Senate bill S.939), that denied all federal funds to universities that failed to meet new ground rules on CIs they hosted.[85]

Those bills forced universities to choose between continuing to receive federal money and operating a CI, a choice that really was no choice at all. Their purpose, moreover, was based on false premises. From personal research I can attest that none of the accusations against Confucius Institutes in the United States are supported with facts.[86] With rare exception, CIs performed as promised, bringing cultural and language learning to many US communities and promoting mutual understanding. More than a hundred interviews of school officials and community participants turned up no evidence of Chinese teachers propagandizing on behalf of the CCP or interfering with academic freedom.[87] What makes the accusations directed at CIs so obviously politically motivated is that no mention is made of homegrown and other foreign efforts to influence school curricula, such as professorial chairs and research institutes established by authoritarian governments, the Koch Foundation's intrusions into university hiring practices, and foreign governments' financing of university chairs and speaking events.[88] Other than speaking events, Confucius Institutes have not financed any of these activities.

Similarly with scientific exchanges, Trump came down hard on applications by US scientists for Chinese research grants and on Chinese scientists engaged in collaborative research in US institutions:

> Before he left office in January, Trump issued a memorandum describing the US government's responsibility to protect the country's research. Simultaneously, the White House Office of Science and Technology Policy (OSTP) published research security guidelines for universities and funding agencies. And in March, the US National Institutes of Health announced new requirements for information that scientists applying for grants must disclose—becoming the first US agency to act on OSTP's guidelines.[89]

The underlying political purpose of the new rules was to prevent Chinese spying and theft of research data. The Justice Department and the FBI, under a so-called China Initiative launched in 2018, was given the job of rooting out Chinese visitors suspected of economic espionage, which the department said in 2021 amounted to about "80 percent of all economic espionage prosecutions" it brought. While it functioned—the China Initiative was terminated in 2022, as discussed below—it encompassed a good deal more than protecting trade secrets, however. Its mandate was expansive and included "potential threats to academic freedom," watching over Chinese registered as foreign agents, preventing threats to supply chains, and identifying possible corruption in Chinese companies that compete with US companies.[90] The Justice Department listed many arrests, indictments, and imprisonments of Chinese nationals and US citizens under the China Initiative, but the list was overblown. It consisted almost entirely of people who had vague connections to the PLA, lied to federal investigators, or failed to disclose research ties to Chinese institutions. The sole conviction in a jury trial was for the latter two offenses; otherwise, no spies, no economic espionage, and no real threats to national security were uncovered. A number of government cases were thrown out for lack of evidence.[91] But the harm to academic freedom, reputations, and personal privacy was substantial.

Despite Biden's tough posture on China, the impact on US-China educational exchanges was very uncertain when he took office. After all, Biden was surely well aware of the benefits to the United States of those exchanges: advances in science and technology, patents, goodwill for Americans, lessons on academic freedom for the Chinese to take back home, and billions of dollars spent by Chinese students and visiting scholars on tuition and other expenses. Would Biden therefore undo all the Trump-era regulations, or would he see the educational exchanges as one-sided, evidence of a Chinese threat and therefore another area of strategic competition? The latter proved correct, as I discuss in the next chapter.

Chapter 6

Biden's China Policy

DEMOCRACY VERSUS AUTOCRACY

It is an extraordinary shift, emblematic not just of China's rise but also of America's insecurity: Where China once looked to the United States as the standard of economic power, now the United States measures itself against China's economic power. *US economic policy, and a good deal of overall foreign policy, is linked to competition with China.* By making China the top challenger, Biden gave policy a Cold War face, enabling him to appeal to both sides of the aisle in Congress—a rare instance in which he encountered no real resistance. China policy produced an unspoken division of labor: Democrats, normally focused on human rights, pushed for government support of high-tech industries and protection of supply chains in strategic materials and semiconductors, using competition with China as the wedge issue. Republicans pressed for preserving Trump-era trade barriers, cutting exchange programs with China, and (with plenty of liberal support) providing more defense money to stem Chinese "aggression" in Asia.[1]

Biden initially dismissed the idea of competition with China but later said China "seeks to establish itself as a hegemon and a global power player." The United States, he said, finds itself in "an ideological struggle . . . a competition of systems [and] a competition of values" with Beijing and other authoritarian powers.[2] Jake Sullivan put China policy this way: "The goal is not to contain China. It's not to start a new Cold War. It's not to get into conflict. It's to compete vigorously and to push back in service of our values and what we believe to be universal values."[3] By thus defining the competition with China as fundamentally ideological—democracy versus autocracy, our universal values versus their authoritarian values—and not merely technological or commercial, the Biden administration established common ground for a new bipartisan consensus.

At the end of his first year in office, Biden called for a Summit for Democracy, saying it would "bring together the world's democracies to strengthen our democratic institutions, honestly confront the challenge of nations that are backsliding, and forge a common agenda to address threats to our common values." China, of course, was not invited, leading it to ridicule the event as a "false narrative" (democracy/autocracy) that would only hinder China-US cooperation.[4] After all, it was America's democracy that was backsliding. By the time the summit was held, in December 2021, Freedom House rated US democracy at 83 (pre-Trump it had been in the mid-90s) and a third of the participating countries were rated "partly free" or "not free."[5]

Biden's top national security officials added to the China threat theme. The CIA director, William J. Burns, said on establishing a new intelligence-gathering center, that China is "the most important geopolitical threat we face in the 21st century, an increasingly adversarial Chinese government."[6] Antony Blinken's speech on China policy in May 2022 likewise spoke of China as "the most serious long-term challenge to the international order."[7] The official US strategy paper on Asia published early in 2022 highlights China's "coercion and aggression," though it adds that the US objective is "not to change the PRC" but to "manage competition" and seek China's collaboration on "climate change and nonproliferation."[8] The paper is a kitchen sink of challenges, intentions, and capabilities, covering just about every imaginable threat and promising every part of the region both protection and assistance. If there is a common thread in the report, it is coalition building, with notable attention to the Quad and AUKUS. It's largely a Cold War–style document, designed for bipartisan appeal. While the paper does not refer to an ideological contest with China, Blinken's speech did: "Beijing's vision would move us away from the universal values that have sustained so much of the world's progress over the past seventy-five years."

Biden's injection of an ideological element into the competition with China is wrong on several counts. First, it is a needless provocation, irrelevant to making the United States more economically competitive. Could the winner of the competition on, say, artificial intelligence or solar power credibly claim it shows the superiority of one political philosophy over another? Moreover, China's economy is in the throes of major changes, no longer a model of unqualified success. It remains to be seen if its economy can overcome low productivity, high debt, excessive construction, and Xi's attack on entrepreneurial excesses. Biden's effort to revitalize the US economy makes sense in its own right; he doesn't need China to justify it.

Second, adding an ideological element to the relationship with China narrows the room for accommodation and diplomacy, inviting the kind of hostile rhetoric practiced in the Mao era and during the Trump administration. Biden consistently emphasized "leading first with diplomacy" when responding to international problems, yet he seemed to make an exception of China.[9] Sullivan's effort, like Blinken's, to revive American exceptionalism with talk about "universal values" and the "unique [US] capacity and responsibility to help make the world a better place" surely antagonizes the Chinese.[10] Third, an ideological contest with China raises questions about US relations with other countries. One is that some are not democracies. Another is that countries in, say, Southeast Asia and Africa may not want to choose sides and would prefer to have positive relations with both the United States and China. Fourth, an ideological battle muddles the message each side sends and receives about its intentions, for example on Taiwan and the South China Sea, increasing the possibility of miscalculations.

Fifth, and potentially most concerning, putting ideology at the top of the list of US aims is raising alarm bells in Beijing about US interference in its domestic affairs—specifically, seeking to undermine the CCP's leadership. The CCP leadership pointed to several ways in which Western political norms and values were a threat to party supremacy.[11] As Chas Freeman, a senior US diplomat in China during the 1970s and 1980s, said of Biden's China policy, it looked like "a more sophisticated effort to do exactly what the Trump administration tried to do, namely, bring them [the Chinese] down." (By "sophisticated," Freeman was referring to the United States forming a "united front [of allies] against China.")[12] The result has been to feed Chinese nationalism. Leading PRC officials have responded to the ideological challenge by making bravado statements such as this one by Chen Yixin in January 2021: "The rise of China is a major variable [in world affairs] . . . while the rise of the East and the decline of the West has become [a global] trend, and changes of the international landscape are in our favor."[13] "Time and momentum are on China's side," Xi Jinping told senior CCP officials the same month.[14] In orienting US foreign and domestic policy so strongly around China, yet also taking a hard line on Russia, Biden was encouraging the old two-camps, divided-world idea that was central to the earlier Cold War.

The anti-China consensus in the United States led to several pieces of legislation designed to shape a new China policy based on the assumption of a threat to US economic, political, and military ascendancy. Senate majority leader Chuck Schumer and Senator Todd Young of Indiana, for example, co-sponsored the Endless Frontier Act, which would commit more than $100 billion to promote research and development of artificial intelligence, quantum computing, robotics, and other cutting-edge technologies in which China is already a leader. The bipartisan sponsors of the bill ran the gamut of conservative-to-progressive senators. A typical comment came from Congressman Ro Khanna, Democrat representing the Silicon Valley of California: "It's a positive answer to a lot of the anxieties about the rise of China."[15] Or take the Senate's "U.S. Innovation and Competition Act" (USICA), introduced by senators from both parties in 2021.[16] The bill, intended to promote scientific research and subsidize semiconductor chip production, portrays China as an aggressive power determined to "displace" the United States in Asia-Pacific and go on to make China the pivotal economic and technological power in the world. In contrast, the bill describes the United States as a great power that merely wishes to maintain rules and order so that the values of "liberal norms and values" may be preserved for all other countries. Long-standing policy on Taiwan would be abandoned in favor of closer US-Taiwan political and military ties. Like Cold War documents of long ago, the USICA enumerates US aims vis-à-vis China as including maintaining a favorable balance of power, sustaining the US "global leadership role," and preserving the "free flow of commerce."[17]

American public opinion, already reshaped by Trump's China policies, was unprecedentedly hostile to China by the time Biden took office.[18] Republicans were only slightly more concerned than Democrats about the "China threat," but together they accounted for about two-thirds of the public that held negative views of the PRC. By the end of 2021, however, the divide on China between Republicans and Democrats had widened, with Republicans far more committed to considering China an adversary, limiting its global influence, and cutting back on commercial, scientific, and educational exchanges.[19] As a whole, the US public supports sanctions on Chinese officials responsible for human rights violations and prohibitions on the sale of high-tech equipment to China as well as on Chinese involvement in US communications networks. If there is a silver lining in these attitudes, it is that seven in ten Americans still believe in seeking cooperation with China on climate change and arms control. Most do not view China as a *strategic* threat.[20] But like most Congress members, public opinion does not endorse making engagement the core of US-China policy.

Sanctions remain, as under Trump, Biden's preferred way to express US displeasure with China's internal policies. How sanctions are supposed to change China's behavior is never explained. Nor is there an explanation for why direct US-China dialogue should be downgraded, such as occurred when the US treasury secretary, Janet Yellen, reportedly said she would not revive the Strategic and Economic Dialogue with China. Lower-level meetings between US and Chinese officials did go on, but official high-level dialogues were few and far between until the war in Ukraine: a meeting in April 2021 between John Kerry and his Chinese counterpart on climate change, which emerged with a loose pledge of cooperation and a Chinese qualification;[21] a visit to China by Wendy Sherman, the deputy secretary of state, in July 2021, again without improving relations (see below); and a second telephone conversation between Biden and Xi in September, apparently to try to calm the waters ahead of a virtual summit meeting that took place in November. Even then, the official readouts from the September conversation differed considerably, with Biden's very brief reference to "managed competition" contrasting with Xi's emphasis on "engagement and dialogue."

EDUCATIONAL EXCHANGES WITH CHINA:
A SELF-DEFEATING APPROACH

The Biden administration has, with few exceptions, followed and reinforced Trump's crackdown on educational exchanges with China. Like Trump, Biden has supported legislation to force Confucius Institutes to close. His administration initially gave the China Initiative its full support, but in the wake of widespread criticism of the program, the Justice Department ditched it early in 2022 and narrowed the range of prosecutions in order to focus on the most serious espionage cases.[22] Biden made obtaining J-1 and F-1 visas very difficult for Chinese graduate students and researchers, denying them based not on individual cases but on any possible connection they might have to any Chinese "entity" doing "military-civil" research.[23] Chinese-language programs in US schools started moving to Taiwan.[24] A House bill, the America Competes Act of 2022, softened some programs aimed at China but was criticized by those who voted against it because it wasn't harsh enough on China.[25]

Though the FBI insists that China's economic espionage in the United States is a major problem—its director said that every day the bureau finds two new cases and it views Chinese researchers as a "whole-of-society" threat[26]—the Biden administration encountered plenty of pushback against such claims and the China Initiative as a whole. The protests seem to have been the main reason for the China Initiative's termination, and those protests remain important. University administrators cited racial profiling and unfair spotlighting of Chinese scientists. A large group of Stanford University faculty wrote to Attorney General Merrick Garland on September 9, 2021: "the China Initiative disproportionally targets researchers of Chinese origin. Publicly available information indicates that investigations are often triggered not by any evidence of wrongdoing, but just because of a researcher's connections with China." Faculty at Columbia University and the University of Michigan did the same. A University of Arizona survey found that 40 percent of scientists of Chinese descent at US research universities felt racially profiled and under US government surveillance.[27]

The negative consequences for research and the economy also drive American scientists' concerns. One group wrote to say that while the government has a legitimate need to tighten rules governing research security, "a response that chokes off legitimate scientific contacts only compounds the problem it seeks to solve." That group was especially disturbed by FBI arrests, writing that "many of those now accused are accomplished scientists engaged in university research in fundamental science, with close collaborations in China." Putting Chinese science students under scrutiny, the group added, defied the facts and "could deprive our country of some of its most talented future scientists."[28] Indeed, China's "Thousand Talents" program has succeeded at luring back many China-born scientists in the United States who are frustrated and frightened by the undeserved scrutiny.[29] Critics point out that while US universities and laboratories have been "careless about theft of intellectual property. . . . it is an exaggeration to blame China's rise on IP [intellectual property] theft. Some Chinese companies, notably Huawei, have been more innovative than their Western competitors."[30]

Biden's approach is clearly self-defeating, for as numerous educators have said, the US economy needs young Chinese scientists. The China Initiative surely hindered future scientific collaboration. Attending conferences in the United States, for instance, might no longer be attractive to China if its scientists have trouble getting visas and then are watched while in the United States. All the more so if the collaborations with US scientists involve industrial or military applications.[31] Restricting scientific collaboration stifles innovation and undermines the very competitiveness that President Biden is depending on for US economic recovery. As one specialist writes:

> The US government's scrutiny of Chinese Americans and Chinese scholars runs up against the value of open scientific exchange. My research on international collaboration in science has shown that open nations have strong science. Nations that accept visitors and send researchers abroad, those that engage richly in cross-border collaborations and fund international projects produce better science and excel in innovation. Closing doors inhibits the very trait that makes the US innovation system the envy of the world.[32]

In response to complaints from academic and Asian American groups, some Democratic Congress members urged the Justice Department to investigate "the repeated, wrongful targeting of individuals of Asian descent for alleged espionage." Their letter reminded the department of America's long history of anti-Asian prejudice and its contemporary consequences—the increased violence against people of Asian ethnicity.[33] What they failed to call out was the official hostility toward China that had influenced the violence. Still, the letter gave voice to the view of Chinese researchers in the United States, *including those with American citizenship*, who believe they are being targeted for having any connection with China, however ordinary.

The goal of country-to-country transactions should be fairness and mutual benefit. That has not been the goal of recent US policy on educational exchanges with China. Politics has taken command, and in ways that undercut America's own interests. If considered objectively, US officials and Congress members would decide that competitive coexistence with China demands exceptional support of Chinese language and cultural learning, if not with help from Confucius Institutes then directly from the federal budget as proposed in the America Competes Act. Likewise, if competition with China sets the bar, the distinct contribution of science and technology students and researchers from China should be recognized. Blinken, in his May 2022 speech, did so, mentioning 100,000 visas granted to Chinese STEM students in 2021 and saying, "We're thrilled that they've chosen to study in the United States—we're lucky to have them." Upholding the Chinese principle of equality and mutual benefit would require that China treat US educational institutions there as well as Chinese language teachers, students, and visiting scholars in the United States are treated—which is to say, with respect, with ordinary visa requirements, and without biased assumptions about intentions.

DEALING WITH THE REAL CHINA

A realistic China policy for the United States involves several reconsiderations: the role of sanctions; evaluation of the China threat; the equating of China with Russia; and assessment of China's strengths and weaknesses.

Sanctions and other negative incentives fail to project the best of American society and democratic values—not to mention doing nothing to alleviate China's repressive policies. Policy-specific criticism of and competition with China, on the other hand, are certainly in order—for instance, on human rights violations, accountability on the origins of COVID-19, and China's bullying of governments that criticize it—as well as actions against unfair Chinese practices, such as harassing journalists, receiving low-interest World Bank loans, and ignoring foreign investors' intellectual property rights. But "reciprocity" and fairness should be clearly separated from a containment strategy based on exaggerated threat projections.

Mao Zedong once said that "having an enemy is a good thing." Washington and Beijing officials all seem to be following that line. The Biden administration's initial national intelligence estimate (NIE) published in April 2021 ranked China first among threats to the United States: "China increasingly is a near-peer competitor, challenging the United States in multiple arenas—especially economically, militarily and technologically—and is pushing to change global norms."[34] The NIE did not predict a US-PRC military clash but rather a persistent effort by China to "spread China's influence, undercut that of the United States, drive wedges between Washington and its allies and partners, and foster new international norms that favor the

Chinese authoritarian system." As noted, the 2022 Indo-Pacific strategy paper and various national security officials echoed those themes. Thus, Biden's China-watching community evidently had no disagreements with its counterparts in the Trump years.

In the United States, the China threat made the Pentagon's job of refurbishing alliance relationships that much easier, not to mention sustaining high military budgets. Both houses of Congress support legislation to significantly increase US military spending in Asia and upgrade Taiwan's strategic role in US policy. The Defense Department endorses that view. An assistant defense secretary, Ely Ratner, told a Senate committee late in 2021 that Taiwan is "critical to the region's security and critical to the defense of vital U.S. interests in the Indo-Pacific."[35] China's military was similarly engaged in expanding its budget and reach: Its 2021 military budget rose by more than 6 percent, assertedly to improve training and show confidence in the PLA's ability to meet the "strong enemy."[36] In 2022 China will officially spend about $229 billion, compared with a US military budget of around $850 billion. Each country's military establishment benefits from having a main enemy to deter or defeat in a war neither surely wants.

Dealing with the real China requires realism about its capabilities. It is one thing to say that China is a "challenge," another to make it out to be a behemoth. To be sure, China aims to be "a leading power on the world stage, a country with greater ability to shape rules, norms, and institutions toward its preferences. China's leaders have consistently made clear their desire to have their political and economic models respected."[37] In short, like any great power, China seeks to shape an international environment conducive to its internal security and development. That means making its own rules on, for example, the environment, human rights, trade, and aid to developing countries. China is doing so through the BRI, regional trade and financing organizations, and multilateral international groups such as the BRICS (Brazil, Russia, India, China, South Africa). But Beijing faces significant obstacles.

Elizabeth Economy writes that China's role as an international leader is limited by at least three factors: its unwillingness to subordinate its interests to "the general global good," its inability to initiate a major international agreement, and its failure to convince other governments that a Chinese-led world is desirable.[38] To those points I would add failure to match words with deeds, common among followers of power politics, for example when it comes to abiding by its own principles of nonintervention and respect for territorial integrity. In short, China has a leadership deficit, as I argued in the discussion of Chinese policy in the Ukraine war. Beijing's assault on human rights, the backlash against the BRI by some governments, and inconsistencies in environmental policies are among the other weak points in China's international standing.

Noteworthy is that prominent Chinese experts add to the criticism. Professor Yan Xuetong, dean of the Institute of International Relations at Tsinghua (Qinghua) University, cites China's lack of *moral* authority:

> Many people wrongly believe that China can improve its foreign relations only by significantly increasing economic aid. But it's hard to buy affection; such "friendship" does not stand the test of difficult times. How then can China win people's hearts across the world? According to ancient Chinese philosophers, it must start at home. Humane authority [王道, literally "the kingly way"] begins by creating a desirable model at home that inspires people abroad.[39]

Professor Shi Yinhong at Renmin University mentions other constraints on China's influence: "The appeal of China's 'soft power' in the world, the resources and experiences available to China, are quite limited, and the domestic and international obstacles China will encounter, including the complexities created by the coronavirus pandemic, are considerable."[40]

What is particularly relevant about all these comments is the unspoken reference point: the post–World War II international leadership role of the United States. At that time the United States possessed the economic and military capabilities, the political attractiveness, and the moral authority to lead the West out of the dark days that followed the defeat of the Axis powers. That leadership was reflected in the pivotal role of the United States in creating the United Nations, in the Marshall Plan for European recovery, and in the Bretton Woods system of global finance and commerce. While Xi's China hopes to offer the world an alternative leadership model, it has a long way to go in all of those leadership categories save, perhaps, economic strength, which happens to be the one area in which China benefits enormously from the global capitalist order.

In sum, we need a more realistic assessment of China, not one looked at through the lens of the Cold War with Russia or of power politics. Realism here means a balanced assessment of China's strengths and weaknesses, intentions, and capabilities. It should not mean an "inescapable . . . competition and conflict" that makes a new Cold War not only inevitable but "more likely [than the Cold War with the Soviet Union] to turn hot."[41] I'm partial to the kind of realism expressed in an open letter to President Trump in 2019, signed by numerous China and international affairs specialists (myself included). The letter called for rethinking US-China relations on the basis that, first, China's threat to US interests was exaggerated and, second, US efforts to contain China or thwart its rise would be counterproductive. "We do not believe Beijing is an economic enemy or an existential national security threat that must be confronted in every sphere; nor is China a monolith, or the views of its leaders set in stone. . . . The fear that Beijing will replace the

United States as the global leader is exaggerated. Most other countries have no interest in such an outcome, and it is not clear that Beijing itself sees this goal as necessary or feasible." The letter called for a "balance of cooperation and competition" in US policy on China.[42]

THE MILITARY COMPETITION

The military competition with China has become a heated topic in the wake of China bashing. Besides assertions about a Chinese threat to Taiwan, official US attention focuses on continuing Chinese investments in air and naval power, nuclear weapons, and cyber capabilities. China's naval modernization has drawn the most attention: It is said to challenge the US Navy's predominance in Asia-Pacific since before World War II. The chief aim of China's navy seems to be to deny or delay US forces' access to Taiwan and nearby areas.[43] Other Chinese maritime forces—the coast guard and maritime militia—have been especially active in the South China Sea. To counteract China's presumed strategy of deterrence and denial, Biden has emulated Obama's pivot to Asia, shifting air and naval forces from the Middle East to Asia. At a briefing of the Pentagon's annual global posture review, an official said the purpose of the force redeployments is "to enable improved warfighting readiness and increased activities" in the Indo-Pacific. The Pentagon announced new air deployments to Australia and "infrastructure improvements" in Guam and elsewhere in the region. The briefing also indicated that the United States is "seeking greater regional access for military partnership activities."[44] Analysts in friendly non-allied countries such as Indonesia, Philippines, and Vietnam are suggesting greater US attention to China's military power and the military aid to match it, even as they caution against overreliance.[45] Here again, nothing is said about engaging China diplomatically or assessing how US actions may be provoking Chinese counteractions. Thus do the parallel buildups of US and Chinese forces in the Asia-Pacific fuel talk about a new Cold War.

The same mutual force increases hold for nuclear weapons. The authoritative 2021 Stockholm International Peace Research Institute states that "China is in the middle of a significant modernization and expansion of its nuclear arsenal."[46] At present China is believed to have 350 nuclear weapons, far below the nearly 6,000 in the US arsenal.[47] The US capability for delivering such weapons by air or sea, moreover, far exceeds China's. But the Pentagon reports that China's arsenal could rise to 1,000 nuclear weapons by around 2030 and that China's ability to deliver nuclear weapons is rapidly increasing, for example by deploying sea-based ballistic missiles.[48] A report from a Monterey, California, research organization, based on satellite observations, suggests that China is constructing more than one hundred new missile silos in the western desert province of Gansu.[49] That means China's intercontinental ballistic missiles (ICBMs) and therefore its nuclear warhead numbers are likely to increase significantly, though some silos may be deliberately kept empty to make detection more difficult.

Beijing has consistently refused to take part in strategic weapons talks on the argument that an agreement would freeze its second-tier status. Will that position change once its nuclear numbers and delivery systems start to catch up with those of the United States and Russia? One writer suggests that the United States should acknowledge "mutual nuclear vulnerability with China." Recalling "the 1985 Reagan-[Mikhail] Gorbachev joint statement that 'a nuclear war cannot be won and must never be fought,'" the writer argues that a "similar mutual commitment by U.S. and Chinese leaders would help defuse today's emerging arms race."[50] It might also pave the way to talks on mutual nuclear arms reductions. The Biden administration is reportedly worried about another nuclear arms race getting out of control, yet the new hotline that was set up by Xi and Obama to prevent a misreading of intentions is apparently not being used by the Chinese.[51] And strategic arms talks between these adversaries still seem a long way off.[52]

Why is China, once a strong advocate of "no first use" of nuclear weapons, now investing heavily in nuclear weapons and delivery systems? One view is that "by limiting the vulnerability and increasing the numbers of its nuclear forces, Chinese strategists may grow more confident that the Chinese military can challenge the United States or its allies conventionally, with little fear that the United States would resort to nuclear escalation."[53] This is a very old argument, once made to explain how Soviet nuclear strategy would neutralize US forces and facilitate Moscow's interventions in the Third World. Yet these days it is the United States that, post-Afghanistan, is redistributing military forces to Asia. The same authors mention a more convincing alternative explanation of China's motives: that it seeks to increase the survivability of its nuclear weapons and deterrence of a theoretical US nuclear first strike. The preponderance of US nuclear weapons, anti-missile defenses, and security alliances that ring China may finally have persuaded Chinese strategists that their country has to respond beyond conventional military preparedness.

The urgency of nuclear arms talks became even more apparent in fall 2021, when Pentagon sources expressed alarm over reports that China had tested a hypersonic missile. That missile, if armed with a nuclear weapon and able to fly in low orbit over the South Pole, would be a less detectable and more accurate weapon than an ordinary ballistic missile. The Chinese denied the reports, saying it had carried out a routine test of a space vehicle. General Milley said the Chinese test was "very close" to a "Sputnik moment." Little was said about US plans to deploy a hypersonic weapon.[54] But just as the

"Sputnik moment" in 1957 turned out not to be a missile gap in the Soviets' favor—the reverse was actually true—this hypersonic moment will not alter the US-China military balance. In contrast with China, the US military has a far-flung network of bases and allies—by one count, eighty-one bases on every continent except Antarctica, compared to one for China (in Djibouti, east Africa)[55]—a military budget roughly three times China's, and an overall power-projection capability that is without peer—not to mention the large gap in nuclear arsenals. The Chinese, with an eye to how the Soviet Union bankrupted itself by trying to catch up to the United States in strategic weapons, most likely are aiming at strengthening their nuclear deterrent.[56]

But weapons, money, and strategy are not the only elements in the military equation. The PLA, like the military in all countries, operates in a political environment; it is one piece in a vast bureaucracy under the CCP's leadership. "The Party controls the gun," as Mao said. The PLA's budget, mission, and operations are subject to a decision-making process that surely involves debate over party priorities and bureaucratic self-interest, which in turn will be affected by the state of the economy, society, and of course relations with the United States and (especially in light of the war in Ukraine) Russia. For example, the PLA and its offshoot, the People's Armed Police, are likely to be preoccupied in coming years with domestic security problems. Control of ethnic minorities comes immediately to mind, but another may be environmental crises, as Michael Klare points out.[57] The PLA's perspective may be affected by Russia's conduct of the war in Ukraine. Russia's failure to achieve its territorial objectives, as seems likely, may incline PLA leaders to request significant budgetary increases on the argument that the Chinese military must not repeat the errors of Russian war planning and performance.

The chief US concern with China's military should be about misreading of intentions and miscalculation of actions. Ever since Chinese entry in the Korean War, failure to communicate has occasionally led to serious confrontations of the kind mentioned previously, such as the mistaken Belgrade embassy bombing or the aircraft collision over Hainan. During Trump's last days in office, we learned that General Milley was so worried about the president's mental state that he twice called his Chinese counterpart to reassure him that the United States was not going to attack. The hypersonic missile presents another situation with the potential for a US-China miscalculation. Instead of seeking to curb further testing and ban deployment of that missile, Washington and Beijing seem headed for another, and extremely expensive, arms race.[58]

The United States and China cannot afford the unforeseen consequences of reliance mainly on high-level, spur-of-the-moment interventions when air and sea incidents occur. The US Defense Department asserts that it is engaged with China's military on conflict prevention:

The pace and scope of the PLA modernization and expansion provides opportunities as well as challenges for U.S.-PRC defense relations. As the PLA develops and expands its reach globally, the risk of an accident or miscalculation also increases, putting a premium on risk reduction efforts and highlighting the need to ensure the safety of U.S. forces operating in close proximity. This evolving condition has further emphasized the importance of establishing timely communications during a crisis, and to maintaining regular communication channels to prevent crisis and conduct post crisis assessments.[59]

Yet Biden has not seemed in a rush to deal with military-to-military relations: He decided in summer 2021 to resume military-to-military talks with China but limited them to low-level officers. Both Chinese think-tank specialists and some former US officials criticized Biden's decision. Rosh Doshi writes that the United States and China have "no framework to effectively manage escalation risks emanating from conventional challenges like intercepts or emerging challenges in new domains."[60] And Max Baucus, a former US ambassador to China, said: "We're making a mistake by not trying to find some way to properly, carefully deal with China. The more we shift toward a decoupling, the more we stand to risk falling into deeper problems."[61]

"STALEMATE": THE CHINESE PERSPECTIVE

Mere contact is not engagement, and contact without proposals or incentives to promote further contact is unlikely to improve relations. That is why Biden's China policy is deeply disappointing to the Chinese, since they had every reason to expect a significant departure from Trump's attempted bullying. Other Chinese officials echo that view, suggesting that the best China can hope for is that, compared with the Trump years, Biden will come around to paying China more attention and finding areas of common ground. Chinese public opinion likewise is only slightly less negative about prospects for an improvement in relations with the United States since Biden took over for Trump.[62] The visit to China of Wendy Sherman in mid-2021 illustrates the US-China divide. Her visit was an attempt to lower the temperature in US-China relations, but all that apparently happened was an exchange of want lists, leading Sherman's Chinese counterpart, Xie Feng, to say the two countries were at a "stalemate."[63]

The Chinese perspective also reflects defensiveness in reaction to the Biden administration's tough posture. The analyses of two of China's most prominent America watchers, Yan Xuetong and Wang Jisi,[64] are representative. Both claim that post-pandemic China is now economically and technologically on par with the United States, and both seem buoyed by the divisions in American politics and society. But they do not gloat and do not claim the title for China of global leader. Instead, they argue that Beijing will no longer be "intimidated" by Washington; China is now a global power, entitled to "equal footing." The United States is still seen as driving the relationship, pressing on China to conform to its worldview and still seeking to "contain" China. Thus, "it is up to the US" to change course, they say; its China policy stems from arrogance and conceit; it is using its allies to gang up on China ("isolating China with a multilateral club strategy," Yan writes); it is the "hidden hand" that constantly meddles in China's internal affairs; it fails to take China's core interests into consideration; it is wrongly depicting China as another Soviet Union or Japan; it is still playing the hegemon, seeking to thwart China's rise and stay on top of the world.

Although such comments are intended to project China's new self-confidence and play to certain domestic and foreign audiences, the vocabulary conveys a different message. Using language such as "push back," "deter," "correct its mistakes," and "retaliate" points to reactiveness and suggests that China is still operating from insecurity about its place in the world and its status in relation to the United States. Thus, for example, China's crackdowns on human rights are explained as responses forced on the leadership by US interference in China—part of what Wang Jisi describes as "a comprehensive, long-term strategy to safeguard the CCP leadership." Similarly, Yan Xuetong says the Biden's administration's strategy "has brought about much more difficulties to China's economic development and pressure on China's diplomatic relations than Trump's unilateral strategy."[65]

Thus, long after the "century of humiliation" by the West, the China-as-victim narrative is still in vogue. To be sure, the newly assertive China (the one of the "Chinese Dream") is also apparent—the China that acts boldly when its core interests are at stake. Yet on the whole, outward toughness may mask inward uncertainty. Beijing's responses to US actions have largely been defensive and reactive—sanctions, military maneuvers, wolf-warrior diplomatic aggressiveness, and complaints about unacceptable interference in China's internal affairs. Even the BRI, which many observers consider a prime example of a Chinese *initiative* in foreign affairs, for some Chinese analysts is another defensive move to offset Western aid programs and supply chain disruptions.

To illustrate, I present below two Chinese views, one from a senior official—Wang Yi, the foreign minister—the other from a CCP insider, Jin Canrong, a senior professor and dean in the School of International Studies at Renmin University. Wang Yi's remarks came during his meeting with Wendy Sherman and were reported on the foreign ministry's home page.[66]

Wang Yi says, the new US administration by and large is continuing the extreme and mistaken China policy of the preceding administration. It is constantly challenging China's bottom line and tightening its containment of China. China firmly opposes this. All the issues I have posed at bottom rest on US perceptions of China, on regarding China as the most important opponent and even more toward being an enemy. It is attempting to block and interrupt China's progress of modernization. This attempt neither now nor even more in the future will not be realized.

Wang then gave the standard history lesson on China's development and its popular approval, its peaceful intentions, and its desire to aim for the good life just like the United States. Wang assured Sherman that China's development "does not challenge America and does not wish to replace America." In a clear response to Biden's ideological challenge, Wang said: "We do not export ideology and a development model, because we have a basic standpoint, which is that every country should seek its own development road in keeping with its national conditions."

As to how to manage US-China differences, Wang offered three conditions. Again, note the defensive language: *Stop doing* certain things. "First, the US must not challenge, undermine, or even attempt to overthrow China's road and system of socialism with special characteristics." Second, the United States must not interfere with China's development, specifically by imposing unilateral sanctions, high tariffs, and technology blocks. Third, with reference especially to Taiwan among other territorial issues, "the US must not invade China's national sovereignty" or "destroy its territorial integrity." (On Taiwan, Wang said that if Taiwan were to declare independence, "China has the right to take any steps necessary to prevent it.") Wang ended with the hope that the United States would "return to a rational and pragmatic" China policy. "Peaceful coexistence" and, "even better," win-win cooperation, would keep the two countries from a "great calamity."

Here are excerpts from a talk Jin Canrong is said to have given early in 2021, evidently to a non-Chinese audience:

I think the fundamental contradiction in Sino-US relations is that the US cannot accept the rise of China and does not recognize the right of the 1.4 billion people to grow and develop. Once this nation [the United States] recognizes you as an opponent it is useless to pray for a compromise. Frankly speaking, surrender is not the way out. You have to stand up and fight him so he [the United States] is convinced. . . . From China's perspective, we certainly have some expectations for the Biden administration in the US. What do we expect? We expect stability in China-US relations. The US-China relationship is very important to China. And in fact, it is also important to the US. However, from my observation, the US is still a bit arrogant. The US still attaches far less importance to China than vice versa. It is not reciprocal. . . . So, my bold projection should be that overall the US-China relationship in the Biden era will be better than the last three years of the Trump era, especially better than the one in 2020. But to what extent it will improve we do not know. . . . So how to face this problem? Dialogue is necessary and both sides must work together to find ways to control these problems. . . . Solidify the dialogue through one or more breakthroughs and then include other areas so that the whole relationship can be stabilized. . . . if we can stabilize the US-China relationship during the next four years of the Biden administration stopping downward spiral that would be a good achievement.[67]

Jin Canrong's narrative jibes with the Chinese leaders' concern about arousing public anger by appearing to make concessions to the United States. But underlying that concern is a deeper reality. The United States is depicted as being in the driver's seat in the relationship; China is not as important to the United States as the United States is important to China. Thus, China is *awaiting a change in America's behavior* and hoping, as Jin says, that relations "will not deteriorate further." Such remarks suggest that while China's leaders have ambitions to claim global leadership parity with the United States, they lack confidence in their ability to "stabilize" relations. All Jin can suggest is more dialogue, but no specific agenda—a telling admission of the limits of nationalist bravado on display these days by wolf-warrior diplomats.[68]

Chapter 7

Four Cases of
US-China Competition

The stumbling blocks to US-China engagement extend beyond national security and human rights. The two countries have dueling policies on many issues; here I discuss the pandemic's origins, aid to developing countries, climate change and energy, and commercial relations. The competition is taking place across the global map, though politics in the United States and China importantly shapes it. Here again, however, opportunities for cooperative US-PRC projects exist if their leaders are engagement-minded.

PANDEMIC DIPLOMACY

China's refusal to grant WHO's request in July 2021 for another site visit to obtain more data made clear that the Chinese feared the lab leak theory would be born out. That and other unresolved questions about the origins of the coronavirus helped shape Biden's early response to China's role in the pandemic. About a half year into his administration, he directed another round of investigations of the origins, leading some observers to infer that Biden, like Trump, suspected a lab leak in Wuhan as the source. But the report proved inconclusive.[1] COVID's origin endures, not only as a political issue in the United States, but also as another in a long list of US-China problems. As Francis Collins, Biden's former director of the National Institutes of Health, said: "The Chinese government should be on notice that we have to have answers to questions that have not been answered about those people who got sick in November who worked in the lab and about those lab notebooks that have not been examined. If they really want to be exonerated from this claim of culpability, then they have got to be transparent."[2]

When the omicron variant of COVID became prominent in 2021, China's approach—"zero COVID"—raised serious doubts among medical professionals abroad.[3] The policy imposed severe restrictions, including quarantines and frequent testing of populations in about forty cities, most prominently Hong Kong and Shanghai, in a possibly futile attempt to eliminate infections altogether. Omicron is so readily transmissible that complete eradication would seem impossible; the variant just kept popping up, revealing the lower effectiveness of Chinese vaccines. China's economy took a major hit as consumer demand went down and supply chains were disrupted. Popular protests ensued. Police and health authorities relied on a ubiquitous cell phone health code app to monitor people's movements, using it to identify anyone who might spread the disease but also making the health code another element of the surveillance state for nabbing fugitives and tracking dissidents.[4] Yet Americans cannot be self-righteous about China's extreme approach—not when, by the spring of 2022, US deaths from the pandemic reached one million.

FOREIGN AID: BRI OR B3W?

China's BRI represents an ambitious approach to global trade and investment, mainly by foreign aid in the form of loans to low- and middle-income countries. The consequences, intended and otherwise, may be illustrated with two recent stories. In Gambia, west Africa, there sits a Chinese fish-processing plant that is a major employer and producer of fishmeal, which is crucial to aquaculture. The Golden Lead plant, one of three in Gambia, is also an environmental hazard; the waste endangers numerous varieties of plants, birds, and animals in a nearby wildlife reserve.[5] China's BRI in Gambia includes debt cancellation and major Chinese investments in agriculture and fishing. Global aquaculture is gradually displacing the traditional fishing industry, and China is not only deploying fishing vessels in Gambian waters and pulverizing local fish for export to China and other countries; it is also shipping more expensive fish from China back to Gambia. A second story: Under the BRI in the Czech Republic, China granted Home Credit the first license for a foreign firm to offer home loans in China. In return for this lucrative arrangement, China got back a great deal: a pro-China public relations campaign led by the Czech Republic's president, Home Credit's chief executive, and various Chinese-invested companies, culminating in an official visit by Xi Jinping in 2016. But the romance didn't last as the Czech security services, among others, criticized the kowtowing to China and rejected adoption of the Huawei 5G network.[6] China issued its usual thinly veiled warning, a foreign ministry spokesman saying he hoped the Czechs will "correct their wrongdoing as soon as possible and not recklessly damage overall China-Czech relations. Otherwise, their own interests will be harmed at the end of the day."[7]

The BRI in Gambia and the Czech Republic are just two of thousands of cases of Chinese-financed projects that span the globe, from the poorest African nations to relatively well-off Europeans. Chinese loans and investments are offered in exchange for raw materials, acceptance of Chinese workers, access to transportation links, and usually well-hidden political concessions. The brainchild of Xi Jinping in 2013, BRI (actually comprised of several "Silk Roads" that reflect its global reach and specializations[8]) is touted by China as a generous development assistance program which, unlike aid from Western-dominated institutions such as the World Bank and the International Monetary Fund, has no strings attached—no human rights requirements of recipients, no environmental constraints, no heavy interest payments, and no infringements of sovereignty. All these claims have been challenged by scholars and other investigators.

One of the most ambitious studies of BRI, by the research lab AidData, examined more than 13,000 Chinese aid projects over an eighteen-year period.[9] The study found declining interest in the BRI due to the onerous terms of engagement, starting with the debt burden and problems in project implementation. These latter include China's insistence on mainly using Chinese labor on major development projects, the dominant position it sometimes acquires in critical areas of the host country's economy (such as telecommunications and transportation), and the corruption and environmental damage occasioned by BRI projects. Other studies show that China is not always able to promote its economic, political, and security interests in return for loans. The Czech case above is one example. Governments in Southeast Asia also have agency when dealing with the BRI. When political, business, and other local elites assess the costs and benefits of partnering with China, they have sometimes decided against it.[10]

Critics who cite the "debt trap" say Chinese state-owned commercial banks foist large loans on recipient countries that have little to no chance of repaying, thus giving China leverage to expand its political influence, garner support for its foreign policies (such as on Taiwan or the South China Sea), and demand repayment in resources, as in the Gambia example above. Here are four other examples, starting with the most-cited one in Sri Lanka:

- China's unrepaid loans to Sri Lanka forced its government to surrender control of Hambantota Port, operated by China Merchants Group, on a 99-year lease. The port sits nearly idle.[11] In 2022 Sri Lanka is near bankruptcy, unable to pay a total foreign debt estimated at $38 billion, with its government under assault from popular protests. China accounts for about 10 percent of the debt, as does Japan, but China charges much higher interest (3.3 percent versus Japan's 0.7 percent). Before the protests, additional Chinese loans were under discussion, essentially to help repay existing loans.[12]

- Muslim Pakistan's endorsement of Chinese policies in Xinjiang came at a time when the BRI's signature project, the China-Pakistan Economic Corridor (CPEC), was providing Pakistan with up to $60 billion.[13]
- China has acquired a dominant position in Laos, achieved in large part with a $6-billion high-speed railway that runs more than 600 miles between Kunming (Yunnan Province) and Vientiane, the Laotian capital. No other country, including the United States, has paid Laos much attention. The railway will benefit Laotian exports and tourism, but it will probably be an even greater economic (and perhaps strategic) advantage for China. To get the railway, Laos had to add to its high indebtedness with a $1.5 billion Chinese loan and provide tax breaks and space for Chinese and other foreign corporations in a special economic zone.[14]
- In Montenegro there is a partially built highway, lampooned as a highway to nowhere, that was financed by the China Export-Import Bank with a $1-billion loan. The current government of Montenegro, already burdened with debt, sees no way to repay the loan—in which case, under terms of the contract signed by Montenegro's previous administration, China may seize land, just as happened in Laos.[15]

Such practices have often been labeled neocolonialism, which Malaysia's prime minister warned about in deciding to back out of the BRI in 2018.[16]

A more favorable assessment of the BRI and the debt issue comes from the Johns Hopkins University–based China Africa Research Initiative (CARI). It studied World Bank data on China's loans from 2014 to 2018 to seventy-two low-income developing countries. The study offers two important findings: first, most BRI recipients are not as deeply trapped by China's debt as is often charged, and second, China has stepped in where Western aid has retreated, especially in Africa, and has cancelled the debt of a number of the poorest countries.[17] While the AidData study mentions ten developing country recipients whose debts to China amount to more than 10 percent of their GNP, the CARI study offers qualifications. The seventy-two countries "owed Chinese creditors $104 billion out of a total disbursed and outstanding debt of $514 billion. $64 billion of this Chinese debt, or 62 percent, was disbursed in Africa, putting China second only to the World Bank." Only two countries, Angola and Pakistan, accounted for substantial portions of both debt to China (34 percent) and debt servicing payments (50 percent). Nor was China the only debt holder; Japan, Saudi Arabia, and various bondholders typically account for around 80 percent of a lender's debt. And China's portion of the debt of those countries in the worst debt circumstances is low (15 percent).[18]

"That is to say, their debt problems are largely caused by lenders other than China," the authors of the CARI report conclude.

Debts aside, some Chinese aid projects under the BRI, such as training programs in Africa for civil service, media, and business, do seem to yield practical skills as well as a positive impression of China's economy.[19] One even-handed study of the multibillion-dollar CPEC project finds that while it has not met specific community needs in some parts of Pakistan and has damaged local environments, it has promoted jobs and diverse energy sources.[20]

Beijing may be reevaluating the scope and size of the BRI, at least in Africa, judging from the Forum on China-Africa Cooperation, which meets every three years. At the most recent gathering, in Dakar, Senegal, in December 2021, the Chinese announced that aid would be reduced significantly, both in worldwide total (from the usual $60 billion to $40 billion for the cycle) and in specific programs, such as scholarships and training. Infrastructure development wasn't mentioned at all, and some key projects, such as public health, were also severely cut back. Only projects that promote African exports will receive additional funds, reflecting China's effort to reduce the huge surplus in its favor in Africa trade. In sum, China may be responding to two concerns: sensitivity over criticism of loans that have created indebtedness and rising costs without commensurate gains.[21]

Security is another issue China faces as BRI projects spread. Take the CPEC, for example: One careful study has found that while the project is welcomed by Pakistan's elites, it thrusts China into a highly insecure environment where, like some other BRI projects in politically unstable countries, Chinese can become targets of militant groups—in Pakistan's case, Baloch insurgents—that do not benefit from the CPEC.[22] From another angle, China faces growing kickback from Pakistan's military, which is reportedly upset with the political leadership over the country's distancing from the United States.[23] China's budding relationship with the Taliban in Afghanistan is another example. Mining projects face resistance from the main Taliban opposition, the Islamic State Khorasan, which has already carried out one suicide bombing in retaliation for Chinese repression of Uyghurs.[24] In fact, it might be said that the greater the involvement of Chinese in BRI projects—as investors, officials, workers, and engineers—the more likely are they to stir up local anger and force Beijing to rethink some of its BRI projects, especially those that involve resource extraction.

In sum, the best and the worst that can be said of the BRI, when judged as a foreign aid program, is that it has sometimes promoted a country's economic development and environment, sometimes harmed it, and sometimes done little either way. It has loaned money for good reasons and wasted money on unsound ideas. Politically, China has won friends and alienated others, especially when it bumps up against local nationalism. The verdict is out on how sustainable the BRI is given its costs and, quite possibly, criticism back home—again, no different from the politics of Western aid programs.[25] From the Chinese leadership's point of view, the costs may be worth the soft-power influence the BRI creates, especially in poor countries that are of little interest to the United States and Europe. AidData reports that Chinese aid to developing countries is now twice as much as Western aid, though overwhelmingly in loans rather than outright grants. China is winning the aid game hands down, all the more so in Africa—"the central human story of the century," the veteran journalist Howard French maintains, and "one that the US has a profound and all but unrecognized interest in."[26]

The US view of the BRI is captured in the Senate's USICA, which, as previously noted, follows the bipartisan view of a monolithic Chinese threat. The act says the BRI "increases the economic influence of state-owned Chinese firms in global markets, enhances the PRC's political leverage with government leaders around the world, and provides greater access to strategic nodes such as ports and railways. Through BRI, the PRC seeks political deference through economic dependence."[27] The Biden administration asked the G7 group to rally around an alternative aid program, Build Back Better World (B3W), a takeoff on the president's Build Back Better domestic program. The G7 agreed to add hundreds of billions of dollars in economic aid to developing countries.[28] "Strategic competition with China" was the announced aim. Biden expressed the hope that, "together with the private sector, other U.S. stakeholders, and G7 partners, B3W will collectively catalyze hundreds of billions of dollars of infrastructure investment for low- and middle-income countries in the coming years."[29]

This competitive approach to foreign aid takes developing countries back to the Cold War era. If US-China engagement were the underlying aid philosophy, the two countries would find common cause to help alleviate developing country poverty and promote market opportunities. Energy, science and technology, and environmental protection were among the areas of US-China cooperation that Xi Jinping proposed to Biden in their third conversation.[30] Secretary Blinken, in the administration's first take on an Africa policy, made a good start. He rejected Cold War competition with China, proposed a "race to the top" instead, and did not repeat the Trump administration's criticism of the BRI as a debt trap. Blinken's emphasis was on transparency and the quality of aid projects.[31]

These points are germane to an emerging, and potentially avoidable, competition in Africa over a highly valuable mineral: cobalt.

The Democratic Republic of Congo (DRC) holds most of the world's cobalt mines.[32] Cobalt is an essential mineral in electric car batteries as well as cell phones, a fact that has not escaped both China and the United States. In 2016 the American multinational Freeport McMoRan sold one of the main cobalt mines in the DRC to China Molybdenum, a Chinese state bank–supported company. US officials in Washington, preoccupied with other world problems, evidently disregarded warnings of the sale and took no steps to support a US stake in the mines. Additional mine sales followed. China Molybdenum now either owns or finances fifteen of nineteen DRC cobalt mines, leaving US officials wondering how to get back in the game and US automakers worrying about supply sources and substitutes for cobalt.

Here, then, is a case study of how the climate crisis and the clean energy competition intersect with the US-China competition for strategic metals. China's dominant position in cobalt mining poses the challenge of controlling the electric car market, thwarting or at least complicating US prospects for transitioning away from gas-guzzling autos. One factor in America's favor: the Chinese firm's conduct in the DRC, which includes charges of cheating and failing to deliver on contracts, safety and environmental violations, and corrupt practices with Congolese officials. US-based companies such as Tesla and Apple, as part of the supply chain, are caught up in child labor abuse suits by various NGOs. Hence, both US and Chinese companies as well as the DRC government and mine workers would benefit from a cooperative approach to cobalt mining.[33]

The larger picture on US-China cooperation in developing countries would see the United States joining the Chinese-initiated RCEP and China joining (and the United States rejoining) the CPTPP. This is not an entirely novel idea when we recall that in June 2020, Xi Jinping gave a speech at a COVID-19 event in which he said: "We encourage Chinese financial institutions to respond to the G-20's Debt Service Suspension Initiative (DSSI) and to hold friendly consultations with African countries according to market principles to work out arrangements for commercial loans with sovereign guarantees."[34] Such a collaborative effort would bring in the World Bank and conceivably the United States, Europe, and Japan to help the most debt-distressed countries. The first order of business, however, is a change in Washington's attitude, from aiming to outcompete China to joining forces with it.

THE GLOBAL ENVIRONMENTAL CRISIS

China is on pace to be simultaneously the world leader in renewable energy production and carbon dioxide emissions. Its extraordinary economic rise has created both a huge and seemingly unquenchable demand for energy, thereby also establishing the rationale for scientific advances in energy research and development. Thus, rising China is both an environmental victim and beneficiary—putting more and more pollutants into the air and ground while also becoming a world leader in wind, solar, and hydroelectric power.

Xi Jinping has promised to make China carbon neutral by 2060, meaning China will remove from the environment as much carbon as it introduces. That would be an extraordinary achievement given that China is now responsible for about 27 percent of global carbon emissions (versus 11 percent for the United States) and continues to depend heavily on coal, consuming more than the rest of the world combined. Even though coal as a percentage of China's total energy *capacity* was less than 50 percent in 2021, its *reliance* on coal for energy still stood at about 60 percent, compared with 24 percent reliance on renewable sources. Investments in renewable sources—wind, solar, and hydroelectric power—are admirably high and rising fast, but investment in new coal-fired plants is far higher.[35] Investment in nuclear power is rising, too, but still only accounts for roughly 5 percent of China's total electricity generation.[36]

Abroad, China until recently was financing coal plant construction, notably in Africa (Zimbabwe), under the BRI.[37] Overall, "Chinese financing was involved in 13 percent of the [world's] coal power capacity operational or under development between 2013 and mid-2019," with 43 percent of the financing going to low- and middle-income countries.[38] The China Development Bank and the Export-Import Bank of China together funded $474 million worth of coal projects outside China in 2020 alone.[39] China has sold nuclear power plants to a number of BRI countries, mainly to Pakistan and Turkey, as well as to a few countries outside the BRI, such as Romania. But opposition from the United States and within some recipient countries based on the usual concerns about nuclear power plants—safety and cost—has put the brakes on these sales. Still, China is in the highly competitive nuclear game and will continue to promote nuclear exports as an extension of its climate-change posture.[40]

China does not count carbon emissions from overseas-funded coal plants in its emissions figures. The omission is significant, "about 3.5% of the annual CO2 emissions from the entire global power sector outside of China." The two Chinese overseas development banks do not yet have environmental restrictions on their loans. On the positive side, Chinese investments in energy sources overseas in recent years has been shifting to non–fossil fuel sources, primarily hydroelectric power.[41] And in September 2021 at the opening session of the UN General Assembly, Xi promised to end Chinese financing of overseas coal plants. Therein lies a possible US-PRC and multilateral collaboration: jointly investing in renewable energy projects in energy-poor countries, even those under the BRI.

Coal investments abroad, which would include plants being built before Xi's promise, along with planned coal power construction at home—which would be around six times Germany's coal capacity—make China less of a leader on climate change than would appear. Those and related investments abroad in steel and coal amount to exporting climate change. Politics, moreover, interferes with even the best intentions, as is true everywhere: Power outages and an energy shortage in winter 2021 forced China to reopen coal mines, just when the COP26 international conference on climate change was getting under way in Scotland. As John Kerry said after a visit to China, "Can the world afford to have China, as already the number one emitter, continuing to grow in those emissions over the next 10 years? No."[42] In short, Xi's climate change plans are likely to be too little, too late.

Still, China is well ahead of the United States in technological innovations to transition from the fossil fuel–dependent economy, such as in battery cells, solar panels, and wind power. Biden pledged to reduce carbon emissions by 50 percent by 2030, a notable goal but one that would require major changes in America's transportation and energy patterns. Many of the country's major corporations, including some that had pledged to be carbon neutral down the road, lined up against Biden's green energy plan in the fractious debate of fall 2021. Ultimately, unlike China, changes of that magnitude are a matter of American politics, which includes jobs for workers in industries that rely on fossil fuels. They would need to find employment in "green" sectors, such as electric cars and solar power. And affording the latest high-tech, energy-saving devices and machines will surely be a major obstacle for all but the wealthiest Americans.

TRADE, INVESTMENT, AND TECHNOLOGY: WHAT DECOUPLING?

In Asia specifically, China is the lead trade partner for every country, including US allies such as Japan and South Korea. China has roughly three times the regional trade volume of the United States. China also has a healthy lead over the United States and Japan in regional direct investment. Thus, while by one power index the United States leads China in defense networks and diplomatic and cultural influence, it follows well behind China on the commercial side.[43] For instance, in 2020 China's total trade with Southeast Asia, about $685 billion, was nearly twice that of the United States. One would think that the trend in China's favor in trade and investment would be accompanied by a downward arc in US-China commercial relations, but that has not been the case except in certain advanced technologies as described below.

Despite the pandemic, unresolved trade issues with China, and supply chain bottlenecks, trade and investment between the United States and China have been unexpectedly positive. For all the speculation about a decoupling of the two economies, including a flight of capital away from China, nothing of the sort has happened. As two writers reported, "bilateral trade in goods is

an area of stability in a relationship that has otherwise continued to deteriorate," even though the large US trade deficit in goods has not changed significantly.[44] In 2019, US merchandise exports to China came to $163 billion,
while imports from China were $471 billion, for a US deficit of $308 billion.
In 2020, the United States exported $110 billion worth of goods to China
and imported $393 billion for a deficit of $283 billion. China remains the
third most important export market for the United States (after Canada and
Mexico) and the top source of imports. Among those Chinese imports is US
liquefied natural gas (LNG). Despite US-China tensions, US LNG exports
to China are booming, and in many instances their contracts with China's oil
import firm are long-term. US firms are second only to Australia's in LNG
exports to China.[45]

On the investment side, China became the leading destination for all foreign direct investment (FDI) in 2020, increasing by 4 percent over 2019, at
the same time that overall foreign investment in the United States decreased
by 49 percent.[46] As for Chinese investments abroad, David Dollar reported
that they moved from Europe to Southeast Asia in response to EU restrictions.[47] That fact would help explain China's large advantage over the United
States in Asia-related FDI. Still, US-China investments remain substantial
despite COVID and political tensions. From 2010 to 2020, US investors put
nearly $150 billion into China, with 2012 the peak year ($15.4 billion) and
2020 and probably 2021 among the low points (around $8 billion in both
those years). Chinese FDI in the United States has climbed rapidly, with a
peak year in 2016 when it jumped to more than $40 billion, before dropping
the following year to just less than $30 billion.[48] If a bipartisan group of US
legislators has its way, however, US investments in China may well drop significantly. A proposed new law, again a product of the bipartisan consensus
on China," requires advance scrutiny of those investments, supposedly to prevent technology transfers to the Chinese military. As much as 40 percent of
US investments in China could be affected. Business groups naturally object
to such legislation, arguing that it would reduce both the size and substance of
investments in China as well as US firms' competitiveness globally.[49]

The Biden administration took many months to come up with a China
trade policy, and when it did, it mostly resembled Trump's. With both countries maintaining high tariffs on more than 50 percent of their imports from
each other, US businesses across the spectrum sought to spur a return to
trade talks, pointing out in a letter to top trade officials that maintaining the
Trump-era tariffs was hurting business: "Due to the tariffs, U.S. industries
face increased costs to manufacture products and provide services domesti-
cally, making their exports of these products and services less competitive
abroad."[50] They might have added that American consumers were feeling the
pinch. The fact that China was not living up to the last 2020 Phase I trade

deal with the United States—specifically, not having purchased $200 billion worth of US goods and services in 2020 or 2021[51]—required *more* engagement with China so far as business was concerned. But the administration, while excoriating China for failing to live up to its promises, doggedly kept to its strategy of postponing talks with China until "unfair trade practices" such as insufficient protection of intellectual property rights and subsidies of key industries were resolved.[52]

The US trade representative, Katherine Tai, said the "million-dollar question" was how to improve China's performance on the trade deal. Rather than negotiate, her approach seemed to consist mainly of warnings of retaliation, such as when Tai said, preparatory to a trip to China late in 2021, that the United States would "hold their [China's] feet to the fire," meaning still higher tariffs.[53] But the trade imbroglio is not just a matter of Chinese duplicity. For one thing, the Trump trade deal set Chinese purchasing targets, such as on farm products, far too high. For another, certain strategic technologies, such as semiconductors, have sold well but (see below) carry restrictions. And the Biden administration was increasing trade with Europe in those same technologies rather than sell to China.[54]

While Biden dithered, the Chinese made a very smart move. In September 2021 it applied to join the CPTPP. All eleven member-countries trade more with China than with the United States. Trump had rejected this trade pact, formerly the Trans-Pacific Partnership, and Biden made no effort to revive US interest. So Beijing acted, seeking to become the pact's largest and most influential member. Not that it will easily gain entry: Australia and Japan are among the countries opposed to China's application, citing China's barriers to intellectual property and labor rights and weak environmental protection. Strong rules in those areas are among the liberalizing features of the CPTPP.[55] Still, the prospect of Chinese tariff reductions may make its entry irresistible, all the more so given that the United States has no better offer.[56]

With respect to technology research and development (R&D), decoupling *is* a reality. Late in 2020 the CCP leadership decided to promote greater technological self-reliance, starting with increased funding of basic research.[57] Import self-reliance, expansion of the domestic market, and export promotion are parts of a strategy that came to be known as "dual circulation" (*shuang xunhuan*: 双循环). As Kevin Rudd points out, dual circulation reflects a Mao-like determination to "develop firm domestic control over the technologies that are key to future economic and military power, all supported by independent and controllable supply chains." But Rudd adds another factor: demographic change, "the horrifying prospect China may grow old before it grows rich."[58] As I have mentioned earlier, China's falling birth rate and population growth rate have led to predictions of major adverse consequences for the economy, such as fewer workers, a large elderly population needing support, and a smaller tax base. Yet China's leaders so far are paying far more attention to the high-tech side of the economy than they are to those problems, as well as to women who are not having children, to insufficient childcare, and to women's rights generally.[59]

Studies suggest that in key industries where the Chinese have made exceptional progress, such as solar panels, telecommunications equipment, and high-speed railways, mercantilist practices limit foreign innovation. In a word, the more market share China controls, the fewer the patents and research worldwide, to the detriment of advances in (for example) health care and environmental protection.[60] The counterpart trend is that China's push for greater technological independence still must rely on external sources of equipment, investment, and even talent—meaning Chinese researchers abroad who choose to stay abroad. As two analysts write, "China's economic and military strategy is fueled by technology. Although the Chinese economy has made impressive gains by promoting innovation at home, the resources that drive its technological progress are still largely sourced from abroad—a trend that will likely continue well into the 2020s."[61]

Semiconductors illustrate the nature of Chinese self-reliance and the challenge it poses for the United States and other countries. China has sought for several years to produce its own chips and avoid reliance on outside sources that can disrupt the supply chain. China has spent billions of dollars subsidizing R&D, training, and thousands of start-ups, with the goal of 70 percent self-reliance in semiconductors. Local governments and high-tech industries such as Alibaba have also invested heavily in chip manufacture. To combat US or other country restrictions on selling semiconductors to China, a 2021 law imposes sanctions on foreign companies that abide by those restrictions, putting those companies in a vise between US and PRC regulations.[62] According to one study, the sanctions, along with other Chinese policies to promote homegrown chip production, greatly reduce semiconductor innovation in foreign companies.[63]

Washington complains that China's goal of world leadership in the production not just of semiconductors but also photovoltaic solar panels and steel reduces US market share and employment.[64] We met this argument in the discussion of cobalt mining, but in the case of semiconductors, the United States has cited national security to prevent Chinese high-tech firms from acquiring chips. That argument was fortified by a major chip shortage in 2022 and legislation in Congress that would subsidize chip production.[65]

In reality, complete Chinese self-sufficiency in semiconductors is highly unlikely, since (as one expert writes) "the sector is still dependent on equipment from abroad, lacks adequate talent, and has not yet mastered sophisticated manufacturing processes."[66] Moreover, the Biden administration has formed its own technology network among allies in Europe and Asia. One goal is to keep China from participating in making the trade rules, given its protectionist stance. Thus, we have a tension between Beijing's aim to protect against American and European export controls and the US aim, shared for example by Japan, to control access to advanced technologies. These different directions affect not only US-China relations but also the possibility of China's joining the CPTPP, which would presumably call into question all restrictions on the semiconductor trade. In short, we have another situation that cries out for negotiations aimed at mutual benefit.

Chapter 8

Engaging China

COMPETITIVE COEXISTENCE

In 2020 the US National Intelligence Agency (NIA) issued a forecast of possible changes in world affairs twenty years ahead. Regarding US-China relations, the report offered five scenarios, ranging from catastrophe to a "renaissance of democracies." In the middle is "competitive coexistence," a phrase I also use but with a meaning very different from the NIA's. The NIA projects that in that scenario, in the 2030s the United States and China agree:

> to protect their most vital common economic interests. China and the United States formed rival "communities of common values" that compete for markets and resources under opposing domestic systems . . . The United States, China, and like-minded states belonging to their respective camps intervened to prevent small conflicts from escalating to the point that they would threaten global economic progress and stability. Nevertheless, geopolitical competition, such as in the South China Sea, remained a persistent threat to economic relations . . . The central security challenge is how to keep the geopolitical competition between the United States and China from undermining the economic cooperation upon which their prosperity and the global economy depends.[1]

Essentially, the NIA report portrays a post–Cold War world that looks very much like the former Cold War, with two camps vying for supremacy while the rest of the world holds its collective breath. The difference is that NIA's new Cold War will not feature arms racing and major interventions abroad; the competition is mainly economic and technological. But to read the NIA's depiction is to forget what the planet will look like if the two greatest powers are scouring the world for resources: out-of-control climate change, widening rich-poor gaps between and within nations, and huge populations in flight across borders. Coexistence there may be, but at what cost?

"Competitive coexistence" in my understanding means US-China economic and technological competition, but also coexistence as great powers with planetary responsibilities alongside conflicting values and interests. Frictions are inevitable and conflict *resolution* is unlikely; but conflict *management* is necessary and possible. Coexistence is far more difficult than competition. The United States must face the reality that today's China has deeply offensive internal policies that defy American notions of human rights. Other than consistently raising the issue in diplomatic give-and-take, and improving its own human rights performance, the United States can do little to influence what happens in China, for any outside interference is much more likely to engender hostility and even worsen oppression than bring about policy change. Moreover, American self-righteousness on human rights has worn thin at a time of "Black Lives Matter," "#MeToo," LGBTQ rights, and other movements for equality at home.

Besides, China today is not mainly a study in repression. The China story is one of a gigantic population whose quality of life has, in most of the country, measurably and dramatically improved since the start of the economic reforms in 1978. Outside ethnic minority areas, the post-Mao regimes have achieved economic success mainly through increased professionalism, limitations on party interference in policy making, educational and scientific advances, and early acceptance of foreign involvement in the economy. Enforced social stability has, of course, been a key part of China's rise, but the leadership has compensated China's masses by delivering on several vectors of human security and providing avenues for individual initiative.

As for the competitive side of engaging China, the US intelligence community reportedly determined in 2020 that Beijing "believes there is a bipartisan consensus against China in the United States that leaves no prospect for a pro-China administration regardless of the election outcome."[2] That understanding has proven accurate. The bipartisan consensus on China has trapped a liberal US administration into departing from the consistent US policy, pre-Trump, of finding ways to overcome differences. Adding an ideological element to the mix not only is unnecessary and provocative; it neglects that the spread of democracy is best helped by example, not by empty crusading. Taking aim at the China threat, moreover, encourages tit-for-tat behavior and makes overtures for cooperation less likely to be accepted. It may also undermine US interests beyond China, such as on the North Korea nuclear issue and China-Russia partnership in the Ukraine war. Jia Qingguo of Beijing University, a leading commentator on foreign affairs who values the US-China relationship, bluntly addressed the last point when he said that US "containment" of China "is pushing us into a bifurcated world. In China, more people are thinking we need to form our own closer security relationships with certain countries, and there are others who worry about this road we may have to take."[3] By "certain countries," Jia surely meant Russia. His warning has added weight since the invasion of Ukraine. It can also be considered a plea for the United States to move from containment of China, as Beijing sees it, to a policy that approximates engagement.

In the National Interest

Strategic engagement of China in the early 1970s led to normalization of US-China relations and demonstrated that engagement is in the US national interest. Today, engaging China has many other advantages, including avoidance of dangerous confrontations and decreased likelihood of misperceptions and miscommunications; recruitment of scientific talent from China; reduction of tariff barriers that result in lower costs to consumers and increased competitiveness for trading firms; opportunities to reduce military spending due to force reductions in Asia and termination of new weapons acquisitions; more opportunities for people-to-people exchanges; participation in each other's trade networks and a variety of other multilateral fora; promotion of public health research and climate change mitigation; a larger, less pressured NGO and journalistic presence in China; wider cooperation in UN peacekeeping operations, environmental protection, and other programs; opportunities for reduction of nuclear weapons; a greatly improved security climate across Asia; and cooperative efforts on aid to developing countries. In a larger sense, engagement also promotes a positive image of the United States among the Chinese people and specifically among China's reform-minded officials, intellectuals (including students), and cosmopolitan citizens. The hyper-nationalism among some Chinese officials and analysts, and in China's emerging middle class,[4] might lose its saliency if engagement were the cornerstone of US policy. As engagement bears fruit, those Chinese who yearn for a more open and transparent political and legal system might gain new support.

Most of these advantages for the United States are also positives for the world. As Anne Marie Slaughter writes, "Competition itself [as with China] is fine and natural, but it needs to be competition to achieve a goal that benefits us all." Deep US-China engagement can fulfill that aim, but these days it takes political courage to address planetary as much as national security. She provides an excellent example: global distribution of the COVID-19 vaccine. Unfortunately, when Xi proposed a global initiative on the vaccine, the United States decided once again to go it alone.[5] Indeed, health security cooperation, such as in 2003 with the severe acute respiratory syndrome (SARS), in the 2009 H1N1 pandemic, and in the Ebola epidemic in Africa in 2014, is one of the most enduring examples of successful US-China engagement.[6]

One has to ask: Are US national security objectives served by *not* engaging China? Or, put another way, can the United States promote changes to its benefit in Chinese policies by containing, constraining, or confronting China? Pressure tactics have not led China to change its human rights policies or withdraw its military installations from the South China Sea. China's tense relations with the United States have sharply limited opportunities to influence North Korea missile and nuclear tests. High tariffs on Chinese exports have not caused China to change its trade policies, and in some cases—take solar technology—actually undermined US policy on climate change.[7] Upgrading political and military ties with Taiwan have made its defense more problematic. To be clear, naming and shaming China's repression of human rights, criticizing its unilateral takeover of some South China Sea islands, reducing the trade deficit with China, and maintaining "strategic ambiguity" on defense of Taiwan are all appropriate policies. But those policies are not served, and in fact are undermined, by following a hard-line approach. History informs us that the Chinese response to confrontation is not to back off. "American-threat" advocates in Beijing gain influence, hyper-nationalism fuels tensions, and bad situations get worse.

Critics of a US engagement policy on China will sometimes cite comments attributed to Xi Jinping that demonstrate an implacable hostility toward the United States—for example, that "the United States is the biggest threat to our country's development and security" and "the US is the greatest source of chaos in the world today." Those may be Xi's convictions, but we should keep in mind the context in which they may have been conveyed (in those cases, a pep talk to local party cadres); and they may be no more valid as indicators of operative Chinese policy than the private comments about China of a US president.[8] I attach greater meaning to Xi's public comments, such as those he made to Biden at their 2021 virtual summit. Xi emphatically welcomed deeper engagement with the United States. He said the two countries needed a "sound and steady" relationship and should engage in "win-win cooperation." He cited several areas of mutual interest, from the economy to the environment, said he hoped for more extensive contact with Biden, and urged "injecting momentum" (*zhuru dongli*) into the relationship so that China and the United States can "make a great China-US cooperative 'cake'" (*zuo da Zhong-Mei hezuo de "dangao"*).[9] The Chinese foreign ministry, in its response to the summit, had this to say: "The key is that both sides should meet each other halfway and use actions to create a good atmosphere to ensure that the meeting achieves positive results. . . . China is open to all options that are conducive to the development of Sino-US relations."[10] Notably, that statement was delivered by the ministry's leading wolf warrior, Zhao Lijian, who usually makes vitriolic comments on US policies. Here,

Zhao toed the line, though separately the next day he denounced US policy on Taiwan.

Xi would not have spoken positively about engagement if he did not believe it is in China's national interests. And it is. Engaging the United States may eliminate or ease sanctions on access to US technology, lower tariffs on Chinese exports, reduce tensions over (for example) Taiwan and thus one rationale for a large US military presence in Asia, remove restrictions on visas, restore Chinese educational and research opportunities in the United States, improve military-to-military communications, possibly move American criticism on human rights from the public to the private arena, and enable collaboration on mutually beneficial research.[11] Hostile rhetoric in official exchanges and the media will be toned down. Stereotyping of Americans may be lessened. Perhaps most importantly, the Chinese government will have greater resources to devote to real security at home—not for intensifying repression, one hopes, but for addressing the rising expectations of young people, people living in rural areas, environmental refugees, and human rights activists.

EVALUATING CHINA'S POWER

If engagement is to emerge as central to US China policy, it must overcome the bipartisan consensus on China that repeats a fundamental Cold War–era analytical error mentioned earlier: magnifying the adversary's capabilities and strategic ambitions while minimizing or neglecting its failures and weaknesses. Those administration officials, Congress members, and journalists who reject engagement out of fear that China is overtaking the West may want to investigate Chinese realities. Beijing's leaders know very well that competing with the United States is significantly hampered by China's large menu of internal problems and economic needs that constrain what they might wish to accomplish abroad. China's astute America watchers probably also recognize US advantages in areas such as research, higher education, and human security—areas that are as relevant to national security as the military budget. Even in tightly controlled societies such as China, politics counts: Leaders must pay attention and devote resources to addressing domestic problems that can become sources of instability. I have pointed to many of those. China is not going to fall apart, but its leaders know very well that rapid economic and social change amid an internet-savvy population can be destabilizing. The wise leader will try to get ahead of the curve, but if insecurity drives social policy, as I believe it presently does in China, those internal problems will only multiply.

Weaknesses in China's conduct of foreign affairs, including its public diplomacy, also deserve more attention by those who consider China a Goliath. Its diplomacy has often been clumsy and arrogant, its BRI not as unconditional as advertised, its model of governance not widely admired, its human rights policies widely condemned, and its economic and environmental policies less consistent and sustainable than claimed. The reach of China's soft power keeps increasing, but its impact seems to be fairly modest—cause for dismay among Chinese specialists, who believe (to quote one of them) that "the strength of our voice does not match our position in the world."[12] Chinese classical culture, for instance, is world renowned, yet its modern version has not resonated globally—in, for example, art, music, novels, and film—though China is doing its best to make its Hollywood investments promote all things Chinese.[13] (Confucius Institutes, after all, have nothing to do with Confucius.) Nor can its news sources and advertising compete with the global reach of Western counterparts. Authoritarian leaders may envy China's surveillance state, but they have limited capability to copy it. Fourth, China's educational, legal, and science communities do not attract people to China; talented Chinese often look abroad, typically to the West, for inspiration, the freedom to learn, and the space to do independent and collaborative research. In short, in global perspective, China stands as a country whose way of life and sociopolitical systems are neither widely admired nor readily adapted.[14] And its capability to promote autocracy abroad is about as limited as US capability to promote democracy.

Nor has China had smooth sailing in fulfilling other elements of its international agenda. China may claim leadership on economic development, the environment, and energy, but when it comes to matters of war and peace, it has little to offer beyond soldiers in UN peacekeeping missions.[15] As China's response to war in Ukraine showed, Beijing could not even be faithful to its own core principles, nonintervention and nonaggression, let alone mediate or respond to a humanitarian disaster in a meaningful way. In fact, China rarely shows up in international conflict resolution, such as in recent wars in Syria, Yemen, Libya, South Sudan, Myanmar, and Mali.

Some of China's domestic demands have had unwelcome effects abroad. Examples include dam building on waters used by India, Vietnam, and Thailand; soy imports from Brazil that add to Amazonian deforestation and the climate crisis; overfishing and illegal fishing in Pacific and Atlantic waters; and coal imports from Australia. The BRI, as discussed, has generated criticism on environmental and economic grounds in a number of countries. China's aggressive push to control the South China Sea islets has been contested by several Southeast Asian countries, notably the Philippines in an arbitral court ruling in 2016 that found against Chinese territorial claims under the UN Convention on the Law of the Sea. The reaction to Chinese repression in Xinjiang and other human rights violations, and China's ham-handed defense of it, has alienated the EU, among others. Beijing has allowed the wolf warriors in its foreign service to garner attention with their outbursts, diminishing the effectiveness of an otherwise very professional group of ambassadors. In general, China has had a very inconsistent record when it comes to adherence to international law, notably the UN human rights covenants and maritime law.

Finally, China's ability to project power is far less than the US bipartisan consensus suggests. Military capabilities aside, China is at a major disadvantage in comparison with the United States in one other respect: allies. This is a weakness that the Biden administration is seeking to exploit, but with an unfortunate emphasis on the China threat. The Quad is an example: Each member has serious strategic, economic, and political differences with Beijing. Whether or not it becomes a military bloc—China's foreign minister has accused the Quad of being an "Indo-Pacific NATO"—it has moved Beijing to try driving a wedge between the four, depicting the Quad as a Cold War weapon.[16] The fact that the Biden administration emphasizes the restoration of alliances makes the Quad much more threatening to China than it had been in the Trump years.

AN ENGAGEMENT MENU

As the UN secretary-general said in the speech cited at the beginning of this book, the rules of the road are much less clear now between China and the United States than they were in the era of US-Soviet rivalry. They are even less clear since Russia's invasion of Ukraine, which will force China to adjust to the reemergence of the Cold War in Europe along East-West fault lines. The new situation makes a US-China engagement menu all the more necessary. The principle underlying the menu below is *cooperative security*: improving both countries' (and therefore the world's) opportunities for peace, interaction, and prosperity, rather than gaining security for one at the expense of the other. Cooperative security is not on either country's menu, but that does not foreclose consideration of specific items on it.

Track IA: Official-level Diplomacy

- Resumption of collaborative research on pandemics
- "Strategic Partnership" on climate change
- Trade talks to reduce tariffs and barriers to global research innovation
- Normalization of visa processing and removal of political obstacles to entry

- Confidence-building talks on AUKUS and the Quad
- Reopening of consulates in Houston and Wuhan
- Renewal and strengthening of the 2016 cybersecurity agreement
- Regular human rights dialogues
- Creation of a Security Dialogue Mechanism for Northeast Asia, a permanent multilateral body with an open common-security agenda, ranging from environmental to military security issues, and with the possibility of creating a nuclear-weapon-free zone in that region[17]
- Mutual membership in Asia-Pacific regional trade and development groups: RCEP, CPTPP, and AIIB
- Expansion of renewable energy cooperation
- Counternarcotics cooperation[18]
- Strengthening of November 2021 bilateral agreement on greenhouse gas emissions and removal of subsidies to fossil fuel producers
- Agreement to reduce threatening and hostile official statements
- Collaboration on climate and energy development projects in developing countries
- Restoration of those Obama-era US-China dialogue groups considered most effective

Track IB: Military Relations

- Restoration of US pledge under 1972 Shanghai Communique to gradually reduce weapons sales to Taiwan in return for Chinese reduction of air and naval activity in the Taiwan Strait area
- Agreement to promote transparency on military spending and deployments
- Regularization of military-to-military talks
- Initiation of talks on hypersonic weapons and reduction of nuclear weapons

Tracks II and III (Semi-official and Non-official Levels)

- Resumption of educational and scientific exchange programs, without prejudice to science graduate students and researchers and with safeguards for academic freedom
- Reciprocity on student and university exchange agreements
- Loosening of China's rules governing foreign NGO activities
- Taiwan: dialogue on tension-reducing, trust-building steps by scholars and others from China, Taiwan, and the United States[19]
- Establishment of climate and energy research centers, either collaborative or parallel
- Further development of city and state partnerships in energy conservation[20]

MANAGING DIFFERENCES

If a serious effort by the United States and China at fulfilling the engagement menu were to occur, we might expect a common desire to focus on trust-building moves. What does each government want, what are the possibilities and limits of acceptability, and how do we get from here to there? Having that kind of exchange would mark a critical inflection point in the relationship, because essential to successful engagement is *sustainability*: functional groups comprised of issue specialists who are dedicated to making engagement work, meet regularly, have the support and respect of political leaders, and together make policy *stable and predictable*.

But therein lies the rub: domestic politics in both countries, which is often the central obstacle to engagement.[21] As I have observed earlier, for Xi and Biden, foreign policy begins at home: social stability and economic performance set the agenda for national security and the pursuit of external goals. It goes without saying that both countries are experiencing serious disruptions to their political and economic order, partly the result of the pandemic but mainly due to deprivation of human rights, social and economic inequities, and deficiencies in governance. So long as these problems fester, leaderships in China and the United States are going to be preoccupied with insecurity on the home front, devoting increasing resources and political capital to dealing with them. One possibility is that they will be less inclined, or politically enabled, to make the kinds of concessions and offer the kinds of incentives that might reduce tensions with their key international adversary. But another possibility is that an engagement strategy will be *more* appealing precisely because, by reducing the mutual sense of threat, it will facilitate focusing on domestic needs and transnational sources of insecurity such as climate change.

China critics have good reason to underscore China's blatant disregard for human rights and democratic (which is to say, accountable and transparent) rule, its pretense at being a world leader on the environment, the manipulation of aid programs such as the BRI to win favor in developed and developing countries alike, and its sanctions against individuals and foreign governments that dare to take issue with Chinese policies. My analysis incorporates many of those criticisms. They should remain part of any dialogue with China, just as the US side should anticipate Chinese criticisms of American deficiencies. Moreover, both governments should be called to account when they reject criticism with flimsy justifications, such as China's insistence on "sovereignty" or "internal matters" and US assertions of "universal values" and exceptionalism.

Mutual criticisms do not, however, negate the central importance of finding common ground between the world's most important, and dangerous, adversaries. The criticisms are very unlikely to promote an adversary's shifts in policy and even less in values, but they *are* likely to reinforce resistance to change and hostile perceptions. At least in US-China relations, the case for constant criticism of the adversary so as to be true to one's own principles pales beside the opposing case for coexistence founded on mutual respect and mutual gain.

Beijing has played the tit-for-tat game when challenged, but it has also tried to communicate that dialogue and cooperation remain desirable and preferable to continued recriminations. That message is a necessary supplement to the "America in decline" theme of Chinese specialists mentioned in chapter 3. The official Chinese view entails both an assertive nationalism *and* hopes for a cooperative relationship with the United States. For instance, in a lengthy article in the *Global Times*, often a virulently nationalist outlet, Yang Jiechi, the CCP politburo member, made "equality and mutual respect" the main theme: "China and the US should avoid strategic miscalculation and manage well their differences. Cooperation and win-win is the only right choice for the two countries. The US must abandon its Cold War mentality and the misguided zero-sum game approach. The two countries need to engage in dialogue and communication in all areas."[22] Foreign Minister Wang Yi said following the contentious Alaska meetings with Blinken and Sullivan in 2021 that while the Chinese are "masters" of their own circumstances and will brook no outside interference, "a checklist of necessary cooperation [in China-US relations] is before us, including fighting the coronavirus, economic recovery, climate change, etc."[23] Wang Dong, a Beijing University professor, argues for US-China agreement on "G2RS"—that is, they "would continue to hedge against each other, but they would manage their differences and compete in a calibrated, constructive manner. Rather than engaging in a rivalry that divides the world, the two powers would lead the world as responsible stakeholders."[24]

Critics dismiss such statements, arguing either that they merely repeat standard Chinese themes, offer highly impractical notions (such as global power-sharing under G2RS), or—most insidiously—mask China's real motive, which is to displace the United States as global leader.[25] But I take the statements as reflecting an honest Chinese interest not to let tensions with the United States boil over, and to want deeper cooperation with the United States so long as the United States stops "attacking" China or trying to transform it.[26] Or, as Xi put it to Biden in their telephone exchange, the two countries should "bring China-U.S. relations back to the right track of stable development as soon as possible."[27] Consider again the quotations from Wang Yi and Jin Canrong in chapter 6. Reading between the lines, and with due recognition of their external audiences, the texts seem to me to convey a traditional Chinese defensiveness about their development project and their security concerns—traditional, because from the Mao era on, Chinese officials have often depicted the economy and territory as subject to foreign interference. On both those overriding matters, the United States has always been regarded as standing in the way of economic achievement and security priorities. Neither Wang nor Jin nor any senior Chinese official is threatening Washington, however; they want the United States to correct its perceptions of China and understand that we are in a new era in which China will not be moved from its chosen path. Ali Wyne and Ryan Hass thus conclude: "Beijing is neither on the precipice of disintegration nor on a path to hegemony; it is an enduring yet constrained competitor."[28]

Put that way, finding common ground should in theory be more effective than trading threats and insults, avoiding communications, and deploying military forces as though prepared for battle—in short, behaving like Russia and the United States in early 2022. We should not assume that China's rise and America's decline are linear or permanent. Nor should we assume that hostile relations will endure—that America's "China threat" consensus is unchangeable or that Xi Jinping and his inner circle will forever believe, like Chairman Mao in the 1950s, that the East will prevail over the West. As Swaine writes, "it would be a mistake for the U.S. government to adopt policies based on that viewpoint. Such an approach would almost certainly close off many options that might exist for moderation and mutual accommodation between the two powers, and simply reinforce the existing Sino-U.S. security competition, most likely in hostile, zero-sum ways."[29]

The Three Main Obstacles

At least three fundamental obstacles exist to lasting accommodation. The first is structural: the great divide between a newly empowered China and a United States used to being number one. Bridging that divide requires addressing different notions about the international order—*what* is its essential aspect, *who* should define it, and *how* should it be maintained. For the United States, the international order is "rules-based," it is defined by the post–World War II institutions that the United States led in creating, and it should be led first and foremost by Washington. Biden told Xi in their second telephone conversation that the United States seeks to "responsibly manage the competition" so that it "does not veer into conflict."[30] My concern is that when the Americans speak of managed competition, the Chinese understand them to mean that *China* must be managed, whereas when the Chinese (such as Yang Jiechi above) urge that China-US differences be "managed well," they assume (as I do) equal status at the table.

Similarly when it comes to the question of "responsible" behavior: The Chinese have their own notion of responsibility, and they reject the idea of being a stakeholder in an America-defined system. For them, the international order is multipolar, demanding creation of a "new kind of great power relationship" in which China plays a role second to none. As President Xi said to Biden, how the US-China relationship fares "is a question of the century to which the two countries must provide a good answer. When China and the United States cooperate, the two countries and the world will benefit; when China and the United States are in confrontation, the two countries and the world will suffer. Getting the relationship right is not optional, but something we must do and must do well."[31] "We" is the key word: China is as essential as the United States to world peace and progress, Xi is insisting. Differences over global responsibility and rule making will persist for some time, and while they need not inhibit finding common ground, they will be a constant source of friction that can be overcome only through the experience of cooperation on specific issues. China's rise is irreversible, and the model of economic growth without political liberalization is going to have its appeal—and failures—regardless of American criticisms or insistence on forever being Number One. The proper US response is to compete with China—in trade, development assistance, accountable governance, respect for human rights, and protection of the environment, for example—rather than punish it for deflating American dreams.

Second, qualities of leadership may make a difference in what policies can accomplish and at what cost. What brought Xi and Trump together was a common deficiency in those qualities normally associated with a successful national leader: empathy, respect for diversity, acceptance of responsibility for mistakes, and reasoned responses to critics. Trump is gone, but Xi, known for his decisiveness but also for his pursuit of a personality cult and resistance to criticism, suffers from an arrogance of power. He has sometimes overplayed his hand, jailing human rights activists and critics of his leadership at the cost of antagonizing relations with the EU, Japan, South Korea, and Australia. Joe Biden is in many respects about as far apart from Donald Trump as one can imagine—a man who prides himself on being empathetic and fair-minded. Yet he has his blind spots, and China seems to be one of them. Professions of friendship with Xi cannot hide an unwillingness to learn about China. To the Chinese, Biden is a great disappointment—another US president seeking to contain China—while to Biden, Xi is not an "old friend" but someone with whom "it's pure business."[32]

The third factor may be the most problematic: a dangerous insecurity in both countries' leaderships. Chinese leaders often seem to operate out of *fear*—fear of democracy and accountability, fear of social protests, fear of foreign influences, fear of economic downturns that create instability, fear of (and contempt for) the rule of law, fear that the United States will take advantage of perceived weakness, and fear to put the global interest in peace ahead of Chinese interests. American leaders are plagued by homegrown problems that are eating away at democratic authority: domestic terrorism, conspiratorial groups, racism, and assaults on voting and other basic freedoms. To many observers, the political future of the United States looks increasingly violent. This mutual insecurity breeds mutual mistrust: China bashing has emerged directly from this social divide, and nationalistic Chinese have had a field day mocking American democracy. Though a US-China clash may seem unlikely in the immediate future, tit-for-tat responses such as have been taking place with increasing regularity raise the possibility of a military confrontation down the road—a confrontation, we must always keep in mind, between nuclear-weapon states. In the meantime, demonizing the other as disputes multiply is becoming commonplace in each other's media.

Mutual insecurity also diminishes reliance on diplomacy to deal with differences. It becomes easier to fall back on stereotypes and bad-faith models than strive for agreement. A case comparable to the US-China imbroglio might be the US-Iran divisions in the Obama years, before the nuclear deal was consummated. As portrayed by Trita Parsi, few people around Obama believed diplomacy would work with Iran, leading Obama to decide not to spend political capital on attempting a breakthrough. The more tensions rose with Iran, and the more hostility to dealing with Iran increased in Congress, the less inclined Obama was to take political risks in diplomacy with Iran. In Tehran the ayatollah followed much the same course.[33] Shift now to Biden and it becomes easy to see how, given his domestic priorities and rising hostility to China inside and outside the Beltway, the political risks of engagement are abnormally high. Xi Jinping may be in a very similar place, reluctant to accommodate America and thus appear to be an appeaser.

But the fact is that Obama did persevere with Iran and achieved a historic nuclear deal in company with Iran's foreign minister. With China, diplomacy—the Strategic and Economic Dialogue (S&ED) as it expanded in the Obama years—was productive. Critics assert that those talks produced more process than substance, but one serious study of them shows that while nothing on the order of the Iran nuclear deal occurred, significant agreements were realized. "On many shared interests," say the study's authors

—stabilizing the international financial system after the Global Financial Crisis; combating climate change; addressing global safety issues including disease prevention, nuclear waste, and illegal trafficking; clarifying domestic rules and regulations; managing a robust program of people-to-people relations; and capacity building as China moved from a developing to a developed country—the US and China were able to make substantial and measurable progress through the S&ED.[34]

To these modest accomplishments should be added the benefits of greater mutual understanding of bureaucratic and decision-making processes and regularized contact on specific issues even in the midst of tensions.

The United States and China probably will never agree on some matters, such as the origins of COVID-19, ownership and demilitarization of the South China Sea islands, Taiwan's status, and respect for the civil liberties of all citizens. But engagement means regularly addressing matters of common concern, where agreement is possible. Disagreements with China need not spell the end of cooperation. Territorial claims regarding the South China Sea, for instance, can be put aside while agreements are worked out on the undersea environment and naval maneuvers. The origins of COVID-19 may always be contentious, but that need not prevent collaborative research on pandemics and perhaps even agreement on new rules governing research procedures and disclosure of data. China will not forswear the use of force against Taiwan, but in return for a reduction or limitation on weapons sales to Taiwan, Beijing might accept limits on naval and air maneuvers near Taiwan.

Exercising mutual restraint and refocusing on common ground allows for recognizing that there was a time when cooperation worked on public health, climate change, and even trade. Accordingly, a priority for Beijing and Washington should be to reestablish working-level groups focused on those issues that seem most amenable to agreement. Crisis management, climate change, pandemics, and military relations would be the top candidates.[35] This view, once well accepted and now in the minority, also argues for a US-China policy that, as one specialist puts it, is not "China-centric" but rather relies on US strengths. He writes: "A durable cohabitation between the United States and China will require each to accept the reality of the other's resilience. Instead of signaling insecurity by undertaking to contest Beijing's maneuvers on a reciprocal basis, Washington should invest anew in its unique competitive strengths, thereby projecting confidence in its ability to recalibrate effectively and sustainably."[36] Part of that perspective is rejecting the notion of a world divided between us and them, since China is well integrated in the economies and societies just about everywhere and is an influential force in areas once the unique province of the United States: economic globalization, alternative energy, regional trade, and foreign aid. That situation presents challenges, to be sure, but *strategic* competition should not be among them.

Accepting China as a global leader need not mean embracing the notion of G2. That notion would require a degree of common action that seems far down the road. It also would probably be unacceptable to many governments, which would regard G2 as amounting to global hegemony. Instead, the

United States might accept the Chinese-proposed "new model of great-power relations," in which the two countries, acting as equals, would avoid conflict and seek "win-win" cooperation. The US side never fully embraced that model when Xi first proposed it, but times are different now and the possibility of open conflict between the two most powerful nations on the planet is greater than in many years. Joint membership in regional organizations, such as the CPTPP and RCEP, is another model. As one study of regional organizing suggests, in certain issue areas such as trade, regional groups may work better than global multilateral organizations, or at least improve the work of global organizations through coordinated effort.[37]

To some China watchers, therefore, the implication of an engagement strategy is clear: Cultivate your own garden. As the former US ambassador to China, Jon Huntsman, writes, "the single greatest challenge facing the United States this century is the rise of an emboldened China with the elements of power—economic, military and diplomatic—to shape a world that is antithetical to our values. We can neither disengage nor wish it away. Our best defense is to continuously improve our system at home that speaks to the American Dream, which still remains aspirational for many around the world—even in China."[38] Another writer similarly urges that "the U.S. should redouble its commitment to repairing its liberal model, confident in its attractiveness, if not to all the governments of the world, then to most of the world's people."[39]

Will the United States hold together as a stable, prosperous society committed to liberal values? Or will blue-red divisions, racism, and the rich-poor gap end the American experiment? Will China hold together as a prosperous and stable society under a one-party state? Or will corruption, authoritarian rule, and social demands end the China dream? The future of US-China relations will depend more than anything on whether or not each country *remains governable.*

What If Engagement Fails?

I have tried to make the case that re-engaging China avoids the costs and risks of inaction, whereas continuing a policy of confronting China raises the risks of conflict by design or miscalculation. However, a serious US engagement strategy may not work, either because mistrust cannot be overcome, one side simply rejects engagement, or the strategy is inconsistently implemented. China's determination to fulfill its "dream" of reunifying with Taiwan, the insufficiency of incentives to engage, a military clash in the South China Sea, another tariff war—these are the sorts of events, planned or otherwise, that can easily disrupt or kill an engagement strategy. Much depends, moreover, on how smoothly and effectively the engagement process is proceeding before a potential spark is set off. The greater the investment of both sides in engagement, and the more that investment pays off, the less likely that it will be derailed by an incident, a misunderstanding, or a deliberate effort to sabotage engagement by its opponents inside one or the other government.

From the US perspective, a strategy of engagement should be seen as a *test* of China's intentions. The president would make clear to China's leader that the United States will be taking specific steps—for example, reassuring Beijing on the one-China policy by reducing military aid to Taiwan, proposing the resumption of collaborative research on pandemics, or eliminating onerous visa restrictions—that he expects will be matched by China. The ball will be in China's court to measure up to the cooperative appeal in Xi Jinping's remarks to Biden at their inaugural summit. Xi will understand that failure to do so will force the president to harden US policy if only because of pressure from members of Congress.

Engaging China is also the preferred US option if Xi's ambitions are thwarted by both domestic crises and international obstacles. Michael Beckley and Hal Brands have predicted just such a Chinese future.[40] They argue that China's rise is about over as resource scarcity, an aging population, a water crisis, and other domestic problems bring slower growth, productivity, and innovation. Abroad, China is being hemmed in by the United States and its allies. The real China threat then arises from a dissatisfied China whose reach exceeds its grasp. I don't agree with this scenario, which casts China as potentially being on the same path to self-destruction as Germany before World War I and Japan before World War II. But if they are right, engagement would remain the correct remedy—surely preferable either to preparing for war with China or strengthening containment of it. The Chinese Dream should not be replaced by China's Revenge.

Right now, the United States and China are not in Cold War II. Nothing comparable to the stark division of the world during Cold War I into two ideological and economic blocs, with consequent proxy battles from Africa to Latin America, has occurred.[41] But the Ukraine crisis creates the disturbing possibility that East-West lines are reforming in Europe, pitting US security partners in Europe and Asia against Russia and its authoritarian sphere. Engaging China is the only way to prevent its joining with Russia and precipitating a global crisis far more dangerous than the earlier Cold War. Yet leaderships in China and the United States might well be blinded into believing, just as in the 1950s and 1960s, that they have no other choice, that their cause is just, with the result being high-risk decision making and disastrous miscalculations.[42] That prospect alone should provide incentives for the United States and China to keep seeking common ground.

Notes

CHAPTER 1

1. Antonio Guterres, interview with the Associated Press, September 19, 2021, https://thehill.com/policy/international/572978-un-chief-warns-of-potential-new-cold-war-between-us-china.

2. See Thomas Fingar, "The Logic and Efficacy of Engagement: Objectives, Assumptions, and Impacts," in Anne F. Thurston, ed., *Engaging China: Fifty Years of Sino-American Relations* (New York: Columbia University Press, 2021), pp. 32–55.

3. Kurt M. Campbell and Jake Sullivan, "Competition without Catastrophe: How America Can Both Challenge and Coexist with China," *Foreign Affairs*, vol. 98, no. 5 (September–October 2019), pp. 96–110.

4. Mel Gurtov, *Engaging Adversaries: Peacemaking and Diplomacy in the Human Interest* (Lanham, MD: Rowman & Littlefield, 2018), p. 9.

5. Gurtov, *Engaging Adversaries*, p. 48.

6. On risk and obligation in trust between nations, see Aaron M. Hoffman, "A Conceptualization of Trust in International Relations," *European Journal of International Relations*, vol. 8, no. 3 (2002), pp. 375–401.

7. Wang Jisi, "The Understanding Gap," *China-US Focus*, March 11, 2021, https://www.chinausfocus.com/foreign-policy/the-understanding-gap.

8. Jake Sullivan, "What Donald Trump and Dick Cheney Got Wrong about America," *The Atlantic*, January 2019, https://www.theatlantic.com/magazine/archive/2019/01/yes-america-can-still-lead-the-world/576427/.

9. Two prominent organizations that periodically assess democracy's progress worldwide—the International Institute for Democracy and Electoral Assistance in Stockholm and Freedom House in the United States—both portray significant backsliding in the United States. See Miriam Berger, "U.S. Listed as a 'Backsliding' Democracy for First Time in Report by European Think Tank," *Washington Post* [hereafter, *WaPo*], November 22, 2021. See also Richard Wike, Laura Silver, Janell Fetterolf, Christine Huang, and J. J. Moncus, "What People around the World Like—and Dislike—about American Society and Politics," Pew Research Center,

November 1, 2021, https://www.pewresearch.org/global/2021/11/01/what-people
-around-the-world-like-and-dislike-about-american-society-and-politics/. Thomas B.
Edsall ("How to Tell When Your Country Is Past the Point of No Return," *New York
Times* [hereafter, *NYT*], December 15, 2021) offers a comprehensive review of the
literature on America's democracy at the breaking point. On the possibility of a repeat
of the January 6, 2021, insurrection at the Capitol, see the essays in *The Atlantic* by
Barton Gellman, George Packer, and Jeffrey Goldberg at https://www.theatlantic.com
/magazine/toc/2022/01/.

10. On corruption and its possible consequences for the Chinese Communist
Party's survival, see Minxin Pei, *China's Crony Capitalism: The Dynamics of Regime
Decay* (Boston: Harvard University Press, 2016).

11. Noteworthy is the comment at that time by China's vice president, Wang Qis-
han, to Henry Paulson, the US treasury secretary: "You were my teacher, but now
here I am in my teacher's domain, and look at your system, Hank. We aren't sure
we should be learning from you anymore." Quoted by Daniel H. Rosen, "China's
Economic Reckoning: The Price of Failed Reforms," *Foreign Affairs*, vol. 100, no. 4
(July–August 2021), p. 27.

12. *Xinhua News*, "Xi Jinping Holds Video Call with US President Biden" (in
Chinese), March 18, 2022, https://xhpfmapi.xinhuaxmt.com/vh512/share/10669343.

CHAPTER 2

1. Rosh Doshi, *The Long Game: China's Grand Strategy to Displace American
Order* (New York: Oxford University Press, 2021).

2. Among studies that do see the domestic-foreign policy connection are Christopher W. Bishop, "To Understand China's Aggressive Foreign Policy, Look at Its
Domestic Politics," Council on Foreign Relations, October 8, 2020, https://www
.cfr.org/blog/understand-chinas-aggressive-foreign-policy-look-its-domestic-politics;
and a RAND Corporation study that says: "The most-critical factors that will determine the outcome of U.S.-China competition are fundamentally domestic." Yet the
authors, who commendably say they "seek to present competitive strategies from a
Chinese perspective," decided that domestic factors are "beyond the scope" of their
analysis. Timothy R. Heath, Derek Grossman, and Asha Clark, *China's Quest for
Global Primacy: An Analysis of Chinese International and Defense Strategies to
Outcompete the United States* (Santa Monica, CA: RAND Corporation, 2021), p.
xviii. Hereafter, RAND Study.

3. Wang Jisi, "Inside China," *Global Asia*, June 10, 2010, https://www.globalasia
.org/v5no2/cover/inside-china-a-note-from-the-guest-editor-wang-jisi_wang-jisi.

4. Ministry of Foreign Affairs of China, "State Councilor and Foreign Minister
Wang Yi Gives Interview to Xinhua News Agency and China Media Group on International Situation and China's Diplomacy in 2021," December 30, 2021, https://www
.mfa.gov.cn/mfa_eng/zxxx_662805/202112/t20211230_10477324.html.

5. Yeling Tan, for example, describes the tussle between opposing local and state
interests in China over economic and legal reforms that were required once it joined

the World Trade Organization. See "How the WTO Changed China," *Foreign Affairs*, vol. 100, no. 2 (March–April 2021), pp. 90–102. Cheng Li's study of Shanghai vividly brings out the political importance of China's nearly half-billion-strong middle class: *Middle Class Shanghai: Reshaping U.S.-China Engagement* (Washington, DC: Brookings Institution, 2021).

6. Songying Fang, Xiaojun Li, and Adam Y. Liu, "Chinese Public Opinion about US-China Relations from Trump to Biden," *Chinese Journal of International Politics*, 2022, https://doi.org/10.1093/cjip/poac001.

7. An exception: internal debate over China's loans to developing countries under the Belt and Road Initiative. See Yun Sun, "The Domestic Controversy over China's Foreign Aid and the Implications for Africa," Brookings Institution, October 8, 2015, https://www.brookings.edu/blog/africa-in-focus/2015/10/08/the-domestic -controversy-over-chinas-foreign-aid-and-the-implications-for-africa/.

8. Kenneth Lieberthal and Wang Jisi, "Addressing U.S.-China Strategic Distrust," Brookings Institution, John L. Thornton China Center, No. 4 (March 2012).

9. A well-publicized example is Cai Xia, a professor at the Central Party School whose vigorous criticisms of the communist party and its leaders led to her expulsion from the CCP and eventually to her leaving China. See her autobiographical account at "The Party That Failed: An Insider Breaks with Beijing," *Foreign Affairs*, vol. 100, no. 1 (January–February 2021), pp. 78–96.

10. Stacie E. Goddard, "The Outsiders: How the International System Can Still Check China and Russia," *Foreign Affairs*, May–June 2022, https://www .foreignaffairs.com/articles/ukraine/2022-04-06/china-russia-ukraine-international -system-outsiders.

11. Alastair Iain Johnston, "The Failures of the 'Failure of Engagement' with China," *The Washington Quarterly*, vol. 42, no. 2 (Summer 2019), pp. 99–114.

12. William Clinton, *A National Security Strategy for a New Century* (Washington, DC: The White House, October 1998), https://www.whitehouse.gov/WH/EOP/NSC/ html/documents/nssr/pdf.

13. Evan Medeiros, "How to Craft a Durable China Strategy," *Foreign Affairs*, March 17, 2021, https://www.foreignaffairs.com/articles/united-states/2021-03-17/ how-craft-durable-china-strategy#author-info.

14. Gurtov, *Engaging Adversaries*, pp. 61–90.

15. Kenneth Lieberthal and Susan Thornton, "Forty-Plus Years of U.S.-China Diplomacy: Realities and Recommendations," in Thurston, ed., *Engaging China*, pp. 376–77.

16. "Remarks of President Obama and President Xi Jinping of the People's Republic of China after Bilateral Meeting," June 8, 2013, www.whitehouse.gov/the -press-office/2013/06/08/remarks-president-obama-and-president-xi-jinping-peoples -republic-china-.

17. "Remarks by President Obama and President Xi of the People's Republic of China before Bilateral Meeting," September 6, 2013, www.whitehouse.gov/the-press -office/2013/09/06/remarks-president-obama-and-president-xi-peoples-republic -china-bilatera.

18. See my "The Uncertain Future of US-China Relations," *The Asia-Pacific Journal*, vol. 11, Issue 52, No. 1 (December 30, 2013), http://japanfocus.org/-Mel-Gurtov/4052.

19. Ben Rhodes, *The World as It Is: A Memoir of the Obama White House* (New York: Random House, 2019), p. 165.

20. US National Security Council, "National Security Strategy," February 2015, https://obamawhitehouse.archives.gov/sites/default/files/docs/2015_national_security_strategy_2.pdf.

21. Yeling Tan, "How the WTO Changed China."

22. John J. Mearsheimer, "The Inevitable Rivalry: America, China, and the Tragedy of Great Power Politics," *Foreign Affairs*, vol. 100, no. 6 (September–December 2021), p. 48. [48–58]

23. Fingar, "The Logic and Efficacy of Engagement," p. 39.

24. Quoted by Dali L. Yang, "The COVID-19 Pandemic and the Estrangement of US-China Relations," *Asian Perspective*, vol. 45, no. 1 (Winter 2001), p. 10.

25. For an overview of the trade war's costs, see "New Research Counts the Costs of the Sino-American Trade War," *The Economist*, January 1, 2022, https://www.economist.com/finance-and-economics/2022/01/01/new-research-counts-the-costs-of-the-sino-american-trade-war.

26. US Department of Defense, *Indo-Pacific Strategy Report: Preparedness, Partnerships, and Promoting a Networked Region*, June 1, 2019, https://media.defense.gov/2019/Jul/01/2002152311/-1/-1/1/DEPARTMENT-OF-DEFENSE-INDO-PACIFIC-STRATEGY-REPORT-2019.PDF. In a related strategy document, the Trump administration asserted as one of its "presumptions" about China that it aims to "dissolve U.S. alliances and partnerships in the [Indo-Pacific] region. China will exploit vacuums and opportunities created by these diminished bonds." US National Security Council, "U.S. Strategic Framework for the Indo-Pacific," n.d., https://trumpwhitehouse.archives.gov/wp-content/uploads/2021/01/IPS-Final-Declass.pdf.

27. Further on Trump's China policy, see my "The China Conundrum," *China-US Focus*, September 26, 2018, https://www.chinausfocus.com/foreign-policy/the-china-conundrum.

28. US Office of the Secretary of State, Policy Planning Staff, *The Elements of the China Challenge*, November 2020, https://www.state.gov/wp-content/uploads/2020/11/20-02832-Elements-of-China-Challenge-508.pdf.

29. Michael Pompeo, "Communist China and the Free World's Future," Nixon Library, July 23, 2020, https://www.state.gov/communist-china-and-the-free-worlds-future/.

30. See Pompeo's speech to students at Georgia Tech University, "The Chinese Communist Party on the American Campus," December 9, 2020, https://www.state.gov/the-chinese-communist-party-on-the-american-campus.

31. Ana Swanson and Keith Bradsher, "U.S.-China Trade Standoff May Be Initial Skirmish in Broader Economic War," *NYT*, May 11, 2019.

32. Anna Fifield, "China Wasn't Wild about Mike Pompeo before the Virus; It's Really Gunning for Him Now," *WaPo*, April 30, 2020.

33. Robert O'Brien, "The Chinese Communist Party's Ideology and Global Ambitions," June 26, 2020, https://trumpwhitehouse.archives.gov/briefings-statements/chinese-communist-partys-ideology-global-ambitions/. See also Edward Wong and Steven Lee Myers, "Officials Push U.S.-China Relations toward Point of No Return," *NYT*, July 25, 2020.

34. See "Remarks by Vice President Pence at the Frederic V. Malek Memorial Lecture," October 24, 2019, https://vn.usembassy.gov/remarks-by-vice-president-pence-at-the-frederic-v-malek-memorial-lecture. Examples of Pence's misstatements: "Much of [China's economic] success was driven by American investment in China"; "we rebuilt China over the last 25 years"; and "President Trump has stood strong for free and fair trade."

35. See Mel Gurtov and Mark Selden, "The Dangerous New US Consensus on China and the Future of US-China Relations," *The Asia-Pacific Journal*, August 1, 2019, https://apjjf.org/2019/15/Gurtov-Selden.html.

36. Ratcliffe, who had no background in intelligence when he was appointed, also made the astounding claim that "US intelligence shows that China has even conducted human testing on members of the People's Liberation Army in hope of developing soldiers with biologically enhanced capabilities." John Ratcliffe (director of National Intelligence), "China Is National Security Threat No. 1," *Wall Street Journal*, December 3, 2020, https://www.wsj.com/articles/china-is-national-security-threat-no-1-11607019599.

37. "United States Strategic Approach to the People's Republic of China," www.whitehouse.gov/U.S.-Strategic-Approach-to-The-Peoples-Republic-of-China-Report-5.20.20(1).pdf. "Given the strategic choices China's leadership is making," the paper reads, "the United States now acknowledges and accepts the relationship with the PRC as the CCP has always framed it internally: one of great power competition."

38. This was the advice given by the National Republican Senatorial Committee in a memo to candidates. See Katie Edmondson, "Faced with Crisis and Re-election, Republican Senators Blame China," *NYT*, June 13, 2020.

39. *Renmin wang*, "How Will China's Economy Fare? A Close Look at the Friction in China-US Trade" (in Chinese), October 2019, http://politics.people.com.cn/GB/8198/426918/index.html. See also Associated Press, "China Voices Strength, Pushes Nationalism around Trade War," *NYT*, May 15, 2019.

40. Xinhua, "American Bullying Can Only Be Dealt with Calmly" (in Chinese), May 12, 2019, https://news.ifeng.com/c/7mbmnHOI9ia.

41. *Renmin Ribao* editorial at www.cnbc.com/2019/05/29/dont-say-we-didnt-warn-you---a-phrase-from-china-signals-the-trade-war-could-get-even-worse.html.

42. Amy Qin, "To Many Chinese, America Was Like 'Heaven'; Now They're Not So Sure," *NYT*, May 18, 2019.

43. Keith Bradsher and Steven Lee Myers, "China Orders U.S. to Shut Chengdu Consulate, Retaliating for Houston," *NYT*, July 24, 2020.

44. *Renmin Ribao*, "Commentator," May 25, 2019.

45. Jungkun Seo, "Strange Bedfellows and US China Policy in the Era of Polarized Politics," *The Korean Journal of Defense Analysis*, vol. 29, no. 1 (March 2017), pp. 47–69.

46. Further on the anti-China consensus, see Gurtov and Selden, "The Dangerous New US Consensus on China and the Future of US-China Relations." See also Ellen Nakashima, "China Specialists Who Long Supported Engagement Are Now Warning of Beijing's Efforts to Influence American Society," *WaPo*, November 28, 2018. Significant exceptions include Stephen Wertheim, "Is It Too Late to Stop a Cold War with China?" *NYT*, June 8, 2019; Jessica Chen Weiss, "A World Safe for Autocracy? China's Rise and the Future of Global Politics," Foreign Affairs, vol. 98, no. 4 (July–August 2019), pp. 92–102. An open letter to President Trump by China specialists M. Taylor Fravel, J. Stapleton Roy, Michael D. Swaine, Susan A. Thornton, and Ezra Vogel, "Making China a U.S. Enemy Is Counterproductive," WaPo, July 3, 2019, signed by major figures in China scholarship, is the most thoughtful challenge to the consensus to date.

47. Adam Schiff, "The World," September 30, 2020, https://www.pri.org/stories/2020-09-30/schiff-us-power-confront-hard-targets-china-has-really-atrophied.

48. Robert Kuttner, "The China Challenge," *The American Prospect*, September–October 2021, https://prospect.org/world/china-challenge/.

49. "[A]ll China's subsidies, protectionism, cheating on trade rules, forced technology transfers and stealing of intellectual property since the 1970s became a much greater threat. If the U.S. and Europe allowed China to continue operating by the same formula that it had used to grow from poverty to compete for all the industries of the future, we'd be crazy. Trump is right about that." Thomas Friedman, "China Deserves Donald Trump," *NYT*, May 21, 2019.

50. Office of Senator Tom Cotton, "Beat China: Targeted Decoupling and the Economic Long War," February 2021, https://www.cotton.senate.gov/imo/media/doc/210216_1700_China%20Report_FINAL.pdf.

51. Office of Senator Chuck Grassley, "News Releases: Grassley to Schools: Confucius Institutes Are Fronts for Chinese Propaganda; Just Ask FBI Mar 11, 2020."

52. The bill was co-sponsored by Republican senator John Kennedy of Louisiana and Democratic senator Doug Jones of Alabama. Their specific argument was that Chinese-trained teachers are approved by the communist party and are therefore party hacks; that Confucius Institutes (CI) must agree to be governed by both Chinese and US law; that the party must approve all CI events and speakers; that CIs must agree that "certain topics will be off-limits"; and that CI teachers teach communist party versions of "Chinese history, culture and current events." The bill, S.939, is in the *Congressional Record* at https://www.congress.gov/bill/116th-congress/senate-bill/939.

53. U.S.-China Economic and Security Review Commission, *2021 Annual Report to Congress*, https://www.uscc.gov/sites/default/files/2021-11/Chapter_1_Section_1--CCPs_Ambitions_and_Challenges_at_Its_Centennial.pdf.

54. Larry Diamond and Orville Schell, "Chinese Influence & American Interests: Promoting Constructive Vigilance," Hoover Institution and Asia Society, November 2018, https://www.hoover.org/research/chinas-influence-american-interests-promoting-constructive-vigilance.

55. In 2017, when Trump took office, positive views of China were about equally shared by Democrats and Republicans at 44 percent and 47 percent respectively. Kat

Devlin, Laura Silver, and Christine Huang, "U.S. View of China Increasingly Negative Amid Coronavirus Outbreak," Pew Research Center, April 21, 2020, https://www.pewresearch.org/global/2020/04/21/u-s-views-of-china-increasingly-negative-amid-coronavirus-outbreak/.

CHAPTER 3

1. Jude Blanchette, "Xi's Gamble: The Race to Consolidate Power and Stave Off Disaster," *Foreign Affairs*, vol. 100, no. 4 (July–August 2021), pp. 10–19.

2. Susan L. Shirk, "China in Xi's 'New Era': The Return to Personalistic Rule," *Journal of Democracy*, vol. 29, no. 2 (April 2018), https://muse.jhu.edu/article/690071.

3. Elizabeth Perry makes a convincing case that "ideology in the PRC has reclaimed an explicit primacy and global ambition" under Xi, just as had been true under Mao. Xi's "China Dream," his references to the historical past, and the elevation of his "thought" must be taken seriously, she argues. See "Debating Maoism in Contemporary China: Reflections on Benjamin I. Schwartz, Chinese Communism and the Rise of Mao," *The Asia-Pacific Journal*, January 1, 2021, https://apjjf.org/2021/1/Perry.html.

4. Deng Xiaoping, *Fundamental Issues in Present-Day China* (Beijing: Foreign Languages Press, 1987), p. 165.

5. Paul Mozur, "Coronavirus Outrage Spurs China's Internet Police to Action," *NYT*, March 16, 2020.

6. See the scathing critique by the legal scholar Xu Zhangrun, "Xi's China, the Handiwork of an Autocratic Roué," *New York Review of Books*, August 9, 2021, https://www.nybooks.com/daily/2021/08/09/xis-china-the-handiwork-of-an-autocratic-roue/?lp_txn_id=1269942.

7. Committee to Protect Journalists, "Number of Journalists behind Bars Reaches Global High," December 13, 2021, https://cpj.org/reports/2021/12/number-of-journalists-behind-bars-reaches-global-high/.

8. Paul Krugman, "This Might Be China's 'Babaru' Moment," *NYT*, September 24, 2021; Phillip Inman, "Xi Jinping's Drive for Economic Equality Comes at a Delicate Moment for China," *The Guardian*, September 2, 2021, https://www.theguardian.com/world/2021/sep/02/xi-jinpings-drive-for-economic-equality-comes-at-a-delicate-moment-for-china.

9. "Announcement of the Full Meeting of the 19th Central Committee, 6th CCP Plenum," Xinhua Net, November 11, 2021, http://www.news.cn/politics/2021-11/11/c_1128055386.htm.

10. Just one example: A guideline introduced in August 2021 by China's education ministry entitled "Curriculum Guide to Include Xi Jinping Thought on Socialism with Chinese Characteristics for the New Era," issued by the National Textbook Committee. As reported in the Chinese press, schools at every level must "fully integrate" Xi Jinping's thoughts on socialism into every part of their curricula, including "philosophy, the social sciences and natural sciences; and be incorporated into every aspect

and the whole process of ideological and moral education, cultural knowledge education, and social practice education," *Renmin Ribao*, August 24, 2021.

11. Javier C. Hernández, "As China Cracks Down on Coronavirus Coverage, Journalists Fight Back," *NYT*, March 14, 2020; Chris Buckley, "Incendiary Essay Ignites
Guessing over Xi's Plans for China," *NYT*, September 11, 2021.

12. Gerry Shih, "China Detains Xu Zhangrun, Leading Critic of President Xi Jinping," *WaPo*, July 6, 2020.

13. Swedish officials have not been allowed access to Gui, and the Xi government
has threatened Sweden over its continued support of him, notably after Gui received
a human rights award in 2019 from Swedish PEN. *The Guardian*, November 18,
2019, and February 25, 2020. CGTN, the Chinese news station that apparently is
under the CCP's control, was fined £100,000 for that episode. "CGTN Sanctioned
on Multiple Counts for Airing Forced Confessions," *Safeguard Defenders*, August
26, 2021, https://safeguarddefenders.com/en/blog/cgtn-sanctioned-multiple-counts
-airing-forced-confessions.

14. Javier C. Hernández, "China Detains Activist Who Accused Xi of Coronavirus Cover-up," *NYT*, February 17, 2020; Emily Feng, "Rights Activist Xu Zhiyong
Arrested in China amid Crackdown on Dissent," National Public Radio, February
17, 2020, www.npr.org/2020/02/17/806584471/rights-activist-xu-zhiyong-arrested-in
-china-amid-crackdown-on-dissent.

15. Abutaleb et al. (n. 1); Michael D. Shear, Maggie Haberman, Noah Weiland,
Sharon LaFraniere, and Mark Mazzetti, "Trump's Focus as Pandemic Raged: What
Would It Mean for Him?" *NYT*, December 30, 2020.

16. Yasmeen Abutaleb, Ashley Parker, Josh Dawsey, and Philip Rucker, "The
Inside Story of How Trump's Denial, Mismanagement and Magical Thinking Led to
the Pandemic's Dark Winter," *WaPo*, December 19, 2020.

17. Michael Bender, "Transcript of President Trump's Interview with the Wall
Street Journal," June 19, 2020, https://www.wsj.com/articles/transcript-of-president
-trumps-interview-with-the-wall-street-journal-11592501000.

18. Dali L. Yang, "The COVID-19 Pandemic and the Estrangement of US-China
Relations," pp. 7–31.

19. Ian Birrell, "Virus 'Definitely' Began in China, Say US Scientists," *Daily Mail*
(London), January 31, 2021, https://www.dailymail.co.uk/news/article-9205501/IAN
-BIRRELL-Virus-definitely-began-China-say-scientists-outbreak-started-October
-2019.html.

20. Ian Birrell, "New Evidence of China's Coronavirus Cover-up," *Daily Mail*,
June 6, 2020, https://www.dailymail.co.uk/news/article-8395163/China-scientists
-KNEW-virus-lethal-officials-told-world-mystery-outbreak.html.

21. Xinhuanet, February 3, 2020, https://xinhuanet.com/english/2020-02/03/c
_138753250.htm.

22. Raymond Zhong, Paul Mozur, Jeff Kao, and Aaron Krolik, "'No Negative
News': How China Censored the Coronavirus," *NYT*, December 19, 2020.

23. Dake Kang, Maria Cheng, and Sam McNeil, "China Clamps Down in Hidden
Hunt for Coronavirus Origins," *AP News*, December 30, 2020, https://apnews.com/

article/united-nations-coronavirus-pandemic-china-only-on-ap-bats-24fbadc58cee3a
40bca2ddf7a14d2955.

24. "Pension Figures from Hubei Spark Doubts over Virus Deaths," *Radio Free Asia*, February 17, 2021, https://www.rfa.org/english/news/china/doubts-02172021092531.html.

25. Editorial Board, "A Chinese Lawyer Criticized the Regime's Handling of the Pandemic; Then He Disappeared," *NYT*, May 12, 2020. The *Times* story, based on reporting in the *South China Morning Press* in Hong Kong, noted that nearly 500 people had been arrested in the first three months of 2020 for making public comments deemed detrimental to the authorities about the coronavirus.

26. Vivian Wang, "She Chronicled China's Crisis; Now She Is Accused of Spreading Lies," *NYT*, December 25, 2020.

27. For example, a lawyer, Xie Yang, who tried to intervene on behalf of Zhang Zhan: https://twitter.com/ZhouFengSuo/status/1463143875564998660.

28. *Guancha* (Observer), May 1, 2020, https://www.guancha.cn/internation/2020_05_01_548969.shtml.

29. Javier C. Hernández, "As Protests Engulf the United States, China Revels in the Unrest," *NYT*, June 2, 2020.

30. Michael Swaine, "Chinese Views of U.S. Decline," *China Leadership Monitor*, September 1, 2021, https://www.prcleader.org/swaine-2.

31. Fang, Li, and Liu, "Chinese Public Opinion about US-China Relations."

32. Meng Weizhan, "Is China's IR Academic Community Becoming More Anti-American?" *Asian Perspective*, vol. 44 (2020), pp. 139–61.

33. Suisheng Zhao, "Top-level Design and Enlarged Diplomacy: Foreign and Security Policymaking in Xi Jinping's China," *Journal of Contemporary China*, 2022, DOI: 10.1080/10670564.2022.2052440.

CHAPTER 4

1. Mel Gurtov, *Will This Be China's Century? A Skeptic's View* (Boulder, CO: Lynne Rienner, 2013).

2. According to the UN Development Programme's *Human Development Report 2020* (http://hdr.undp.org/en/content/download-data), of 189 countries, China ranks 86th, between Brazil and Ecuador. (The United States ranks 17th.)

3. Over the roughly forty years since China's economic reforms began in 1978, reductions in rural poverty account for about 70 percent of the world total, according to the World Bank. Investment in poverty alleviation at all levels of government during that time amount to about $244 billion, with a drop in the incidence of rural poverty (as of 2017) from 97.5 percent to 3.1 percent. People's Republic of China, State Council Information Office, *Poverty Alleviation: China's Experience and Contribution*, April 2021, https://Xinhuanet.com/English/2021-04/06/c-139860414.htm.

4. Steven Lee Myers and Alexandra Stevenson, "China's Births Hit Historic Low, a Political Problem for Beijing," *NYT*, January 17, 2022.

5. Scott Rozelle and Natalie Hell, *Invisible China: How the Urban-Rural Divide Threatens China's Rise* (Chicago: University of Chicago Press, 2020). The UN's *Human Development Report 2020* would seem to corroborate the Rozelle-Hell finding. Its data shows that China's mean years of schooling is 8 (in 2019) and expected years of schooling is 14, both well below comparable figures (averaging about 12 and 18 years, respectively) for high human development countries. (Mean years of schooling is defined as: "Average number of years of education received by people ages 25 and older, converted from education attainment levels using official durations of each level.") Interestingly, the UN's report does not include two other important figures relevant to China's education: the percentage of the labor force that is skilled and the ratio of educational and health expenditures to military spending.

6. Private communication from Joe Parker in China.

7. Michael Pettis, "China's Record Trade Gap a Symptom of Struggle to Rebalance Its Economy," *Financial Times*, January 17, 2022, https://www.ft.com/content/a38c83c2-4e1a-45dd-8558-9ff25bd870c8.

8. "Statement by President Xi Jinping at Virtual Event of Opening of the 73rd World Health Assembly, Fighting COVID-19 through Solidarity and Cooperation: Building a Global Community of Health for All," May 18, 2020, transcript.

9. Dali L. Yang, "The COVID-19 Pandemic and the Estrangement of US-China Relations," pp. 17–20.

10. Carl Bildt, "The Post-American World Is Now on Full Display," *WaPo*, May 19, 2020.

11. David Wertime, "'Not the World's Number One': Chinese Social Media Piles on the U.S.," *Politico*, May 4, 2020, www.politico.com/news/magazine/2020/05/04/china-america-struggle-disaster-221741.

12. State Council Information Office of the PRC, "Fighting COVID-19: China in Action," June 2020, http://english.scio.gov.cn/whitepapers/2020-06/07/content_76135269.htm.

13. Lara Jakes, "Despite Big Promises, U.S. Has Delivered Limited Aid in Global Virus Response," *NYT*, June 7, 2020.

14. The figure is 400 million vaccine doses donated. Amy Cheng, Adela Suliman, and Brittany Shammas, "White House Announces 400 Million Vaccine Doses Made to Global Effort," *WaPo*, January 26, 2022.

15. "The Latest on Southeast Asia," Center for Strategic and International Studies, July 22, 2021, https://www.csis.org/blogs/latest-southeast-asia/latest-southeast-asia-july-22-2021.

16. Sui-Lee Wee, "China Wanted to Show Off Its Vaccines; It's Backfiring," *NYT*, January 25, 2021.

17. Heloísa Traiano and Terrence McCoy, "Brazil Battles Coronavirus with a Chinese Vaccine Even the Chinese Concede Could Be Better," *WaPo*, April 15, 2021.

18. Michael Birnbaum, "E.U. Accuses China of Waging Pandemic Disinformation Campaign," *WaPo*, June 10, 2020.

19. Lucien O. Chauvin, Anthony Faiola, and Eva Dou, "Squeezed Out of the Race for Western Vaccines, Developing Countries Turn to China," *WaPo*, February 16, 2021.

20. The Brazilian turnabout reportedly was linked to a decision on Huawei's 5G system. At first the Bolsinaro government had treated Huawei as a threat to privacy, but after obtaining the vaccine Huawei was allowed to compete in the 5G auction. The fact that Bolsinaro's ally, Donald Trump, who had warred against Huawei, was no longer in office also mattered. Ernesto Londoño and Letícia Casado, "Brazil Needs Vaccines, China Is Benefiting," *NYT*, March 15, 2021.

21. Jack Crowe, "Beware China's 'Investigation' into COVID's Origins," *The National Review*, March 25, 2021, https://www.nationalreview.com/2021/03/beware -chinas-internal-investigation-into-covids-origins/. Peter Daszak, the US scientist, had conflicting ties to the Wuhan laboratory that would seem to explain his early insistence that the lab had no part in the spread of the coronavirus.

22. Andrew Harnik, "China Pushes Conspiracy Theories on COVID-19 Origins, Vaccine," *Globe and Mail* (Toronto), January 25, 2021, https://www.theglobeandmail .com/amp/world/article-china-pushes-fringe-theories-on-pandemic-origins-pfizer -vaccine/; Cristiano Lima, "China Is Exploiting Search Engines to Push Propaganda about Origins of Covid-19, Study Finds," *WaPo*, October 5, 2021.

23. Experiments with bats at the Wuhan Institute of Virology are at the center of the transference theory. Jonathan Bucks, "New Cover-up Fears as Chinese Officials Delete Critical Data about Wuhan Lab," *Daily Mail* (London), January 9, 2021, https: //www.dailymail.co.uk/news/article-9129681/New-cover-fears-Chinese-officials -delete-critical-data-Wuhan-lab.html; Glenn Kessler, "Timeline: How the Wuhan Lab-leak Theory Suddenly Became Credible," *WaPo*, May 25, 2021.

24. Amy Maxmen, "Scientists Struggle to Probe COVID's Origins amid Sparse Data from China," *Nature*, March 17, 2022, https://www.nature.com/articles/d41586 -022-00732-0.

25. "Open Letter: Call for a Full and Unrestricted International Forensic Investigation into the Origins of Covid-19," March 4, 2021 [published in *Wall Street Journal* same day]. Also "Open Letter to the World Health Organization and Members of Its Executive Board," April 30, 2021.

26. "Open Letter: Call for a Comprehensive Investigation of the Origin of SARS-CoV-2, If Possible with Chinese Government Participation," June 28, 2021.

27. Among the facts that point to that possibility is a revelation by a leading US epidemiologist with extensive experience in China, Ian Lupkin of Columbia University, that he learned of a "new outbreak" in Wuhan in mid-December 2019, more than two weeks before Chinese authorities notified the WHO about a possible pandemic. Ian Birrell, "Top US Scientist Reveals He First Heard about Virus Outbreak in Wuhan Two Weeks before Beijing Warned the World about Covid," *Daily Mail*, September 4, 2021, https://www.dailymail.co.uk/news/article-9958207/Scientist-reveals-heard -Covid-Wuhan-TWO-WEEKS-Beijing-warned-world.html.

28. On Britain, see David Green, "The U.K.'s Incoherent China Strategy," *World Politics Review*, January 29, 2021, https://www.worldpoliticsreview.com/articles /29387/boris-johnson-s-approach-to-china-uk-relations-is-incoherent.

29. Eurostat, "China-EU International Trade in Goods Statistics," March 2021, https://ec.europa.eu/eurostat/statistics-explained/index.php?title=China-EU_ -_international_trade_in_goods_statistics.

30. Andreas Fulda, "Germany's China Policy of 'Change through Trade' Has Failed," RUSI (Royal United Services Institute), June 1, 2020, https://www.rusi.org/explore-our-research/publications/commentary/germanys-china-policy-change-through-trade-has-failed.

31. Julia Pamilih and Chris Cash, "The UK and China: Next Steps," China Research Group, September 2021, https://static1.squarespace.com/static/5f75a6c74b43624d99382ab6/t/61504b44c2965710d91a7bcd/1632652104633/The+UK+and+China_+Next+Steps.pdf.

32. Stephen Castle, "U.K. Suspends Extradition Treaty with Hong Kong Over Security Law," *NYT*, July 20, 2020. Under Britain's plan, people who hold British National (Overseas) passports would be granted twelve-month renewable visas that would allow them to work in Britain with the possibility of eventual citizenship. Besides the existing passport holders, an additional 2.5 million people from Hong Kong are also to be eligible for the passports.

33. Fulda, "Germany China Policy of 'Change through Trade' Has Failed."

34. Eva Dou, Pei Lin Wu, and Isabelle Khurshudyan, "Huawei Calls on an Old Friend, Russia, as U.S. Sanctions Bite Down," *NYT*, May 28, 2021.

35. "Foreign Affairs Committee Publish Report: 'Never Again: The UK's Responsibility to Act on Atrocities in Xinjiang and Beyond,'" July 8, 2021, https://committees.parliament.uk/committee/78/foreign-affairs-committee/news/156425/fac-xinjiang-detention-camps-report-published-21-22/.

36. *Safeguard Defenders*, "CGTN Sanctioned on Multiple Counts."

37. Pamilih and Cash, "The UK and China"; Julia Pamilih, "Data: Chinese Research Partnerships with UK Universities," China Research Group, June 9, 2021, https://chinaresearchgroup.org/research/data-chinese-research-partnerships-with-uk-universities.

38. Germany's ambassador to the UN, Christoph Heusgen, announced this demand. DW News via Twitter, October 7, 2020.

39. "France Steps Up Calls for Probe into Uighurs," RTHK News, July 29, 2020, https://news.rthk.hk/rthk/en/component/k2/1540464-20200729.htm.

40. "German Universities Move to Reject China's Confucius Institutes," *Taiwan News*, July 28, 2020, https://www.taiwannews.com.tw/en/news/3975526.

41. Keith Johnson, "How Europe Fell Out of Love with China," *Foreign Policy*, June 25, 2020, https://foreignpolicy.com/2020/06/25/china-europe-rival-strategic-competitor-huawei/; Andrew Higgins, "Serbia Hails Chinese Companies as Saviors, but Locals Chafe at Costs," *NYT*, March 27, 2021; Gabriele Carrer, "Italian Alarm as China Eyes Port of Palermo," Center for European Policy Analysis, December 6, 2021, https://cepa.org/italian-alarm-as-china-eyes-port-of-palermo/.

42. Aryaman Bhatnagar, "Is the EU's COVID-19 Response Losing Central and Eastern Europe to China?" *World Politics Review*, May 8, 2020, www.worldpoliticsreview.com/articles/28744/is-the-eu-s-covid-19-response-losing-central-and-eastern-europe-to-china.

43. Emily Rauhala, "Stalled E.U.-China Investment Deal Signals European Skepticism on China, Willingness to Work with Biden," *WaPo*, December 26, 2020.

44. Ministry of Foreign Affairs of China, "State Councilor and Foreign Minister Wang Yi Gives Interview."

45. Emily Rauhala, Lily Kuo, Ellen Nakashima, and Cate Cadell, "How the Ukraine War Has Europe Reassessing Relations with China," *WaPo*, March 31, 2022. Exemplifying the changed mood in Europe was Lithuania's decision to open a "Taiwanese" trade office in Taiwan, a move that drew China's ire.

46. Michael Gardner, "Germany Doubles Funding for China Studies, Collaboration," *University World News*, July 7, 2021, https://www.universityworldnews.com/post.php?story=20210707080823132.

47. "Solidarity Statement on Behalf of Scholars Sanctioned for Their Work on China," in Andreas Fulda and David Missal, "German Academic Freedom Is Now Decided in Beijing," *Foreign Policy*, October 28, 2021, https://foreignpolicy.com/2021/10/28/germany-china-censorship-universities-confucius-institute/.

48. James Panichi, "Australia's 'Spartacus' Moment: Canberra Pushes Back at Beijing," *Global Asia*, vol. 16, no. 2 (June 2021), pp. 90–95.

49. James Grubel, "ANU Helping to Reshape Australia's Ties to China," *ANU Reporter*, n.d., https://reporter.anu.edu.au/anu-helping-reshape-australia%E2%80%99s-ties-china.

50. See Clive Hamilton, *Silent Invasion: China's Influence in Australia* (Melbourne: Hardie Grant Books, 2018), pp. 138–41. As that book's title indicates, the author upholds the second view.

51. According to the *Sydney Morning Herald*, the grievances also included "government funding for 'anti-China' research at the Australian Strategic Policy Institute, raids on Chinese journalists and academic visa cancellations, 'spearheading a crusade' in multilateral forums on China's affairs in Taiwan, Hong Kong and Xinjiang, . . . and blocking 10 Chinese foreign investment deals across infrastructure, agriculture and animal husbandry sectors." Jonathan Kearsley, Eryk Bagshaw, and Anthony Galloway, "'If You Make China the Enemy, China Will Be the Enemy': Beijing's Fresh Threat to Australia," *Sydney Morning Herald*, November 18, 2020, https://www.smh.com.au/world/asia/if-you-make-china-the-enemy-china-will-be-the-enemy-beijing-s-fresh-threat-to-australia-20201118-p56fqs.html.

52. Yan Zhuang and Damien Cave, "Australia Asks: How Far Is Too Far in Making China a Campaign Weapon?" *NYT*, March 10, 2022.

53. Damien Cave and Chris Buckley, "Why Australia Bet the House on Lasting American Power in Asia," *NYT*, September 16, 2021. The submarines will be powered by highly enriched uranium that can be used in weapons. For Washington, the decision also produced an unpleasant surprise: French anger at not having been consulted, going so far as to call the decision a "stab in the back" and a serious setback to alliance relations. The French had tried to reach agreement with Australia for the sale of non-nuclear submarines, but the deal collapsed. Roger Cohen, "France Is Outraged by U.S. Nuclear Submarine Deal with Australia," *NYT*, September 16, 2021.

54. "Joe Biden Announces US, UK and Australia Co-operation on Hypersonic Weapons," *Financial Times*, April 6, 2022, https://www.ft.com/content/b8ddf153-b9ca-4db5-8835-cb8509a9921f.

55. Embassy of the People's Republic of China in the United States of America, "Wang Yi: U.S.-Britain-Australia Nuclear Submarine Cooperation Poses Three Hidden Dangers," September 28, 2021, http://www.china-embassy.org/eng/zgyw/t1911163.htm.

56. Shotaro Tani, "Xi Says China Ready to Sign ASEAN's Nuclear Arms-Free Zone Treaty," *Nikkei Asia*, Novembeer 22, 2021, https://asia.nikkei.com/Politics/International-relations/Xi-says-China-ready-to-sign-ASEAN-s-nuclear-arms-free-zone-treaty.

57. John Fitzgerald, ed., *Taking the Low Road: China's Influence in Australia's States and Territories* (Barton: Australian Strategic Policy Institute, 2022), http://ad-aspi.s3.ap-southeast-2.amazonaws.com/2022-02/Taking%20the%20low%20road.pdf?VersionId=NIkDeFmjPYAxwSb45VMUmOvFuhAkKekk.

58. See Peter Van Ness, "Hitting Reset on the Australia-China Relationship," *East Asia Forum*, February 2, 2022, https://www.eastasiaforum.org/2022/02/02/hitting-reset-on-the-australia-china-relationship/.

59. New Zealand House of Representatives, Justice Committee, "Inquiry into the 2019 Local Elections and Liquor Licensing Trust Elections, and Recent Energy Trust Elections," July 2021, https://www.parliament.nz/resource/en-NZ/SCR_112173/ac05 6d5bfbb02d80f3171b435891330c1ff92bb7.

60. Catherine Churchman, "NZ-China Relations: What's in It for Beijing?" *Newsroom*, July 12, 2021, https://www.newsroom.co.nz/nz-china-relations-whats-in-it-for-beijing.

61. https://twitter.com/crehage/status/1376246590151798792/photo/1.

62. Catherine Tunney, "Spy Agency Warned Trudeau China's Tactics Becoming More 'Sophisticated,' 'Insidious,'" *CBC News*, December 7, 2021, https://www.cbc.ca/news/politics/csis-trudeau-china-media-1.6270750.

63. A Reuters report cited an April 2020 briefing paper by the China Institutes of International Relations, one of several officially sponsored think tanks, that made this argument. See www.reuters.com/article/us-health-coronavirus-china-sentiment-ex-idUSKBN22G19C.

64. Ian Williams, "How China Is Stoking Racial Tensions in the West," *The Spectator*, May 2, 2021, https://www.spectator.co.uk/article/how-china-is-stoking-racial-tensions-in-the-west.

65. Sophie McNeill, "'They Don't Understand the Fear We Have,'" Human Rights Watch Report, June 30, 2021, https://www.hrw.org/report/2021/06/30/they-dont-understand-fear-we-have/how-chinas-long-reach-repression-undermines.

66. German Lopez, "U.S. Institutions Are Increasingly Silencing Themselves to Win Access to China," *NYT*, February 20, 2022.

67. An investigation of the World Bank's annual "Doing Business" survey, which ranked countries by their business climate and therefore openness to foreign investment, found that the bank's leadership in 2018 ordered China's ranking inflated so as to avoid offending Beijing. "Inquiry Finds World Bank Officials, Including now-I.M.F. Chief, Pushed Staff to Inflate China Data," *NYT*, September 16, 2021.

68. Amy Qin and Julie Creswell, "China Is a Minefield, and Foreign Firms Keep Hitting New Tripwires," *NYT*, Oct 9, 2019.

69. Raymond Zhong and Sopan Deb, "Celtics Games Are Pulled in China after Enes Kanter's Pro-Tibet Posts," *NYT*, October 21, 2021.

70. Drew Harwell and Ellen Nakashima, "Federal Prosecutors Accuse Zoom Executive of Working with the Chinese Government to Surveil Users and Suppress Video Calls," *WaPo*, December 18, 2020.

71. Ben Bland, "China Censorship Drive Splits Academic Publishers," *Financial Times*, November 4, 2017, https://www.ft.com/content/b68b2f86-c072-11e7-b8a3 -38a6e068f464.

72. The Spanish NGO Safeguard Defenders is the source of the report. Matthew Loh, "Xi Jinping Forced 10,000 People Who Fled Overseas through an Operation Called 'Sky Net,' Says Human Rights NGO," *Business Insider*, January 19, 2022, https://www.businessinsider.com/china-forced-10000-fugitives-return-operation-sky -net-safeguard-defenders-2022-1. At other times, according to this report, the fugitive, living in a country friendly to Beijing, will be extradited. In March 2022 five Chinese in New York were charged with being PRC agents who allegedly harassed and threatened Chinese critics of Beijing, including a candidate for the US Congress. It is not clear if those agents are part of the Sky Net program. Ellen Nakashima and Shayna Jacobs, "Five People Charged with Acting as Chinese Government Agents to Spy on and Harass U.S. Residents Critical of Beijing," *WaPo*, March 17, 2022.

73. Marco D'Eramo, "Our Daily Sanction," *New Left Review*, January 24, 2022, https://newleftreview.org/sidecar/posts/our-daily-sanction.

74. BBC News, "Xi Jinping Calls for More 'Loveable' Image for China in Bid to Make Friends," June 2, 2021, https://www.bbc.com/news/world-asia-china -57327177.

75. It is not out of the question that Cui's critique was also directed at Xi's tit-for-tat America policy. Katsuji Nakazawa, "Analysis: China's Ex-Washington Envoy Resurfaces with an Important Message," *Nikkei Asia*, January 13, 2022, https://asia .nikkei.com/Editor-s-Picks/China-up-close/Analysis-China-s-ex-Washington-envoy -resurfaces-with-an-important-message.

76. According to a CNN investigation (Jomana Karadsheh and Gul Tuysuz, "Uyghurs Are Being Deported from Muslim Countries, Raising Concerns about China's Global Reach," June 8, 2021, https://www.cnn.com/2021/06/08/middleeast /uyghur-arab-muslim-china-disappearances-cmd-intl/index.html). Three countries— Egypt, the United Arab Emirates, and Saudi Arabia—are cited as having deported Uyghurs to China.

77. "Turkey Summons Chinese Ambassador over Response to Uighur Claims," Reuters, April 6, 2021, https://www.reuters.com/article/turkey-china-diplomacy-int -idUSKBN2BT236.

78. Rayhan Asat and Yonah Diamond, "U.S. China Policy Must Confront the Genocide in Xinjiang First," *Foreign Policy*, January 21, 2021, https://foreignpolicy .com/2021/01/21/uighur-genocide-china-policy-biden-confront/.

79. Russia-China trade came to about $146 billion in 2021. That compares with Russia-US total trade of $34 billion and Russia-EU trade of $220 billion. Eugene Chausovsky, "China Can't Carry the Russian Economy," *Foreign Policy*, February 4, 2022, https://foreignpolicy.com/2022/02/04/china-russia-sanctions-ukraine/.

80. Gerry Shih, "Faced with Sanctions and Condemnation from the West, China Becomes Bedfellows with Russia," *WaPo*, March 24, 2021. In 2021 China and Russia held their first joint naval patrol in the western Pacific.

81. Edward Wong and Julian E. Barnes, "China Asked Russia to Delay Ukraine War until after Olympics, U.S. Officials Say," *NYT*, March 2, 2022. The report cites "Western intelligence."

82. See Harley Balzer, *Axis of Collusion: The Fragile Putin-Xi Partnership* (Atlantic Council, December 2021), https://www.atlanticcouncil.org/event/axis-of-collusion -the-fragile-putin-xi-partnership/.

83. Gurtov and Selden, "The Dangerous New US Consensus on China and the Future of US-China Relations"; Fareed Zakaria, "The New China Scare: Why America Shouldn't Panic about Its Latest Challenger," *Foreign Affairs*, December 6, 2019, www.foreignaffairs.com/articles/china/2019-12-06/new-china-scare.

84. Thomas Christensen, "There Will Not Be a New Cold War," *Foreign Affairs*, March 24, 2021, https://www.foreignaffairs.com/articles/united-states/2021-03-24/ there-will-not-be-new-cold-war.

85. Nicole Perlroth, "How China Transformed into a Prime Cyber Threat to the U.S.," *NYT*, July 19, 2021.

86. In a report of the US intelligence agencies (US National Intelligence Council, "Foreign Threats to the 2020 US Federal Elections," March 16, 2021, https://www.dni .gov/files/ODNI/documents/assessments/ICA-declass-16MAR21.pdf), China was cleared of any serious wrongdoing, in contrast with Russia and Iran, which were judged to have authorized influence operations using prominent Americans.

87. See, for example, the op-ed by China's ambassador to the United States: Qin Gang, "Chinese Ambassador: Where We Stand on Ukraine," *WaPo*, March 15, 2022.

88. Eleanor Olcott, "China Backs Russia's 'Security Concerns' in Crisis with West over Ukraine," *Financial Times*, January 27, 2022, https://www.ft.com/content /51a61659-8caf-4abc-aca7-4a6808917089.

89. Lily Kuo, "China Keeps Walking Its Tightrope between Russia and the West as Tensions Flare in Ukraine," *WaPo*, February 22, 2022.

90. Robin Wright, "Russia and China Unveil a Pact against America and the West," *The New Yorker*, February 7, 2022, https://www.newyorker.com/news/daily-comment /russia-and-china-unveil-a-pact-against-america-and-the-west.

91. "Joint Announcement of the People's Republic of China and the Russian Federation on the New Era in International Relations and Global Sustainable Development" (中华人民共和国和俄罗斯联邦关于新时代国际关系和全球可持续发展的联合声明), *Renmin Ribao*, February 22, 2022, http://politics.people.com.cn/n1/2022 /0204/c1001-32345502.html.

92. "Wang Yi's Telephone Call with the Ukraine Foreign Minister Kuleba" (in Chinese), March 1, 2022, https://www.fmprc.gov.cn/web/wjbzhd/202203/t20220301 _10646886.shtml.

93. Qin Gang, "Chinese Ambassador: Where We Stand on Ukraine."

94. Brendan Ahern, "Vice Premier Liu He's Speech Sends Stocks Flying," *Forbes*, March 16, 2022, https://www.forbes.com/sites/brendanahern/2022/03/16/ vice-premier-liu-hes-speech-sends-stocks-flying/.

95. "Sanctions will affect global finance, energy, transportation and stability of supply chains, and dampen a global economy that is already ravaged by the pandemic," Xi said. "And this is in the interest of no one." CK Tan, "China Signals Shift on Ukraine as Russia Accused of Atrocities," *Nikkei Asia*, March 9, 2022, https://asia.nikkei.com/Politics/Ukraine-war/China-signals-shift-on-Ukraine-as-Russia-accused-of-atrocities.

96. Chausovsky, "China Can't Carry the Russian Economy."

97. "China State Banks Restrict Financing for Russian Commodities," *Bloomberg*, February 25, 2022, https://www.bloomberg.com/news/articles/2022-02-25/chinese-state-banks-restrict-financing-for-russian-commodities.

98. Reuters, "China State Refiners Shun Russian Oil Trades," April 6, 2022, https://www.reuters.com/business/energy/exclusive-china-state-refiners-shun-new-russian-oil-trades-teapots-fly-under-2022-04-06/.

99. Laura He, "4 Ways China Is Quietly Making Life Harder for Russia," CNN, March 17, 2022.

100. Anton Troianovski, "At a Ukrainian Aircraft Engine Factory, China's Military Finds a Cash-Hungry Partner," *WaPo*, May 20, 2019.

101. See news reports at https://www.washingtonpost.com/world/2022/03/07/china-russia-relationship-ukraine/; https://www.cnn.com/2022/03/08/asia/china-russia-invasion-xi-macron-scholz-intl/index.html.

102. Elizabeth Dwoskin, "China Is Russia's Most Powerful Weapon for Information Warfare," *WaPo*, April 8, 2022.

103. For example, this tweet on March 20, 2022, from Hu Xijin, the longtime, now retired, editor of *China Times*: https://m.weibo.cn/status/4749196285969009. Hu's main argument is that Russia augments China's deterrent against the United States, whereas alignment with the United States would wind up pitting China against both Russia and the United States.

104. Among those voices were five Chinese historians who circulated a letter to the leaders that opposed "unjust wars." Twitter post by David Cowhig, February 26, 2022. Of potentially greater significance is an article by Hu Wei, a policy adviser to the Chinese government's State Council or cabinet. Hu urged China's disengagement from Putin's disastrous war lest China be isolated and come under Western sanctions. Doing so, "China will surely win widespread international praise for maintaining world peace, which may help China prevent isolation but also find an opportunity to improve its relations with the United States and the West." "Possible Outcomes of the Russo-Ukraine War and China's Choice," U.S.-China Perception Monitor, March 12, 2022, https://uscnpm.org/2022/03/12/hu-wei-russia-ukraine-war-china-choice/.

105. En route, Sullivan expressed "concern" about Chinese aid to Russia and said "we have communicated to Beijing that we will not stand by and allow any country to compensate Russia for its losses from the economic sanctions." Sam Fossum, Kaitlan Collins, Jim Sciutto, and Kylie Atwood, "Russia Has Requested Military and Economic Assistance from China, US Officials Say," CNN, March 13, 2022.

106. Julian Borger and Helen Davidson, "US Urged China Not to Supply Arms to Russia at 'Intense' Rome Meeting," CNN, March 14, 2022.

107. The Biden administration was widely reported to have shared intelligence with China on the Russian buildup and invasion plans over a three-month period, with the aim to get Beijing to intercede. The Chinese were surprised and evidently unconvinced until the invasion happened—and meantime, let the Russians know of the US intelligence. Edward Wong, "U.S. Officials Repeatedly Urged China to Help Avert War in Ukraine," *NYT*, February 25, 2022.

108. For background and commentary, see Walter C. Clemens Jr., "Triangular Diplomacy in the Age of Putin, Xi and Trump," *Global Asia*, vol. 15, no. 1 (March 2020), https://www.globalasia.org/v15no1/feature/triangular-diplomacy-in-the-age -of-putin-xi-and-trump_walter-c-clemens-jr.

109. The final communiqué from that meeting stated that "China's growing influence and international policies can present challenges that we need to address together as an Alliance. . . . China's stated ambitions and assertive behavior present systemic challenges to the rules-based international order." "Brussels Summit Communique," https://www.nato.int/cps/en/natohq/news_185000.htm.

110. Yun Sun, "Ukraine: China's Desired Endgame," *Carnegie*, March 22, 2022, https://www.stimson.org/2022/ukraine-china-endgame/.

111. According to the Chinese readout of the conversation, Xi said: "China-US relations still haven't escaped from the dilemma created by the previous administration, and instead have encountered more and more challenges." "Xi Jinping Holds Video Call with US President Biden."

112. See, for example, the essay by two Chinese journalists, Xu Zeyu and Zhai Xiang, "The View from Beijing: America's 'Mirage' of Strength," *U.S.-China Perception Monitor*, August 9, 2021, https://uscnpm.org/2021/08/09/the-view-from -beijing-americas-mirage-of-strength/.

113. Laura Silver, Kat Devlin, and Christine Huang, "Large Majorities Say China Does Not Respect the Personal Freedoms of Its People," Pew Research Center, June 30, 2021, https://www.pewresearch.org/global/2021/06/30/large-majorities-say-china -does-not-respect-the-personal-freedoms-of-its-people/.

114. Ministry of Defense of Japan, *Defense of Japan 2021*, n.d., https://www.mod .go.jp/en/publ/w_paper/index.html.

115. Ben Dooley, "Japan Calls for 'Sense of Crisis' over China-Taiwan Tensions," *NYT*, July 13, 2021; William Sposato, "Taro Aso's Taiwan Slip Was Likely Deliberate," *Foreign Policy*, July 12, 2021, https://foreignpolicy.com/2021/07/12/taro-aso -taiwan-japan-china-policy/.

116. See Yasuhiro Matsuda, interview by National Bureau of Asian Research, December 23, 2021, https://www.nbr.org/publication/the-2021-defense-white-paper -and-japans-taiwan-policy/.

117. See Rajaram Panda, "Japan's Military Gets a Boost in Response to Threats from China and North Korea," *Global Asia*, vol. 16, no. 4 (December 2021), pp. 100–104.

118. For example, Sarang Shidore, "De-risking the India Relationship: An Action Agenda for the United States," Quincy Institute Brief No. 10, March 10, 2021, https: //quincyinst.org/report/de-risking-the-india-relationship-an-action-agenda-for-the -united-states/?mc_cid=a0f34e4c69&mc_eid=a890eb89be.

119. Yun Sun, "China's Strategic Assessment of the Ladakh Clash," *War on the Rocks*, June 19, 2020, warontherocks.com/2020/06/chinas-strategic-assessment-of-the-ladakh-clash/.

120. Shidore, "De-risking the India Relationship." Shidore points out that US arms sales to India jumped from nearly zero in 2008 to about $20 billion in 2020.

121. Wang said: "China does not pursue the so-called 'unipolar Asia' and respects India's traditional role in the region. If China and India spoke with one voice, the whole world will listen. If China and India joined hands, the whole world will pay attention." Gerry Shih, Niha Masih, and Eva Dou, "China Woos India as Both Face Western Ire over Ukraine," *WaPo*, March 25, 2022.

122. Rup Narayan Das, "The Galwan Clash: A Landmark Change in India-China Relations," *Global Asia*, vol. 16, no. 2 (June 2021), pp. 78–85.

123. C. Raja Mohan, "China's Two-Ocean Strategy Puts India in a Pincer," *Foreign Policy*, January 4, 2022, https://foreignpolicy.com/2022/01/04/india-china-ocean-geopolitics-sri-lanka-maldives-comoros/.

124. The prime minister denied the deal would mean a Chinese base and said the criticism was demeaning. Yan Zhuang, "Solomon Islands' Leader Calls Concern over Chinese Security Deal 'Insulting,'" *NYT*, March 29, 2022.

125. "Shock China Security Deal Shows Pacific Powers Need to Face Facts," Sydney Morning Herald, March 25, 2022, https://www.smh.com.au/world/oceania/shock-china-security-deal-shows-pacific-powers-need-to-face-facts-20220325-p5a7zw.html. The Solomon Islands prime minister denies that China will be allowed to establish a military base there.

126. Anne-Marie Brady, "How China Is Using Humanitarian Aid to Gain a Foothold in the South Pacific," *Sydney Morning Herald*, February 9, 2022, https://www.smh.com.au/national/how-china-is-using-humanitarian-aid-to-gain-a-military-foothold-in-the-south-pacific-20220209-p59v18.html.

127. Kate Lyons, "China's Foreign Minister Tells Pacific Leaders, 'Don't Be Too Anxious' after They Reject Regional Security Pact," *The Guardian*, May 30, 2022.

128. Rebecca Starting and Joanne Wallis, "Strategic Competition in Oceania," in Ashley J. Tellis, Alison Szalwinski, and Michael Wills, eds., *Navigating Tumultuous Times in the Indo-Pacific* (Seattle, WA: The National Bureau of Asian Research, 2022), https://www.nbr.org/wp-content/uploads/pdfs/publications/strategicasia2021-22_oceania_strating_wallis.pdf.

129. Dorothy Wickham, "Can You Blame Poor Countries Like Mine for Turning to China?" *NYT*, June 27, 2022.

130. Andrei Lankov, "Chinese Aid Strategy Hinders Goals on North Korea," *East Asia Forum*, December 30, 2021, https://www.eastasiaforum.org/2021/12/30/chinese-aid-strategy-hinders-goals-on-north-korea/.

131. Kim Yo-jong, Kim Jong-un's powerful sister, said in a statement: "It is our fixed judgment that it is no longer possible to discuss the North-South ties with such a servile partner engaging only in disgrace and self-ruin, being soaked by deep-rooted flunkyism." Simon Denyer and Min Joo Kim, "South Korea's Moon Was Once Given VIP Welcome by the North; He's Now Mocked as Korean Crisis Deepens," *WaPo*, June 17, 2020.

132. See Scott Snyder and See-Won Byun, "China-Korea Relations: Economic Stabilization, End-of-War Declaration, and the Ongoing 'Joint Struggle,'" *Comparative Connections*, vol. 23, no. 3, pp. 107–16.

133. Ryan D. Martinson and Andrew S. Erickson, "Manila's Images Are Revealing the Secrets of China's Maritime Militia," *Foreign Policy*, April 19, 2021, https://foreignpolicy.com/2021/04/19/manilas-images-are-revealing-the-secrets-of-chinas-maritime-militia/.

134. Derek Grossman, "Duterte's Dalliance with China Is Over," *Foreign Policy*, November 2, 2021, https://foreignpolicy.com/2021/11/02/duterte-china-philippines-united-states-defense-military-geopolitics/.

135. Bonnie Gerard, "Even Duterte Can't Get around the Thorn in China-Philippine Relations," *The Diplomat*, December 1, 2021, https://thediplomat.com/2021/12/even-duterte-cant-get-around-the-thorn-in-china-philippine-relations/.

136. Richard C. Paddock, "Days of Killing and Defiance, with Neither Side Relenting," *NYT*, March 14, 2021.

137. See the United States Institute of Peace report by the Myanmar Study Group, "Anatomy of the Military Coup and Recommendations for U.S. Response," February 1, 2022, https://www.usip.org/publications/2022/02/myanmar-study-group-final-report.

138. Lara Jakes, "U.S. to Declare That Myanmar's Military Has Committed Genocide," *NYT*, March 20, 2022.

139. Owen Bolcott and Rebecca Ratcliffe, "UN's Top Court Orders Myanmar to Protect Rohingya from Genocide," *The Guardian*, January 23, 2020.

140. Timothy McLaughlin, "Why the U.S. Finally Called the Genocide in Myanmar a 'Genocide,'" *The Atlantic*, March 2022, https://www.theatlantic.com/international/archive/2022/03/blinken-myanmar-genocide-rohingya-muslims/627124/.

141. Nandita Bose, "Harris to Push Back on China's South China Sea Claims during Asia Trip," Reuters, August 3, 2021, https://www.reuters.com/world/asia-pacific/harris-will-reject-chinas-claim-south-china-sea-during-trip-asia-2021-08-03/.

142. Farnaz Fassihi and Steven Lee Myers, "China, with $400 Billion Iran Deal, Could Deepen Influence in Mideast," *NYT*, March 27, 2021.

143. Patrick Wintour, "Iran Leaders Pressed to Disclose Details of 25-Year China Pact," *The Guardian*, March 30, 2021, https://www.theguardian.com/world/2021/mar/30/iranian-leaders-pressed-to-disclose-details-of-25-year-china-pact.

144. Dina Esfandiary, "Iran's 'New' Partnership with China Is Just Business as Usual," *World Politics Review*, April 22, 2021, https://www.worldpoliticsreview.com/articles/29593/the-iran-china-deal-isn-t-all-that.

145. Julia Marnin, "China Tells U.S. to Stop Suppressing Its Rights and Interests, Help Wanted in Afghanistan," *Newsweek*, August 17, 2021, https://www.newsweek.com/china-tells-us-stop-suppressing-its-rights-interests-help-wanted-afghanistan-1620117.

146. Ministry of Foreign Affairs of China, "State Councilor and Foreign Minister Wang Yi Gives Interview."

147. "Afghanistan: Taliban to Rely on Chinese Funds, Spokesperson Says," *Aljazeera*, September 2, 2021, https://www.aljazeera.com/news/2021/9/2/afghanistan-taliban-to-rely-on-chinese-money-spokesperson-says.

148. Scott L. Montgomery, "Afghanistan Has Vast Mineral Wealth, but Faces Steep Challenges to Tap It," *Yahoo! News*, August 31, 2021, https://news.yahoo.com/afghanistan-vast-mineral-wealth-faces-191603748.html; Mercy A, Kuo, "China in Afghanistan: How Beijing Engages the Taliban," *The Diplomat*, December 25, 2021, https://thediplomat.com/2021/12/china-in-afghanistan-how-beijing-engages-the-taliban/. The article is an interview of Claudia Chia, a research analyst with the Institute of South Asia Studies at the National University of Singapore.

149. Senate Strategic Competition Act, p. 12.

150. Steven Lee Myers, "China Offers the Taliban a Warm Welcome While Urging Peace Talks," *NYT*, July 28, 2021; Catherine Wong, "US-China Relations: Beijing Takes Pointers from Mao in Protracted Power Struggle with US," *South China Morning Post*, August 2, 2021, https://www.scmp.com/news/china/diplomacy/article/3143505/us-china-relations-beijing-takes-pointers-mao-protracted-power?module=perpetual_scroll&pgtype=article&campaign=3143505.

CHAPTER 5

1. "*Meiguo tongmeng tixi chi zongzui*" (美国同盟体系'七宗罪'), *China Daily*, August 4, 2021.

2. Ana Swanson, Mike Isaac, and Paul Mozur, "Trump Targets WeChat and TikTok, in Sharp Escalation with China," *NYT*, August 6, 2020. Azar's visit came under the 2018 Taiwan Travel Act, which set the stage for official US visits.

3. U.S.-China Economic and Security Review Commission, *2021 Annual Report to Congress*, https://www.uscc.gov/sites/default/files/2021-11/Chapter_4--Dangerous_Period_for_Cross-Strait_Deterrence.pdf.

4. Kevin Liptak, "Biden Says Taiwan's Independence Is Up to Taiwan after Discussing Matter with Xi," CNN, November 16, 2021, https://www.cnn.com/2021/11/16/politics/biden-china-taiwan/index.html.

5. Ned Price, Department Press Briefing, April 7, 2021, https://www.state.gov/briefings/department-press-briefing-april-7-2021/.

6. "Blinken: China Aggression against Taiwan Would Be 'Serious Mistake,'" *The Guardian*, April 11, 2021, https://www.theguardian.com/world/2021/apr/11/antony-blinken-china-aggression-taiwan.

7. See Michael Swaine, "Recent Chinese Views on the Taiwan Issue," *China Leadership Monitor*, December 1, 2021, https://www.prcleader.org/swaine-3.

8. Xi Jinping, "Speech at a Ceremony Marking the Centenary of the Communist Party of China," July 1, 2021, http://en.people.cn/n3/2021/0701/c90000-9867483.html.

9. "Commemoration of the 110th Anniversary of the 1911 Revolution Solemnly Held in Beijing; Xi Makes Important Speech," *Renmin Ribao*, October 9, 2021, http://politics.people.com.cn/n1/2021/1009/c1024-32248605.html (my translation).

10. Ministry of Foreign Affairs of the People's Republic of China, "President Xi Holds Virtual Meeting with US President Biden," November 16, 2021, https://www.fmprc.gov.cn/web/zyxw/t1919210.shtml (in Chinese).

11. "Xi Jinping Holds Video Call with US President Biden."

12. Tsai has said "we will do our utmost to prevent the status quo from being unilaterally altered." See Natasha Kassam, "What Taiwan Really Wants," *NYT*, October 29, 2021. On Taiwan public opinion, see Russell Hsiao, "Taiwanese Preference for Status Quo Remains Constant Even as Views Harden," *Global Taiwan Institute*, July 28, 2021, https://globaltaiwan.org/2021/07/vol-6-issue-15/#RussellHsiao07282021.

13. A Track II (nonofficial) discussion among Chinese, Taiwanese, and American scholars sponsored by the National Committee on American Foreign Policy helps bring out this point. See Susan A. Thornton, "Whither the Status Quo? A Cross–Taiwan Strait Trilateral Dialogue," National Committee on American Foreign Policy, December 2021, https://www.ncafp.org/2016/wp-content/uploads/2021/12/NCAFP-Cross-Strait-Trilat-Report_2021_Final.pdf.

14. In 2021 Daniel Ellsberg released a previously classified RAND Corporation study of the 1958 crisis in which US decision makers debated use of nuclear weapons against the China mainland if China attacked Taiwan and conventional weapons were believed inadequate to defend the island (https://www.nytimes.com/2021/05/22/us/politics/nuclear-war-risk-1958-us-china.html). The military was particularly hawkish in that crisis, talking about a nuclear attack on Chinese airfields first and cities next if necessary. Eisenhower would not hear of it.

15. Reuters, "China Unlikely to Militarily Seize Taiwan in Near Future, Top US General," https://www.reuters.com/world/china/china-unlikely-try-militarily-seize-taiwan-near-future-top-us-general-2021-11-03.

16. Taiwan's defense exercises have stressed these options and stepped up long-range missile production to deter Chinese action on them. Yu Nakamura, "Taiwan Simulates Chinese Biological and Electronic Attacks in War Games," *Nikkei*, September 14, 2021.

17. Heath, Grossman, and Clark, *China's Quest for Global Primacy*, p. 186.

18. www.congress.gov/bill/116th-congress/senate-bill/1838/text.

19. Article 23 gives Hong Kong the power to "enact laws on its own to prohibit any act of treason, secession, sedition, subversion against the Central People's Government." The draft law essentially eviscerates that power. Chris Buckley, Keith Bradsher, and Elaine Yu, "Law Will Tighten Beijing's Grip on Hong Kong with Chinese Security Force," *NYT*, June 21, 2020.

20. Shibani Mahtani and Theodora Yu, "China Uses Patriotism Test to Sweep Aside Last Outlet for Hong Kong Democracy," *WaPo*, February 23, 2021.

21. Shibani Mahtani, Timothy McLaughlin, and Theodora Yu, "With New Mass Detentions, Every Prominent Hong Kong Activist Is Either in Jail or Exile," *WaPo*, February 28, 2021.

22. Vivian Wang, interviewed by David Leonhardt, "The Morning: The New Hong Kong," *NYT*, March 10, 2021.

23. Austin Ramzy, "Hong Kong Policy Arrest Organizers of Tiananmen Square Vigil," *NYT*, September 7, 2021.

24. Jeffie Lam, "Hong Kong Elections," *South China Morning Post*, December 20, 2021, https://www.scmp.com/news/hong-kong/politics/article/3160469/hong-kong -elections-already-dominant-pro-establishment-camp.

25. Vivian Wang and Alexandra Stevenson, "'A Form of Brainwashing': China Remakes Hong Kong," *NYT*, June 29, 2021; Vivian Wang, "'This Drop Came So Quickly': Shrinking Schools Add to Hong Kong Exodus," *NYT*, October 11, 2021.

26. Kurt Tong, "Hong Kong and the Limits of Decoupling," *Foreign Affairs*, July 14, 2021, https://www.foreignaffairs.com/articles/asia/2021-07-14/hong-kong-and -limits-decoupling.

27. "Expert Says 1.8 Million Uyghurs, Muslim Minorities Held in Xinjiang's Internment Camps," Radio Free Asia, November 24, 2019, www.rfa.org/english/news /uyghur/detainees-11232019223242.html.

28. See the collection of leaked documents at www.nytimes.com/interactive/2019 /11/16/world/asia/china-xinjiang-documents.html; China's response is reported by Steven Lee Myers, "China Defends Crackdown on Muslims, and Criticizes Times Article," *NYT*, November 18, 2021.

29. Xi's speech and many other documents not in the *New York Times* "Xinjiang Papers" were obtained by an unprecedented leak to the London-based Uyghur Tribunal (https://uyghurtribunal.com) in September 2021. These later documents are collected in Adrian Zenz, "The Xinjiang Papers: An Introduction" (Washington, DC: Uyghur Tribunal, November 27, 2021), https://uyghurtribunal.com/wp-content/ uploads/2021/11/The-Xinjiang-Papers-An-Introduction-1.pdf.

30. Zenz, "The Xinjiang Papers," pp. 3–6.

31. Associated Press, "Report: Xinjiang Has Sharp Drop in Birthrate," *WaPo*, May 12, 2021. The report cites an investigation by an Australian research institute.

32. This program, temporarily halted when the coronavirus hit, resumed later. Beijing sees the labor assignment as vindication of its reeducation; the "graduates" have supposedly shown that the internment camps really are just schools. "China Plans to Send Uygur Muslims from Xinjiang Re-education Camps to Work in Other Parts of Country," *South China Morning Post*, May 2, 2020, www.scmp.com/news/china /politics/article/3082602/china-plans-send-ugyur-muslims-xinjiang-re-education -camps-work.

33. On destruction of Uyghur culture, see Dale Berning Sawa, "Uyghur Civilisation in China Continues to Be Erased as Part of Chilling Mission," *The Art Newspaper*, November 3, 2020, https://www.theartnewspaper.com/2020/11/03/uyghur -civilisation-in-china-continues-to-be-erased-as-part-of-chilling-mission.

34. Sarah Johnson, "China's Uyghurs Living in 'Dystopian Hellscape,' Says Amnesty Report," CNN, June 10, 2021, https://www.theguardian.com/global -development/2021/jun/10/china-uyghur-xinjiang-dystopian-hell scape-says- amnesty-international-report. The evidence of genocide is by now enormous. Professor Magnus Fiskesjö of Cornell University has compiled a bibliography on behalf of the Uyghur Human Rights Project (https://uhrp.org/bibliography/) that has a long list of sources. Among his many writings is "Bulldozing Culture: China's Systematic Destruction of Uyghur Heritage Reveals Genocidal Intent," *Cultural Property News*, June 23, 2021, https://culturalpropertynews.org/bulldozing-culture-chinas-systematic

-destruction-of-uyghur-heritage-reveals-genocidal-intent/. Among many insider accounts, see Ben Mauk, "Inside Xinjiang's Prison State," *The New Yorker*, February 26, 2021, https://www.newyorker.com/news/a-reporter-at-large/china-xinjiang-prison -state-uighur-detention-camps-prisoner-testimony.

35. On the charge of genocide, the tribunal found "beyond reasonable doubt that the PRC, by the imposition of measures to prevent births, intended to destroy a significant part of the Uyghurs in Xinjiang as such, has committed genocide." The full judgment is at https://uyghurtribunal.com/wp-content/uploads/2022/01/Uyghur -Tribunal-Judgment-9th-Dec-21.pdf and the proceedings are in https://uyghurtribunal .com/wp-content/uploads/2021/11/The-Xinjiang-Papers-An-Introduction-01.pdf.

36. The "Xinjiang police files," as this evidence became known, is a project of the Victims of Communism Memorial Foundation. See https://www.xinjiangpolicefiles .org. The hacked data includes more than 5,000 images of Uyghurs, police spread-sheets, and confidential documents from two counties in Xinjiang.

37. As one extensive Australian study also observes, "in addition to mass internment and coercive labour assignments, Xinjiang residents are also compelled to participate in acts of political theatre, such as mass show trials, public denunciation sessions, loyalty pledges, sermon-like 'propaganda lectures,' and chants for Xi Jinping's good health. In doing so, they're mobilised to attack shadowy enemies hiding among the people: the so-called 'three evil forces' and 'two-faced people.'" Vicky Xiuzhong Xu, James Leibold, and Daria Impiombato, *The Architecture of Repression*, Australian Strategic Policy Institute, October 2021, https://www.aspi.org.au/report/architecture -repression?__cf_chl_jschl_tk__=pmd_mj4ySTi65QZKxNen850h27K8CiUW .363UdjlQ8HQgi0-1634662284-0-gqNtZGzNAiWjcnBszQjR.

38. See the personal experience recounted by Raffi Khatchadourian, "Ghost Walls," *The New Yorker*, April 12, 2021, pp. 30–55.

39. See the interview of the Belgian geneticist Yves Moreau by National Public Radio, December 7, 2019, www.npr.org/2019/12/07/785804791/uighurs-and-genetic -surveillance-in-china.

40. Sui-Lee Wee, "China Is Collecting DNA from Tens of Millions of Men and Boys, Using U.S. Equipment," *NYT*, June 19, 2020.

41. An apologist for China reminded readers that in George W. Bush's "war against terror" the State Department did call one Uyghur group a terrorist organization. Beijing took full advantage of that US mistake. Weijian Shan, "Xinjiang: What the West Doesn't Tell You about China's War on Terror," *South China Morning Post*, April 14, 2021, https://www.scmp.com/comment/opinion/article/3129325/xinjiang-what-west -doesnt-tell-you-about-chinas-war-terror. For an accurate portrayal, see Sean R. Roberts, *The War on the Uyghurs: China's Internal Campaign against a Muslim Minority* (Princeton, NJ: Princeton University Press, 2020).

42. See "Ambassador Zhang Jun Exercises the Right to Reply in Response to the Statement Made by the Representative of the United States at the General Debate of the Third Committee," Ministry of Foreign Affairs of the PRC, October 4, 2021, https://www.fmprc.gov.cn/mfa_eng/wjb_663304/zwjg_665342/zwbd_665378 /t1912680.shtml.

43. For example, Nathan Vanderklippe, "Thousands of Uyghur Workers in China Are Being Relocated in an Effort to Assimilate Muslims, Documents Show," *The Globe and Mail*, March 2, 2021, https://www.theglobeandmail.com/world/article-thousands-of-uyghur-workers-in-china-are-being-relocated-in-an-effort/; BBC News, "New Evidence of China Moving Uighur Minority Workers in Order to Uproot Communities," March 2, 2021, https://www,youtube.com/watch?v=mqga0a6H81 &feature=youtu.be; Cate Cadell, "China Counters Uighur Criticism with Explicit Attacks on Women Witnesses," Reuters, February 28, 2021, https://www.reuters.com /article/us-china-xinjiang-idUSKCN2AT1BA.

44. Patrick Howell O'Neill, "Chinese Hackers Posing as the UN Human Rights Council Are Attacking Uyghurs," *MIT Technology Review*, May 27, 2021, https: //www.technologyreview.com/2021/05/27/1025443/chinese-hackers-uyghur-united -nations/.

45. Amy Qin, "BBC Correspondent Leaves China, Citing Growing Risks," *NYT*, April 1, 2021.

46. Paul Mozur, "Microsoft's Bing Briefly Blocked 'Tank Man' on Tiananmen Anniversary," *NYT*, June 5, 2021.

47. Peter S. Goodman, Vivian Wang, and Elizabeth Paton, "Global Brands Find It Hard to Untangle Themselves from Xinjiang Cotton," *NYT*, April 6, 2021.

48. Jeanne Whelan, "World Bank Unit Is Financing Chinese Companies That Appear to Employ Forced Laborers, Report Says," *WaPo*, February 17, 2022.

49. "UN: Unprecedented Joint Call for China to End Xinjiang Abuses," Human Rights Watch, July 10, 2019, www.hrw.org/news/2019/07/10/un-unprecedented-joint -call-china-end-xinjiang-abuses.

50. A proposed visit by the human rights commissioner, Michelle Bachelet, was greeted with a statement by Zhao Lijian that "the purpose of the trip is to promote exchange and cooperation, not for an investigation." Christian Shepherd, "China Open to U.N. Rights Chief Visiting Xinjiang, as Long as She Doesn't Do Any Investigating There," *WaPo*, January 28, 2022.

51. The UN secretary-general has insisted on a "credible" visit, but if that doesn't happen, "of course the high commissioner [Bachelet] will take the decisions that correspond to her mandate." Voice of America, "UN Chief 'Determined' Human Rights Chief Visit Xinjiang," February 18, 2022.

52. I discuss Bachelet's trip at greater length in my blog post "Co-opted: The UN's Misguided Mission to Xinjiang," June 16, 2022, https://melgurtov.com/2022/06/16/ post-341-co-opted-the-uns-misguided-mission-to-xinjiang/.

53. Reuters, "China Says Door to Xinjiang 'Always Open,' but U.N. Human Rights Boss Should Not Prejudge," https://www.reuters.com/article/us-china-rights-un/ china-says-door-to-xinjiang-always-open-but-u-n-rights-boss-should-not-prejudge -idUSKCN2AU0Z3.

54. These excerpts from Bolton's book were reported by many media, including CNN, June 19, 2020, and Nicholas Kristof, "China's Man in Washington, Names Trump," *NYT*, June 20, 2020.

55. Nike (shoes) and Coca-Cola (sugar) are among the corporations that supposedly support legislation to ban imports produced by forced labor in Xinjiang but

argue the proposed law (the Uyghur Forced Labor Prevention Act) is too broad. Ana Swanson, "Nike and Coca-Cola Lobby against Xinjiang Forced Labor Bill," *NYT*, November 29, 2020, online ed.

56. Pompeo specified Chinese policy in Xinjiang as "the systematic attempt to destroy Uighurs by the Chinese party-state." Chinese officials, he said, were "engaged in the forced assimilation and eventual erasure of a vulnerable ethnic and religious minority group," *NYT*, January 19, 2021. Biden administration officials agreed, though without initially providing a definition. In fact, both those officials and legal scholars in the United States and United Kingdom were divided over whether to call the repression genocide or a crime against humanity.

57. BBC, "US, UK Governments Condemn Reports of Systematic Rape," February 4, 2021, https://www.bbc.com/news/world-asia-55930344.

58. See, for instance, the editorial of *China Times*, "Lithuania Risks Trouble with Geopolitical Move," https://www.globaltimes.cn/page/202105/1224253.shtml.

59. Karadsheh and Tuysuz, "Uyghurs Are Being Deported from Muslim Countries."

60. Andrew Ross Sorkin, "Business Makes the Case for a Post-Trump Reset," *NYT*, January 20, 2021.

61. Apple iPhone suppliers in Xinjiang were identified for using forced labor. See Reed Albergotti, "Apple's Longtime Supplier Accused of Using Forced Labor in China," *WaPo*, December 20, 2020.

62. John Liu, "Intel Apologizes over Its Statement on Forced Labor in Xinjiang," *NYT*, December 21, 2021.

63. Sophie Richardson, "Thermo Fisher's Necessary, but Insufficient, Step in China," Human Rights Watch, https://www.hrw.org/news/2019/02/22/thermo-fishers-necessary-insufficient-step-china.

64. Polysilicon is a key ingredient in the manufacture of solar panels, in which China is the world leader. A US firm led the way in urging companies that rely on polysilicon from Xinjiang, which produces 40 percent of the world total, to look elsewhere. Korean and Malaysian companies picked up the slack. According to one report, "Due to mounting criticism, massive Chinese solar manufacturers such as Longi Solar, JA Solar and Jinko Solar last month signed a pledge with other 172 members of the Solar Energy Industry Association to drive out forced labor from their supply chains." "Xinjiang's Polysilicon Boycott Opens Window for OCI," *Korea Herald*, February 15, 2021, http://www.koreaherald.com/view.php?ud=20210215000887.

65. "FLA Statement on Sourcing in China," December 3, 2020, https://www.fairlabor.org/blog/entry/fla-statement-sourcing-china#.X-jNTiLcdZE.twitter.

66. Bethany Allen-Ebrahimian, "U.S. Sanctions China's Paramilitary in Xinjiang," *Axios*, n.d., https://www.axios.com/us-sanctions-china-paramilitary-xinjiang-xpcc-41e29c92-9649-4e47-9e91-a7f78330d4d8.html; Ana Swanson, "U.S. Bans All Cotton and Tomatoes from Xinjiang Region of China," *NYT*, January 13, 2021.

67. "Forced Labour to Keep Pressure on Chinese Textile Firms as American Firms Cut Orders," *South China Morning Post*, February 16, 2021, https://www.scmp.com/economy/china-economy/article/3121900/us-china-relations-forced-labour-keep-pressure-chinese.

68. Besides criticizing the internment of Chinese Muslims, the AAA statement also pointed to the Chinese government's "clear disregard for academic freedom. We are particularly dismayed by the way the pretext of 'terrorism' and 'countering violent extremism' has resulted in the disappearance of more than 40 Uyghur and Kazakh cultural leaders. These intellectuals, scientists and artists are the carriers of Uyghur and Kazakh Indigenous traditions." "The Assault on Indigenous Peoples in Northwest China Must End," February 26, 2020, www.americananthro.org/ParticipateAndAdvocate/AdvocacyDetail.aspx?ItemNumber=25500.

69. Sui-Lee Wee and Paul Mozur, "China Genetic Research on Ethnic Minorities Sets Off Science Backlash," *NYT*, December 4, 2019.

70. Sui-Lee Wee, "Two Scientific Journals Retract Articles Involving Chinese DNA Research," *NYT*, September 9, 2021. An additional study of about 38,000 men of diverse ethnic backgrounds, published in the journal *Human Genetics*, was also withdrawn from publication in 2021. Again, informed consent was the main objection, although here again most of the co-authors were policemen. See Mara Hvistendahl, "Journal Retracts Paper Based on DNA of Vulnerable Chinese Minorities," *The Intercept*, December 13, 2021, https://theintercept.com/2021/12/13/china-uyghur-dna-human-genetics-retraction/.

71. Mara Hvistendahl, "Mass Resignations at Scientific Journal over Ethically Fraught China Genetics Papers," *The Intercept*, August 4, 2021, https://theintercept.com/2021/08/04/dna-profiling-forensic-genetics-journal-resignations-china/.

72. *Tibet Watch* (International Campaign for Tibet), Spring 2021.

73. The companies are Promega and Thermo Fisher Scientific. In 2019 Thermo Fisher (but not Promega) announced that, in accordance with its "ethics code," it would stop supplying genetic sequencers to the Chinese authorities in Xinjiang. But will these companies still sell the technology to Chinese public security forces elsewhere, and will they obtain assurances concerning their use? See Jessica Batke and Mareike Ohlberg, "China's Biosecurity State in Xinjiang Is Powered by Western Tech," *Foreign Policy*, February 19, 2020, https://foreignpolicy.com/2020/02/19/china-xinjiang-surveillance-biosecurity-state-dna-western-tech/; Natasha Khan, "American Firm, Citing Ethics Code, Won't Sell Genetic Sequences in Xinjiang," *Wall Street Journal*, February 20, 2019, www.wsj.com/articles/thermo-fisher-to-stop-sales-of-genetic-sequencers-to-chinas-xinjiang-region-11550694620.

74. US Department of Commerce Press Release, "Commerce Department to Add Nine Chinese Entities Related to Human Rights Abuses in the Xinjiang Uighur Autonomous Region to the Entity List," May 22, 2020, www.commerce.gov/news/press-releases/2020/05/commerce-department-add-nine-chinese-entities-related-human-rights. Huawei was accused of providing partners with technology used in surveillance systems, specifically ethnicity-tracking technology. Eva Dou and Drew Harwell, "Huawei Worked on Several Surveillance Systems Promoted to Identify Ethnicity, Documents Show," *WaPo*, December 12, 2020.

75. Thermo Fisher Scientific, based in Waltham, Massachusetts, says its decision is "consistent with Thermo Fisher's values, ethics code and policies." "We recognize the importance of considering how our products and services are used—or may be used—by our customers."

76. Dou and Harwell, "Huawei Worked on Several Surveillance Systems."

77. The company said it was merely testing the technology. On discovery, Alibaba reportedly removed references to minority groups, but it never explained why it developed the software to begin with. Raymond Zhong, "As China Tracked Muslims, Alibaba Showed Customers How They Could, Too," *NYT*, December 17, 2020.

78. Jack Nicas, Raymond Zhong, and Daisuke Wakabayashi, "Censorship, Surveillance and Profits: A Hard Bargain for Apple in China," *NYT*, May 26, 2021.

79. Zolan Kanno-Youngs and David E. Sanger, "U.S. Formally Accuses China of Hacking Microsoft," *NYT*, July 19, 2021; Sam Clench, "Beijing Reacts to Microsoft Exchange Hack as Australia and US Allies Blame China," *news.com.au*, July 20, 2021, https://www.news.com.au/technology/australia-us-and-allies-blame-china-for-huge-microsoft-exchange-hack-condemn-countrys-malicious-cyber-activities/news-story/6a6df9a7de7c9a45630cc9d9229a005f#.s150h.

80. See Zach Dorfman, "Beijing Ransacked Data as U.S. Sources Went Dark in China," *Foreign Policy*, December 22, 2020, https://foreignpolicy.com/2020/12/22/china-us-data-intelligence-cybersecurity-xi-jinping/; Dorfman, "Tech Giants Are Giving China a Vital Edge in Espionage," *Foreign Policy*, December 23, 2020, https://foreignpolicy.com/2020/12/23/china-tech-giants-process-stolen-data-spy-agencies/.

81. "China Says U.S. Addresses Used Its Computers to Launch Cyberattacks on Russia, Ukraine," Reuters, March 10, 2022, https://www.reuters.com/technology/chinas-has-faced-continuous-cyber-attacks-united-states-xinhua-2022-03-11/; Ronen Bergman and Kate Conger, "Chinese Hackers Tried to Steal Russian Defense Data, Report Says," *NYT*, May 19, 2022.

82. Joseph S. Nye Jr., "The End of Cyber-Anarchy?" *Foreign Affairs*, vol. 101, no. 1 (January–February 2022), pp. 32–42.

83. Dmitri Alperovitch, "The Case for Cyber-Realism," *Foreign Affairs*, vol. 101, no. 1 (January–February 2022), pp. 44–50.

84. After Trump's departure, it came to light that his Commerce Department had a rogue division that targeted Chinese Americans and other minority groups within the department. The unit used surveillance and investigations that included break-ins of offices based on the suspicion that Chinese Americans were espionage threats. Catie Edmondson, "'Rogue' U.S. Agency Used Racial Profiling to Investigate Commerce Department Employees, Report Says," *NYT*, July 16, 2021.

85. The bill also contends that teachers trained in China are approved by the CCP and therefore are mere political hacks; that CIs must agree to be governed by both Chinese and US law; that the CCP must approve all CI events and speakers; and that CIs must agree that "certain topics will be off limits." Text of the bill is at www.congress.gov/bill/116th-congress/senate-bill/939.

86. My research team interviewed dozens of CI directors, university administrators, advisory board members, and Chinese teachers in a project funded by China's education ministry, which wanted an independent assessment of how well CIs were doing in their mission of teaching Chinese language and culture. Our team operated without interference and with complete respect for academic freedom. See Lee Lu, Mel Gurtov, and Dale Cope, *Confucius Institutes in the U.S.: Final Report*, November 2020, https://www.ciuscenter.org/wp-content/uploads/Confucius-Institutes-in-the-U

.S.-Final-Report-1.pdf. Thanks to Professor Daniel Julius, who was also part of the research team.

87. Concern about academic freedom would be better served by examining cases of threats to Chinese students at American universities who criticize their government. Some of those students are subject to harassment by members of Chinese student associations, and their families in China may receive threats from public security personnel. (See Sebastian Rotella, "Even on U.S. Campuses, China Cracks Down on Students Who Speak Out," *ProPublica*, November 30, 2021, https://www.propublica .org/article/even-on-us-campuses-china-cracks-down-on-students-who-speak-out.) However, the number of such cases may be exaggerated by Americans who are either critical of China generally or who use the cases to promote their culture war position. See Yangyang Cheng, "Cancel Culture Isn't the Real Threat to Academic Freedom," *The Atlantic*, November 23, 2021, https://www.theatlantic.com/international/archive /2021/11/china-academic-freedom-cultural-revolution-cancel-culture/620777/.

88. Jane Mayer, "How Right-Wing Billionaires Infiltrated Higher Education," *Chronicle of Higher Education*, February 2, 2016, https://www.chronicle.com/article /how-right-wing-billionaires-infiltrated-higher-education/.

89. Nidhi Subbaraman, "US Universities Call for Clearer Rules on Science Espionage amidst China Crackdown," *Nature*, April 6, 2021, https://www.nature.com/ articles/d41586-021-00901-7.

90. US Department of Justice, "Information about the Department of Justice's China Initiative and a Compilation of China-Related Prosecutions since 2018," June 14, 2021, https://www.justice.gov/nsd/information-about-department-justice-s-china -initiative-and-compilation-china-related.

91. Two especially glaring cases of FBI misconduct—one at the University of Tennessee, the other at the Massachusetts Institute of Technology—are detailed by Karin Fischer, "Do Colleges Need a Foreign Policy?" *Chronicle of Higher Education*, June 22, 2021, https://www.chronicle.com/article/do-colleges-need-a-foreign-policy. See also Ellen Nakashima and David Nakamura, "In High-Profile Case against MIT's Gang Chen, Prosecutors Seeking to Drop Charges," *WaPo*, January 14, 2022. Perhaps the most celebrated case under the China Initiative is that of Professor Charles Lieber, a renowned research chemist at Harvard. He was arrested in 2020 and convicted at the end of 2021, not for espionage but for lying about financial benefits from his involvement in China's Thousand Talents program. Ellen Barry, "In a Boston Court, a Harsh Spotlight Falls on a Heavyweight of Science," *NYT*, December 21, 2021.

CHAPTER 6

1. When the Senate passed the industrial policy bill by a wide margin in June 2021, the Democratic leader, Chuck Schumer, said the bill's support of high-tech would determine whether the world would be shaped by a "democratic image" or an "authoritarian image like President Xi would like to impose on the world?" *NYT*, June 8, 2021.

2. Thomas Wright, "Democrats Need to Place China at the Center of Their Foreign Policy," Brookings Institution, May 15, 2019, https://www.brchinookings.edu/blog/order-from-chaos/2019/05/15/democrats-need-to-place-a-at-the-center-of-their-foreign-policy/.

3. Quoted by Demetri Sevastopulo, "Biden's 100 Days: Hawkish Approach to China Stokes Beijing Frictions," *Financial Times*, April 31, 2021.

4. Foreign Minister Wang Yi said of the summit, in his final news conference of 2021, "As long as the US gives up its obsession with ideological confrontation, the two systems and paths adopted by China and the US could work in parallel and coexist peacefully on this planet." Ministry of Foreign Affairs of China, "State Councilor and Foreign Minister Wang Yi Gives Interview."

5. See my "Downhill from the Summit for Democracy," December 19, 2021, https://melgurtov.com/2021/12/19/post-321-downhill-from-the-summit-for-democracy/ and "What the End of 'America First' Might Mean for US Foreign Policy," *Global Asia*, vol. 16, no. 1 (March 2021), pp. 18–21.

6. *WaPo*, October 7, 2021.

7. Antony J. Blinken, "The Administration's Approach to the People's Republic of China," Speech at the George Washington University, US Department of State, Washington, DC, May 26, 2022, https://www.state.gov/the-administrations-approach-to-the-peoples-republic-of-china/.

8. The White House, *Indo-Pacific Strategy of the United States* (Washington, DC: February 2022), https://www.whitehouse.gov/wp-content/uploads/2022/02/U.S.-Indo-Pacific-Strategy.pdf.

9. For example, the White House's *Interim National Security Strategic Guidance* (March 2021, https://www.whitehouse.gov/wp-content/uploads/2021/03/NSC-1v2.pdf) says: "China, in particular, has rapidly become more assertive. It is the only competitor potentially capable of combining its economic, diplomatic, military, and technological power to mount a sustained challenge to a stable and open international system."

10. Sullivan, "What Donald Trump and Dick Cheney Got Wrong about America."

11. See Sheena Chestnut Greitens, "China: Two Key Questions," *Democracy*, no. 61 (Summer 2021), https://democracyjournal.org/magazine/61/china-two-key-questions/.

12. Paul Jay, "Biden's China Policy: A More Polite Trump—Amb. Chas Freeman," *The Analysis.news*, March 12, 2021, https://theanalysis.news/interviews/bidens-china-policy-a-more-polite-trump-amb-chas-freeman/.

13. Chen sits atop China's law enforcement hierarchy as secretary general of the party's Central Political and Legal Affairs Commission. See "The Time for China's Rise Has Come, Security Chief Tells Law Enforcers," *South China Morning Post*, January 15, 2021, https://www.scmp.com/news/china/politics/article/3117973/time-chinas-rise-has-come-security-chief-tells-law-enforcers.

14. Quoted by Wang Jisi, "The Plot against China? How Beijing Sees the New Washington Consensus," *Foreign Affairs*, vol. 100, no. 4 (July–August 2021), p. 50.

15. Benji Sarlin and Sahil Kapur, "Why China May Be the Last Bipartisan Issue Left in Washington," NBC News, March 21, 2021, https://www.nbcnews.com/

politics/congress/why-china-may-be-last-bipartisan-issue-left-washington-n1261407?cid=eml_nbn_20210322.

16. US Congress, 117th Cong., 1st Sess., Senate, "Strategic Competition Act of 2021," https://www.congress.gov/bill/117th-congress/senate-bill/1169.

17. Senate Strategic Competition Act, pp. 13–20. By contrast, the House of Representatives considered the EAGLE (Ensuring American Global Leadership and Engagement) Act, which also calls for a tough approach to China but urges collaborative scientific research and improvement in military-to-military communication. The EAGLE Act was criticized by Republicans for being insufficiently anti-China. As of early 2022, efforts to integrate the two bills for a vote had failed.

18. William A. Galston, "A Momentous Shift in US Public Attitudes toward China," Brookings Institution, March 22, 2021, https://www.brookings.edu/blog/order-from-chaos/2021/03/22/a-momentous-shift-in-us-public-attitudes-toward-china/.

19. Craig Kafura and Dina Smeltz, "Republicans and Democrats Split on China Policy," The Chicago Council on Global Affairs, December 10, 2021, https://www.thechicagocouncil.org/research/public-opinion-survey/republicans-and-democrats-split-china-policy.

20. Julian Brave NoiseCat and Thom Woodroofe, "The United States and China Need to Cooperate—for the Planet's Sake," *Foreign Policy*, February 4, 2021, https://foreignpolicy.com/2021/02/04/united-states-china-climate-change-foreign-policy/.

21. The statement proposed "taking enhanced climate actions," mentioning carbon neutrality as an objective. "What we need to do is prove we can actually get together, sit down and work on some things constructively," Kerry said. Steven Lee Myers, "Despite Tensions, U.S. and China Agree to Work Together on Climate Change," *NYT*, April 18, 2021. China's qualification, by Foreign Minister Wang Yi, was: "The US side wants the climate change cooperation to be an 'oasis' of China-US relations," he told Kerry. "However, if the oasis is all surrounded by deserts, then sooner or later, the oasis will be desertified." Quoted by Robert Lewis, "After US Afghanistan Withdrawal Debacle, Huawei CFO Case May Be One Key to Reducing US-China Tensions," Paper, September 16, 2021, https://www.lexology.com/library/detail.aspx?g=0b90c84a-ed1f-4438-acf4-44dbcfd70b15.

22. Katie Benner, "Justice Dept. Is Set to Modify Trump-era Program Aimed at Fighting Chinese Threats," *NYT*, February 20, 2022.

23. Stuart Anderson, "Biden Keeps Costly Trump Visa Policy Denying Chinese Grad Students," *Forbes*, August 10, 2021, https://www.forbes.com/sites/stuartanderson/2021/08/10/biden-keeps-costly-trump-visa-policy-denying-chinese-grad-students/?sh=35b71d103641.

24. Yojana Sharma, "Taiwan Fills Gap Left by Confucius Institute Closures," *University World News*, December 2, 2021, https://www.universityworldnews.com/post.php?story=20211202125025734.

25. The bill, for example, will fund Chinese-language programs in US schools and enable Chinese (and all other) graduate student researchers in the STEM fields to get visas without requiring immigrant status. But it will also impose new reporting requirements for faculty and schools that seek foreign grants and new rules on schools that still have Confucius Institutes (in contrast with the USICA, which bars

certain government funds to schools with Confucius Institutes). The House bill must be reconciled with the Senate's USICA.

26. NBC-TV Evening News interview of FBI director Christopher Wray, February 1, 2022.

27. Karin Fischer, "Chinese Scientists Feel a Chill under U.S. Investigation of Higher Ed's China Ties, a New Survey Shows," *Chronicle of Higher Education*, October 28, 2021, https://www.chronicle.com/article/chinese-scientists-feel-a-chill-under-u-s-investigation-of-higher-eds-china-ties-a-new-survey-shows.

28. Philip H. Bucksbaum et al., "Current US Policy on China: The Risk to Open Science," *American Physical Society News*, August 9, 2021, https://www.aps.org/publications/apsnews/updates/china-risk.cfm. A letter to the attorney general from 430 University of Michigan faculty made the same point; see https://www.apajustice.org/uploads/1/1/5/7/115708039/letter_to_attorney_general_-_um.pdf.

29. Amy Qin, "As U.S. Hunts for Chinese Spies, University Scientists Warn of Backlash," *NYT*, November 28, 2021.

30. David P. Goldman, interviewed in Laure Mandeville and David P. Goldman, "AT Tells Le Figaro Why China Is Winning the Tech War," *Asia Times*, December 14, 2020, https://asiatimes.com/2020/12/at-tells-le-figaro-why-china-is-winning-the-tech-war/.

31. Andrew Silver, "Scientists in China Say US Government Crackdown Is Harming Collaborations," *Nature*, July 8, 2020, https://www.nature.com/articles/d41586-020-02015-y.

32. Caroline Wagner, "Scrutiny of Chinese Researchers Threatens Innovation," *University World News*, January 30, 2021, https://www.universityworldnews.com/post.php?story=20210128141727753.

33. Press release, Congressman Ted Lieu, July 30, 2021, https://lieu.house.gov/media-center/press-releases/rep-lieu-and-90-members-congress-urge-doj-probe-alleged-racial-profiling?utm_campaign=latitude%28s%29&utm_medium=email&utm_source=Revue%20newsletter; Karin Fischer, "Has the Hunt for Chinese Spies Become a Witch Hunt?" *Chronicle of Higher Education*, August 11, 2021, https://www.chronicle.com/article/has-the-hunt-for-chinese-spies-become-a-witch-hunt.

34. Office of the Director of National Intelligence, *Annual Threat Assessment of the US Intelligence Community*, April 9, 2021, https://www.nytimes.com/interactive/2021/04/13/us/annual-threat-assessment-report-pdf.html.

35. The comment was a further erosion of the one-China policy, since "it clearly implies that, in fact, Taiwan should be regarded primarily as a strategic asset to be kept separate from Beijing." Michael D. Swaine, "US Official Signals Stunning Shift in the Way We Interpret 'One China' Policy," *Responsible Statecraft*, December 10, 2021, https://responsiblestatecraft.org/2021/12/10/us-official-signals-stunning-shift-in-the-way-we-interpret-one-china-policy/.

36. Nathan Beauchamp-Mustafaga, "Dare to Face the 'Strong Enemy': How Xi Jinping Has Made the PLA Talk about the United States," *Sinocism*, March 4, 2021, https://sinocism.com/p/dare-to-face-the-strong-enemy-how?r=2e&utm_campaign=post&utm_medium=web&utm_source=twitter&s=09.

37. Ryan Hass, "How China Is Responding to Escalating Strategic Competition with the U.S.," *China Leadership Monitor*, March 1, 2021, https://www.prcleader.org/hass.

38. Elizabeth Economy, "Xi Jinping's Superpower Plans," *Wall Street Journal*, July 19, 2018.

39. Yan Xuetong, "How China Can Defeat America," *NYT*, November 20, 2011. Yan is best known for his "moral realism" theorizing.

40. Quoted by Hass, "How China Is Responding."

41. Mearsheimer, "The Inevitable Rivalry," p. 48.

42. M. Taylor Fravel, J. Stapleton Roy, Michael D. Swaine, Susan A. Thornton, and Ezra Vogel, "China Is Not an Enemy," *WaPo*, July 3, 2019.

43. Congressional Research Service (CRS), "China's Naval Modernization: Implications for U.S. Navy Capabilities—Background and Issues for Congress" (Washington, DC: September 9, 2021), https://crsreports.congress.gov/product/pdf/RL/RL33153/253. China has more total ships than the United States, but as the CRS report makes clear, a comparison is not very useful. "The U.S. Navy, for example, has many more aircraft carriers, nuclear-powered submarines, and cruisers and destroyers, while China's navy has many more diesel attack submarines, frigates, and corvettes."

44. Ellie Kaufman, "Pentagon to Build Up US Bases in Guam and Australia to Meet China Challenge," November 29, 2021, https://www.cnn.com/2021/11/29/politics/global-posture-review-china/index.html.

45. See Bates Gill, ed., *Meeting China's Military Challenge: Collective Responses of U.S. Allies and Security Partners* (Washington, DC: The National Bureau of Asian Research, January 2022).

46. From the *SIPRI Yearbook 2021: Armaments, Disarmament and International Security*, https://www.sipri.org/media/press-release/2021/global-nuclear-arsenals-grow-states-continue-modernize-new-sipri-yearbook-out-now.

47. The US State Department released nuclear weapon figures in fall 2021: 3,750 stockpiled and 2,000 scheduled to be dismantled (https://www.cnn.com/2021/10/06/politics/us-nuclear-weapons-stockpile/index.html). But to judge from Biden's military budget requests, research and development on nuclear weapons will continue. China, as usual, did not release any similar information.

48. A comprehensive accounting of China's nuclear capability is in Hans M. Kristensen and Matt Korda, "Nuclear Notebook: Chinese Nuclear Forces, 2021," *Bulletin of the Atomic Scientists*, November 15, 2021, https://thebulletin.org/premium/2021-11/nuclear-notebook-chinese-nuclear-forces-2021/.

49. Joby Warrick, "China Is Building More Than 100 New Missile Silos in Its Western Desert, Analysts Say," *WaPo*, June 30, 2021.

50. Tong Zhao, "Why Is China Building Up Its Nuclear Arsenal?" *NYT*, November 16, 2021.

51. Kurt Campbell, the White House coordinator on China policy, has said: "So we do have a hotline, it's known to have, the couple of times we've used it, just rung in an empty room for hours upon hours." Quoted in David Brunnstrom and Michael Martina, "Strategic Clarity on Taiwan Policy Carries 'Significant

Downsides'—U.S.," Reuters, May 4, 2021, https://www.reuters.com/world/asia
-pacific/significant-downsides-strategic-clarity-over-taiwan-us-2021-05-04/.

52. David E. Sanger and William J. Broad, "As China Speeds Up Nuclear Arms
Race, U.S. Wants to Talk," *NYT*, November 28, 2021.

53. Abraham Denmark and Caitlin Talmadge, "Why China Wants More and Better
Nukes," *Foreign Affairs*, November 19, 2021, https://www.foreignaffairs.com/articles
/china/2021-11-19/why-china-wants-more-and-better-nukes.

54. David E. Sanger and William J. Broad, "China's Weapon Test Close to a 'Sputnik Moment,' U.S. General Says," *NYT*, October 27, 2021.

55. China might be building a new naval base in Cambodia, in a part of an existing Cambodian base. Cambodians deny a foreign base is being built, saying China
is renovating it for Cambodia's security needs. Ellen Nakashima and Cate Cadell,
"China Secretly Building Naval Facility in Cambodia, Western Officials Say," *WaPo*,
June 6, 2022.

56. Some experts think China's expanding arsenal will require many more weapons
to ensure mutual destruction in a nuclear exchange, among other contingencies, in a
three-superpower world. Forgotten is a lesson from a two-superpower world: diplomacy to prevent use of nukes, reduce their numbers and capabilities, and stop other
nuclear-capable states from going nuclear.

57. As China is increasingly victimized by large-scale floods, forest fires, and other
disasters, the leadership will need to call on the military for help, as it has already
done in recent times. Klare predicts that "by 2049, the Chinese military (or what's
left of it) will be so busy coping with a burning, flooding, churning world of climate
change—threatening the country's very survival—that it will possess scant capacity,
no less the will, to launch a war with the United States or any of its allies." Michael
Klare, "China, 2049: A Climate Disaster Zone, Not a Military Superpower," *TomDispatch*, August 24, 2021, https://tomdispatch.com/china-2049/.

58. See Ellen Nakashima, "China's Test of Hypersonic Vehicle Is Part of a Program
to Rapidly Expand Strategic and Nuclear Systems," *WaPo*, October 19, 2021; Sanger
and Broad, "As China Speeds Up Nuclear Arms Race."

59. US Office of the Secretary of Defense, *Military and Security Developments
Involving the People's Republic of China 2021: Annual Report to Congress* (Washington, DC: Department of Defense, 2021), p. 151. The Defense Department reports
that it has a crisis communication working group with China as well as a maritime
operational safety dialogue group, but how regularly these groups meet is not clear.

60. Rosh Doshi, "Improving Risk Reduction and Crisis Management in US-China
Relations," in Ryan Hass, Ryan McElveen, and Robert D. Williams, eds., *The Future
of US Policy toward China: Recommendations for the Biden Administration* (Washington, DC: Brookings Institution and Yale Law School, November 2020), pp. 69–71.

61. Cissy Zhou, "US-China Economic Talks 'Infinitely Far Away' with 'Emphasis
on Competition over Cooperation,'" *South China Morning Post*, July 19, 2021, https:
//www.scmp.com/economy/china-economy/article/3141700/us-china-economic-talks
-infinitely-far-away-emphasis.

62. Fang, Li, and Liu, "Chinese Public Opinion about US-China Relations."

63. Eva Dou, "Senior U.S. Official Visits China, in Small Thaw in Relations with Beijing," *WaPo*, July 26, 2021. The US list had no surprises: it included various human rights concerns, Taiwan, technology, and trade issues. China's list was in two parts (https://www.fmprc.gov.cn/mfa_eng/wjbxw/t1894983.shtml). Under "US Wrongdoings," China listed visa restrictions and sanctions on CCP members and students. Under "key individual cases," China "urged the United States to stop suppressing Chinese enterprises, stop harassing Chinese students, stop suppressing the Confucius Institutes, revoke the registration of Chinese media outlets as 'foreign agents' or 'foreign missions,' and revoke the extradition request for Meng Wanzhou." Meng was the chief financial officer of Huawei, who was arrested in December 2018 in Canada on the US charge that a Huawei-controlled company had violated sanctions on Iran and that Meng had lied about it. China shortly thereafter arrested two Canadians on spying allegations. The case was not resolved until September 2021 when Meng admitted to a few of the charges on being released and the Canadians were simultaneously released.

64. Yan Xuetong, "Becoming Strong: The New Chinese Foreign Policy," *Foreign Affairs*, vol. 100, no. 4 (July–August 2021), pp. 40–47; Wang Jisi, "The Plot against China?" Yan Xuetong is dean of the Institute of International Relations at Qinghua University in Beijing and is a strong nationalist critic of US foreign policy. He wrote. "This [US] strategy has brought about much more difficulties to China's economic development and pressure on China's diplomatic relations than Trump's unilateral strategy." Wang Jisi, president of the Institute of International and Strategic Studies at Beijing University, has long favored finding common ground between China and the United States.

65. For example, Steven Lee Myers and Amy Qin, "Biden Has Angered China, and Beijing Is Pushing Back," *NYT*, July 20, 2021.

66. Ministry of Foreign Affairs, China, "Wang Yi Meets US Deputy Secretary of State Sherman," July 26, 2021, https://www.fmprc.gov.cn/web/wjbz_673089/zyhd_673091/t1895177.shtml.

67. "Jin Canrong: Defeating the US Is CCP's Main Objective," GNews, March 2021, https://gnews.org/940306/. The reliability of this source is low, since it comes from a right-wing anti-China foundation (Rule of Law Foundation) in Canada, does not indicate the original source (noting only that it comes from a video), and seems to be a poor translation from the original. Nevertheless, I include it here because the quotation does appear to reflect Jin Canrong's nationalistic bent. I have lightly edited the quotation for grammatical correctness.

68. An example is the case of Meng Wanzhou described in n. 63 above. China all along chose to treat Meng as a patriot, never acknowledged her partial admission of guilt, and denied the obvious—that the Canadians had essentially been hostages.

CHAPTER 7

1. Michael R. Gordon and Warren P. Strobel, "New U.S. Intelligence Report Doesn't Provide Definitive Conclusion on Covid-19 Origins," *Wall Street Journal*, August 24,

2021, https://www.wsj.com/articles/biden-to-receive-report-on-coronavirus-origins
-but-challenges-persist-in-how-to-deal-with-china-11629825758.

2. Yasmeen Abutaleb and Shane Harris, "Trump Administration's Hunt for Pandemic 'Lab Leak' Went Down Many Paths and Came Up with No Smoking Gun," *WaPo*, June 15, 2021.

3. For example, Ezekiel J. Emanuel and Michael T. Osterholm, "China's Zero-Covid Policy Is a Pandemic Waiting to Happen," *NYT*, January 25, 2022.

4. Chris Buckley, Vivian Wang, and Keith Bradsher, "Living by the Code: In China, Covid-Era Controls May Outlast the Virus," *NYT*, January 30, 2022.

5. This paragraph relies on the work of Ian Urbina, "The Smell of Money," *The New Yorker*, March 8, 2021, pp. 24–29.

6. Robert Tait, "China Accused of Buying Influence after Czech Billionaire Funds PR Push," *The Guardian*, January 5, 2020.

7. Michael Birnbaum, "China Investing in Europe—but There Are Strings Attached," *WaPo*, August 19, 2020.

8. These are the Maritime Silk Road, the Silk Road, the Green Silk Road (increasing renewable energy capacity), Digital Silk Road (for high-tech and "big data" development in cities), and Silk Road of Innovation (technology transfers). Iran has become the centerpiece for the latter three components. Taylor Butch, "China in the Middle East: Iran's 'Belt and Road' Role," *Middle East Quarterly*, Spring 2021, vol. 28, no. 2, https://www.meforum.org/62067/china-middle-east-irans-belt-and-road
-role.

9. Ammar A. Malik, Bradley Parks, Brooke Russell, Jiahui Lin, Katherine Walsh, Kyra Solomon, Sheng Zhang, Thai-Binh Elston, and Seth Goodman, *Banking on the Belt and Road: Insights from a New Global Dataset of 13,427 Chinese Development Projects.* Williamsburg, VA: AidData at William & Mary, 2021.

10. See the case studies in *Asian Perspective*, vol. 45, no. 2 (Spring 2021), in particular Cheng-Chwee Kuik, "Introduction to the Special Issue," pp. 255–76.

11. "Inside China's US$1 Billion Port in Sri Lanka Where Ships Don't Want to Stop," *Straits Times* (Singapore), April 18, 2018, https://www.straitstimes.com/asia/
south-asia/inside-chinas-us1-billion-port-in-sri-lanka-where-ships-dont-want-to-stop.

12. "Sri Lanka Meltdown Exposes China Loan Policy: 5 Things to Know," *Nikkei Asia*, https://asia.nikkei.com/Spotlight/Sri-Lanka-crisis/Sri-Lanka-meltdown-exposes
-China-loan-policy-5-things-to-know.

13. Pakistan's prime minister, Imran Khan, has said: "Because we have a very strong relationship with China, and because we have a relationship based on trust, so we actually accept the Chinese version. What they say about the programs in Xinjiang, we accept it." Sammy Westfall, "Pakistan Prime Minister Embraces China's Policy toward Uyghurs in Remarks on Communist Party Centenary," *WaPo*, July 2, 2021.

14. Philip J. Cunningham, "As China Brings Laos into Its Fold, Will the U.S. Seek to Reset Relations to Counter Beijing?" *South China Morning Post*, December 9, 2021, https://www.scmp.com/comment/opinion/article/3158751/china-brings-laos-its
-fold-will-us-seek-reset-relations-counter; "China's Southern Railway Expansion Is Not All Good News for Laos," *Hankyoreh* (Seoul), December 19, 2021, https://english

.hani.co.kr/arti/english_edition/e_international/1023847.html?fbclid=IwAR0T3o
-hLH2ztE4hO3wTCgFYnJa9wUsa-IxW-1OwzI3XYaBp68KOEpjPY0Q.

15. China, to be sure, can be taken to task for imposing abnormal conditions for the loan, but the main responsibility for the debt trap would seem to belong to Montenegro for deciding to fall into it—and perhaps to the EU for failing to come to Montenegro's assistance, and thus ceding influence to Beijing in the Balkans. Rob Schmitz, "How a Chinese-Built Highway Drove Montenegro Deep into Debt," National Public Radio (NPR), June 26, 2021, https://www.npr.org/2021/06/28/1010832606/road-deal -with-china-is-blamed-for-catapulting-montenegro-into-historic-debt.

16. "We do not want a situation where there is a new version of colonialism happening because poor countries are unable to compete with rich countries," said Mahathir. Hannah Beech, "'We Cannot Afford This': Malaysia Pushes Back against China's Vision," *NYT*, August 20, 2018.

17. Yufan Huang and Deborah Brautigam, "Putting a Dollar Amount on China's Loans to the Developing World," *The Diplomat*, June 24, 2020, https://thediplomat .com/2020/06/putting-a-dollar-amount-on-chinas-loans-to-the-developing-world/.

18. Huang and Brautigam, "Putting a Dollar Amount on China's Loans to the Developing World."

19. Interview of Professor Maria Repnikova by Jessica Chen Weiss, "Does China Actively Promote Its Way of Governing—and Do Other Countries Listen?" *WaPo*, July 14, 2021. Professor Repnikova found that the training programs are not politically heavy-handed and trainees do not come away with a strong regard for China's political system even as they appreciate China's generosity.

20. Shakir Ullah et al., "Problems and Benefits of the China-Pakistan Economic Corridor (CPEC) for Local People in Pakistan: A Critical Review," *Asian Perspective*, vol. 45, no. 4 (Fall 2021), pp. 861–76.

21. Yun Sun, "FOCAC 2021: China's Retrenchment from Africa?" Brookings Institution, December 6, 2021, https://www.brookings.edu/blog/africa-in-focus/2021 /12/06/focac-2021-chinas-retrenchment-from-africa/. Another study of BRI investments in 2021 similarly found a shift to smaller projects, lower investments, and more emphasis on west Asia and the Middle East. Christoph Nedopil Wang, "China Belt and Road Initiative (BRI) Investment Report H1 2021," Green Finance and Development Center, July 21, 2021, https://greenfdc.org/china-belt-and-road-initiative-bri -investment-report-h1-2021/?cookie-state-change=1638536227352.

22. David F. Gordon, Haoyu Tong, and Tabatha Anderson, "Beyond the Myths: Towards a Realistic Assessment of China's Belt and Road Initiative, the Security Dimension," International Institute for Strategic Studies, Report, September 2020, https://www.iiss.org/blogs/research-paper/2020/09/beyond-the-myths-of-the -bri.

23. The military's upset may be due to Pakistan's having declined the US invitation to the Summit for Democracy and the country's pro-China orientation at a time when US-India relations are improving. See Arif Rafiq, "Why Pakistan's Army Wants the U.S. Back in the Region," *NYT*, January 23, 2022.

24. Kuo, "China in Afghanistan."

25. Audrye Wong, "How Not to Win Allies and Influence Geopolitics," *Foreign Affairs*, vol. 100, no. 3 (May–June 2001), pp. 44–53.

26. French's comment is based in large part on demographic projections: "Today there are approximately 1.4 billion Africans. By 2050 that number will nearly double to 2.5 billion. And by century's end, according to the UN's median projection, there will be 4.4 billion Africans—well more than the combined populations of China and India today." Howard W. French, "Can America Remain Preeminent?" *New York Review of Books*, April 29, 2021, https://www.nybooks.com/articles/2021/04/29/can-america-remain-preeminent/.

27. Senate Strategic Competition Act, p. 12.

28. David E. Sanger and Mark Landler, "Biden Tries to Rally G7 Nations to Counter China's Influence," *NYT*, June 12, 2021. As this report suggests, the funds, components, rules, and other dimensions of Biden's idea were not decided at the G7 meeting.

29. The White House, "President Biden and G7 Leaders Launch Build Back Better (B3W) Partnership," June 12, 2021, https://www.whitehouse.gov/briefing-room/statements-releases/2021/06/12/fact-sheet-president-biden-and-g7-leaders-launch-build-back-better-world-b3w-partnership/.

30. Ministry of Foreign Affairs, China, "Xi Jinping and US President Biden Hold Virtual Summit" (in Chinese), November 16, 2021, https://www.fmprc.gov.cn/web/zyxw/t1919210.shtml.

31. John Hudson, "Blinken Lays Out U.S. Policy toward Africa and Deliberately Avoids Mentioning China," *WaPo*, November 19, 2021.

32. Sources for this case study are Dionne Searcey, Michael Forsythe, and Eric Lipton, "Global Rivalries Are Miring the Clean Energy Revolution," *NYT*, November 20, 2021; Nicolas Niarchos, "Buried Dreams," *The New Yorker*, May 31, 2021, pp. 40–49; Eric Lipton and Dionne Searcey, "How the U.S. Lost Ground to China in the Contest for Clean Energy," *NYT*, November 21, 2021.

33. A similar competition exists over lithium, which is another vital mineral in electric car production. Bolivia has large lithium deposits that are now in competition between Chinese, Russian, US, and other firms. See Clifford Krauss, "Green-Energy Race Draws an American Underdog to Bolivia's Lithium," *NYT*, December 16, 2021.

34. "Keynote Speech by President Xi Jinping at Extraordinary China-Africa Summit on Solidarity against COVID-19," Xinhuanet, June 18, 2020, http://www.xinhuanet.com/english/2020-06/18/c_139147084.htm.

35. Gerry Shih, "Biden's Climate Summit Shows Rivalry with U.S. Complicates China's Green Push," *WaPo*, April 23, 2021. Useful statistics are at BP, "Statistical Review of World Energy, 2021: China's Energy Market in 2020," https://www.bp.com/content/dam/bp/business-sites/en/global/corporate/pdfs/energy-economics/statistical-review/bp-stats-review-2021-china-insights.pdf.

36. World Nuclear Association, "Nuclear Power in China," January 2022, https://world-nuclear.org/information-library/country-profiles/countries-a-f/china-nuclear-power.aspx.

37. Su-Lin Tan, "China's Carbon Neutral Push Gathers Pace," *South China Morning Post*, February 20, 2021, https://www.scmp.com/economy/china-economy/article/3122419/chinas-carbon-neutral-push-gathers-pace-coal-fired-power.

38. Ma Xinyue, "China's Shifting Overseas Energy Footprint," *China Dialogue*, September 8, 2021, https://chinadialogue.net/en/energy/chinas-shifting-overseas -energy-footprint/. Japan, as a source of public financing of overseas coal plants, is about the same as China.

39. Emma Newburger, "China's Emission Exceed Those of U.S. and Developed Countries Combined, Report Says," NBC News, May 6, 2021, https:// www.nbcnews.com/science/environment/chinas-emissions-exceed-us-developed -countries-combined-report-says-rcna852.

40. Zoe Mize, "China's Green Silk Road to Nuclear Power," IISS (International Institute for Strategic Studies), December 21, 2021, https://www.iiss.org/blogs/ analysis/2021/12/chinas-green-silk-road-to-nuclear-power.

41. Ma Xinyue, "China's Shifting Overseas Energy Footprint."

42. Keith Bradsher and Lisa Friedman, "China's Power Crunch Exposes Tensions Ahead of Key U.N. Climate Summit," *NYT*, October 7, 2021.

43. Lowy Institute, *Asia Power Index 2021 Edition*, https://power.lowyinstitute.org /data/economic-relationships/regional-trade-relations/primary-trade-partner/.

44. Eric Martin and James Mayger, "U.S.-China Trade Booms as if Virus, Tariffs Never Happened," *Bloomberg*, July 21, 2021, https://www.bloomberg.com/news/ articles/2021-07-22/u-s-china-goods-trade-booms-as-if-virus-tariffs-never-happened.

45. Justin Jacobs and Derek Brower, "US-China Gas Deals Defy Tensions between World Powers," *Financial Times*, December 20, 2021, https://www.ft.com/content/ c267b3ea-a874-4bea-9105-860ae1847176.

46. Paul Hannon and Eun-Young Jeong, "China Overtakes U.S. as World's Leading Destination for Foreign Direct Investment," *Wall Street Journal*, January 24, 2021, https://www.wsj.com/articles/china-overtakes-u-s-as-worlds-leading-destination-for -foreign-direct-investment-11611511200; Sarah Zheng, "US-China Trade War Did Not Bring American Firms Home, Research Finds," *South China Morning Post*, September 24, 2021, https://www.scmp.com/news/china/diplomacy/article/3149792/us -china-trade-war-did-not-bring-american-firms-home-research?utm_source=Twitter &utm_medium=share_widget&utm_campaign=3149792.

47. David Dollar, "Clear Skies over Asia's New Foreign Investment Landscape," *East Asia Forum*, May 2, 2021, https://www.eastasiaforum.org/2021/05/02/clear -skies-over-asias-new-foreign-investment-landscape/.

48. Thilo Hanemann, Mark Witzke, Charlie Vest, Lauren Dudley, and Ryan Featherston, "An Outbound Investment Screening Regime for the United States?" Rhodium Group and National Committee on U.S.-China Relations, January 2022, https://www.ncuscr.org/sites/default/files/page_attachments/NCUSCR_RHG_TWS _2022_US_Outbound_Investment_1.26.22_FINAL.pdf. Another source puts cumulative US FDI in China, from 2000 to 2020, at about $124 billion—a good deal less than the previous source. "Direct Investment Position of the United States in China from 2000 to 2020," *Statista*, https://www.statista.com/statistics/188629/united-states -direct-investments-in-china-since-2000/.

49. Hanemann et al., "An Outbound Investment Screening Regime."

50. Paul Mozur and David McCabe, "U.S. Business Groups Urge Biden to Restart China Trade Talks," *NYT*, August 6, 2021.

51. Chad P. Bown, "China Bought None of the Extra $200 Billion of Exports in Trump's Trade Deal," *PIIE*, February 8, 2022, https://www.piie.com/blogs/realtime -economic-issues-watch/china-bought-none-extra-200-billion-us-exports-trumps -trade.

52. See the report of the United States Trade Representative, "2021 Report to Congress on China's WTO Compliance," February 2022, https://ustr.gov/sites/default/ files/enforcement/WTO/2021%20USTR%20Report%20to%20Congress%20on %20China's%20WTO%20Compliance.pdf. Among the report's conclusions is that "China's embrace of a state-led, non-market approach to the economy and trade has increased rather than decreased over time, and the mercantilism that it generates has harmed and disadvantaged U.S. companies and workers, often severely."

53. Ana Swanson and Keith Bradsher, "U.S. Signals Little Thaw in Trade Relations with China," *NYT*, October 4, 2021.

54. Ana Swanson, "Biden's China Dilemma: How to Enforce Trump's Trade Deal," *NYT*, December 15, 2021.

55. Su-Lin Tan and Orange Wang, "China's Bid to Join Pacific Rim Trade Pact Heaps Pressure on US to Step Up Regional Economic Strategy," *South China Morning Post*, September 18, 2021, https://www.scmp.com/economy/global-economy/ article/3149192/chinas-bid-join-pacific-rim-trade-pact-heaps-pressure-us.

56. Gary Clyde Hufbauer and Megan Hogan, "Security Not Economics Is Likely to Drive US Trade Engagement in Asia," *East Asia Forum*, January 9, 2022, https:// www.eastasiaforum.org/?p=568999.

57. Sidney Leng, "China Strikes Triumphal Note over Economic Recovery as It Looks to Cut Reliance on US Technology," *South China Morning Post*, December 20, 2020, https://www.scmp.com/economy/china-economy/article/3114652/china-strikes -triumphal-note-over-economic-recovery-it-looks?utm_source=email&utm_medium =share_widget&utm_campaign=3114652.

58. Kevin Rudd, "What Explains Xi's Pivot to the State?" Belfer Center, Harvard University, September 19, 2021, https://www.belfercenter.org/publication/what -explains-xis-pivot-state.

59. Helen Davidson, "China's Population Growth Rate Falls to 61-Year Low," *The Guardian*, January 17, 2022; Michael Schuman, "China Isn't That Strategic," *The Atlantic*, July 1, 2021, https://theatlantic.com/international/archive/2021/07/china -communists-demographics/619312/. Demographers generally seem to doubt that the government's steps to address the declining population, such as later retirement and allowance for a three-child family, will be enough to reverse the trend.

60. Robert D. Atkinson, "Industry by Industry: More Chinese Mercantilism, Less Global Innovation," Information Technology & Innovation Foundation, May 10, 2021, https://itif.org/publications/2021/05/10/industry-industry-more-chinese -mercantilism-less-global-innovation.

61. Ryan Fedasiuk and Emily Weinstein, "Beijing's Strategic Blueprint Is Changing as Tensions Grow," *Foreign Policy*, December 3, 2021, https://foreignpolicy.com /2021/12/03/china-strategic-blueprint-technology/.

62. Adam Segal, "China Moves to Greater Self-reliance," *China Leadership Monitor*, December 1, 2021, https://www.prcleader.org/segal.

63. Paul Mozur, "The Failure of China's Microchip Giant Tests Beijing's Tech Ambitions," *NYT*, July 19, 2021; Atkinson, "Industry by Industry."

64. See Office of the United States Trade Representative, "Remarks as Prepared for Delivery of Ambassador Katherine Tai Outlining the Biden-Harris Administration's 'New Approach to the U.S.-China Trade Relationship,'" October 4, 2021, https://ustr.gov/about-us/policy-offices/press-office/press-releases/2021/october/remarks-prepared-delivery-ambassador-katherine-tai-outlining-biden-harris-administrations-new.

65. Both the 2021 USICA and the pending House of Representatives bill, the "America Competes Act of 2022," provide about $52 billion in support of chip research and production.

66. Segal, "China Moves to Greater Self-reliance."

CHAPTER 8

1. US National Intelligence Council, "Global Trends 2040: A More Contested World," March 2021, https://www.dni.gov/files/ODNI/documents/assessments/GlobalTrends_2040.pdf.

2. US National Intelligence Council, "Foreign Threats to the 2020 US Federal Elections."

3. Gerry Shih, "Faced with Sanctions and Condemnation from the West, China Becomes Bedfellows with Russia," *WaPo*, March 29, 2021.

4. China's middle class, Cheng Li argues, plays a pivotal role in the evolution of US-China competition, moving it either in a nationalistic or a transnational direction. See his *Middle Class Shanghai*, pp. 11–13 and 51–53.

5. Anne Marie Slaughter, "The Biden Doctrine," *NYT*, November 12, 2021.

6. Deborah Seligsohn, "The Rise and Fall of the US-China Health Relationship," *Asian Perspective*, vol. 45, no. 1 (Winter 2021), pp. 203–24.

7. See Peter Beinart, "Biden Thinks He Can Have It Both Ways on China; He's Wrong," *NYT*, November 19, 2021.

8. He Bin, "Speech to County-level Leading Cadres to Study and Thoroughly Implement the Party's Special Topics at the 5th Plenary Session of the 19th Central Committee," *Qilian News*, February 25, 2021, http://www.qiliannews.com/system/2021/02/25/013341147.shtml. Qilian County is in Qinghai Province and is part of Haibei Tibetan Autonomous Prefecture. The reporter cites Xi Jinping's "great judgment" about world affairs, but aside from the quotes of Xi, the speech is entirely devoted to party affairs and is something of a pep talk to local cadres.

9. Ministry of Foreign Affairs, China, "Xi Jinping and US President Biden Hold Virtual Summit."

10. Ministry of Foreign Affairs, China, "The Video Meeting Is Another Instance in China-US Relations of the Two Countries' Leaders Piloting the Ship by Rudder at a Critical Moment" (in Chinese), November 16, 2021, http://world.people.com.cn/n1/2021/1116/c1002-32284196.html.

11. For example, academic research by Americans that has value for Chinese rural areas. See Tianli Feng, "Bringing Evidence-Based Policy Change to Rural China," *Stanford Social Innovation Review*, Fall 2021, https://ssir.org/articles/entry/bringing_evidence_based_policy_change_to_rural_china.

12. Yu Guoming, a leading communications scholar at Renmin University, quoted by Maria Repnikova, *Chinese Soft Power* (Cambridge, UK: Cambridge University Press, 2022), ch. 1 (online version). Yu added: "If our voice does not match our role, however strong we are, we remain a crippled giant." Repnikova's study finds that "Much of this rhetoric [on soft power] appears to stem from a perception of China's inadequacy when it comes to its soft power, especially in comparison with the West."

13. Erich Schwartzel, *Red Carpet:* Hollywood, China and the Global Battle for Cultural Supremacy (New York: Penguin Press, 2022).

14. China's international image, as measured by Pew Research, is much lower than that of the United States, especially since Biden became president. Favorable views of the United States are more than twice as high as they are for China nearly everywhere. See Laura Silver, "China's International Image Remains Broadly Negative as Views of the U.S. Rebound," Pew Research Center, June 30, 2021, https://www.pewresearch.org/fact-tank/2021/06/30/chinas-international-image-remains-broadly-negative-as-views-of-the-u-s-rebound/.

15. As of mid-2020, China had about 2,500 soldiers and police in UN operations, mainly in Africa in line with China's aid and investment interests. The number is small, but still greater than the combined total of the other permanent UN Security Council members. Richard Gowan, "China's Pragmatic Approach to UN Peacekeeping," Brookings Institution, September 14, 2020, https://www.brookings.edu/articles/chinas-pragmatic-approach-to-un-peacekeeping/.

16. Kevin Rudd, "Why the Quad Alarms China," *Foreign Affairs*, August 6, 2021, https://www.foreignaffairs.com/articles/united-states/2021-08-06/why-quad-alarms-china.

17. I discuss the SDM idea in more detail in Gurtov, *Engaging Adversaries*, pp. 84–85.

18. Vanda Felbab-Brown, "China and Synthetic Drugs Control: Fentanyl, Methamphetamines, and Precursors," Brookings Institution, March 2022, https://www.brookings.edu/research/china-and-synthetic-drugs-control-fentanyl-methamphetamines-and-precursors/. China is a major source of fentanyl, a synthetic opioid that is regulated in both countries. But counternarcotics cooperation is limited, Felbab-Brown writes, by "the overall deteriorated geostrategic relationship between the two superpowers. There is little prospect that in the absence of significant warming of the overall U.S.-China bilateral relationship, China would significantly intensify its anti-drug cooperation with the United States."

19. See Thornton, "Whither the Status Quo? A Cross–Taiwan Strait Trilateral Dialogue."

20. A number of such partnerships have already been established, for example at the province level (Hainan's ban on combustible engines, Jiangsi's energy efficiency program, and Guangdong's cap on carbon emissions) and the city level (Shenzhen's electric vehicles and a Los Angeles–Shanghai "green port" initiative. Woodrow

Wilson Center, "Walking the Walk after the New U.S.-China Climate Declaration," January 13, 2021, webcast interview of Fan Dai, director of the California-China Climate Institute, https://www.wilsoncenter.org/event/walking-walk-after-new-us-china -climate-declaration.

21. Gurtov, *Engaging Adversaries*, pp. 18–23.

22. "Respect History, Look to the Future and Firmly Safeguard and Stabilize China-US Relations," *Global Times*, August 7, 2020, https://www.globaltimes.cn/content/1197044.shtml.

23. Ministry of Foreign Affairs, China, March 2021, https://www.fmprc.gov.cn/web/wjbzhd/t1859110.shtml.

24. Wang Dong, "The Case for a New Engagement Consensus: A Chinese Vision of Global Order," *Foreign Affairs*, April 15, 2021, https://www.foreignaffairs.com/articles/china/2021-04-15/case-new-engagement-consensus.

25. On the latter, see Doshi, *The Long Game*.

26. Lewis, "After US Afghanistan Withdrawal."

27. Ministry of Foreign Affairs of the People's Republic of China, "Chinese President Xi Jinping Speaks with U.S. President Joseph Biden by Phone," https://www.fmprc.gov.cn/mfa_eng/zxxx_662805/t1906035.shtml.

28. Ali Wyne and Ryan Hass, "China Diplomacy Is Limiting Its Own Ambitions," *Foreign Policy*, June 9, 2021, https://foreignpolicy.com/2021/06/09/china-wolf-war -diplomacy-foreign-policy/.

29. Swaine, "Chinese Views of U.S. Decline."

30. "Readout of President Joseph R. Biden Call with President Xi Jinping of the People's Republic of China," September 9, 2021, https://www.whitehouse.gov/briefing-room/statements-releases/2021/09/09/readout-of-president-joseph-r-biden-jr -call-with-president-xi-jinping-of-the-peoples-republic-of-china/.

31. Ministry of Foreign Affairs of the PRC, "President Xi Jinping Speaks with U.S. President Joseph Biden."

32. "Let's get something straight," Biden is reported to have said of Xi. "We know each other well, we're not old friends. It's pure business." Chris Jansing, MSNBC, tweet of June 16, 2021. Biden probably said that at least partly in order to avoid repeating Trump's mistake of lauding friendship with Xi and other authoritarian leaders.

33. Trita Parsi, *A Single Roll of the Dice: Obama's Diplomacy with Iran* (New Haven, CT: Yale University Press, 2012), pp. 222–23.

34. Tiffany Barron, Rorry Daniels, M. Patrick Hulme, Daniel Jasper, Craig Kafura, and Kacie Miura, *Engagement Revisited: Progress Made and Lessons Learned from the US-China Strategic and Economic Dialogue* (National Committee on American Foreign Policy, September 2021), p. 2, https://NCAFP_China_Engagement_final _Sept-2021.pdf.

35. See Ryan Hass, Ryan McElveen, and Robert D. Williams, eds., *The Future of US Policy toward China: Recommendations for the Biden Administration* (Washington, DC: Brookings Institution and Yale Law School, November 2020), https://www.brookings.edu/wp-content/uploads/2020/11/Future-U.S.-policy-toward-China

-v8.pdf, in particular Hass, "Designing a New Diplomatic Framework for Dealing with China," pp. 15–19.

36. Ali Wyne, "Competition with China Shouldn't Dictate U.S. Foreign Policy," *World Politics Review*, February 25, 2021, https://www.worldpoliticsreview.com/articles/29450/competition-with-a-rising-china-shouldn-t-dictate-u-s-foreign-policy. See also Wyne and Hass, "China's Diplomacy Is Limiting Its Own Ambitions."

37. See Brahima S. Coulibaly and Elizabeth Sidiropoulos, "Regional Cooperation: A Necessary Complement to Global Multilateralism," in Coulibaly and Kemal Derviş, eds., *Essays on a 20th Century Multilateralism That Works for All* (Washington, DC: Brookings Institution, 2021), pp. 29–39, https://www.brookings.edu/wp-content/uploads/2022/02/21st-Century-Multilateralism.pdf.

38. Jon Huntsman Jr., "Biden's China Relationship: The View from Utah," *Deseret News*, February 5, 2021.

39. Judah Grunstein, "More 'Wolf Warrior' Diplomacy, Please." *World Politics Review*, March 24, 2021, https://www.worldpoliticsreview.com/articles/29517/wolf-warrior-diplomacy-and-the-us-china-relationship.

40. Michael Beckley and Hal Brands, "The End of China's Rise," *Foreign Affairs*, October 1, 2021, https://www.foreignaffairs.com/articles/china/2021-10-01/end-chinas-rise.

41. Christensen, "There Will Not Be a New Cold War."

42. How that result might happen on the China side is discussed by Beckley and Brands, "The End of China's Rise."

Bibliography

BOOKS

Balzer, Harley. *Axis of Collusion: The Fragile Putin-Xi Partnership* (Atlantic Council, December 2021), https://www.atlanticcouncil.org/event/axis-of-collusion -the-fragile-putin-xi-partnership/.

Coulibaly, Brahima S., and Kemal Derviş, eds. *Essays on a 20th Century Multilateralism That Works for All* (Washington, DC: Brookings Institution, 2021), https://www.brookings.edu/wp-content/uploads/2022/02/21st-Century -Multilateralism.pdf.

Doshi, Rosh. *The Long Game: China's Grand Strategy to Displace American Order* (New York: Oxford University Press, 2021).

Fitzgerald, John, ed. *Taking the Low Road: China's Influence in Australia's States and Territories* (Barton: Australian Strategic Policy Institute, 2022), http://ad-aspi .s3.ap-southeast-2.amazonaws.com/2022-02/Taking%20the%20low%20road.pdf ?VersionId=NIkDeFmjPYAxwSb45VMUmOvFuhAkKekk.

Gurtov, Mel. *Engaging Adversaries: Peacemaking and Diplomacy in the Human Interest* (Lanham, MD: Rowman & Littlefield, 2018).

———. *Will This Be China's Century? A Skeptic's View* (Boulder, CO: Lynne Rienner, 2013).

Hamilton, Clive. *Silent Invasion: China's Influence in Australia* (Melbourne: Hardie Grant Books, 2018).

Heath, Timothy R., Derek Grossman, and Asha Clark. *China's Quest for Global Primacy: An Analysis of Chinese International and Defense Strategies to Outcompete the United States* (Santa Monica, CA: RAND Corporation, 2021).

Li, Cheng. *Middle Class Shanghai: Reshaping U.S.-China Engagement* (Washington, DC: Brookings Institution, 2021).

Parsi, Trita. *A Single Roll of the Dice: Obama's Diplomacy with Iran* (New Haven, CT: Yale University Press, 2012), pp. 222–23.

Pei, Minxin. *China's Crony Capitalism: The Dynamics of Regime Decay* (Boston, MA: Harvard University Press, 2016).

Repnikova, Maria. *Chinese Soft Power* (Cambridge, UK: Cambridge University Press, 2022).

Rhodes, Ben. *The World as It Is: A Memoir of the Obama White House* (New York: Random House, 2019).

Roberts, Sean R. *The War on the Uyghurs: China's Internal Campaign against a Muslim Minority* (Princeton, NJ: Princeton University Press, 2020).

Rozelle, Scott, and Natalie Hell. *Invisible China: How the Urban-Rural Divide Threatens China's Rise* (Chicago: University of Chicago Press, 2020).

Schwartzel, Erich. *Red Carpet:* Hollywood, China and the Global Battle for Cultural Supremacy (New York: Penguin Press, 2022).

SIPRI Yearbook 2021: Armaments, Disarmament and International Security, https://www.sipri.org/media/press-release/2021/global-nuclear-arsenals-grow-states-continue-modernize-new-sipri-yearbook-out-now.

Thurston, Anne F., ed. *Engaging China: Fifty Years of Sino-American Relations* (New York: Columbia University Press, 2021).

Zenz, Adrian. "The Xinjiang Papers: An Introduction" (Washington, DC: Uyghur Tribunal, November 27, 2021), https://uyghurtribunal.com/wp-content/uploads/2021/11/The-Xinjiang-Papers-An-Introduction-1.pdf.

ARTICLES

Ahern, Brendan. "Vice Premier Liu He's Speech Sends Stocks Flying," *Forbes*, March 16, 2022, https://www.forbes.com/sites/brendanahern/2022/03/16/vice-premier-liu-hes-speech-sends-stocks-flying/.

Allen-Ebrahimian, Bethany. "U.S. Sanctions China's Paramilitary in Xinjiang," *Axios*, n.d., https://www.axios.com/us-sanctions-china-paramilitary-xinjiang-xpcc-41e29c92-9649-4e47-9e91-a7f78330d4d8.html.

Alperovitch, Dmitri. "The Case for Cyber-Realism," *Foreign Affairs*, vol. 101, no. 1 (January–February 2022), pp. 44–50.

Anderson, Stuart. "Biden Keeps Costly Trump Visa Policy Denying Chinese Grad Students," *Forbes*, August 10, 2021, https://www.forbes.com/sites/stuartanderson/2021/08/10/biden-keeps-costly-trump-visa-policy-denying-chinese-grad-students/?sh=35b71d103641.

Asat, Rayhan, and Yonah Diamond. "U.S. China Policy Must Confront the Genocide in Xinjiang First," *Foreign Policy*, January 21, 2021, https://foreignpolicy.com/2021/01/21/uighur-genocide-china-policy-biden-confront/.

Atkinson, Robert D. "Industry by Industry: More Chinese Mercantilism, Less Global Innovation," Information Technology & Innovation Foundation, May 10, 2021, https://itif.org/publications/2021/05/10/industry-industry-more-chinese-mercantilism-less-global-innovation.

Barron, Tiffany, Rorry Daniels, M. Patrick Hulme, Daniel Jasper, Craig Kafura, and Kacie Miura. *Engagement Revisited: Progress Made and Lessons Learned from the US-China Strategic and Economic Dialogue* (National Committee on American

Foreign Policy, September 2021), https://NCAFP_China_Engagement_final_Sept
-2021.pdf.

Batke, Jessica, and Mareike Ohlberg. "China's Biosecurity State in Xinjiang
Is Powered by Western Tech," *Foreign Policy*, February 19, 2020, https://
foreignpolicy.com/2020/02/19/china-xinjiang-surveillance-biosecurity-state-dna
-western-tech/.

Beauchamp-Mustafaga, Nathan. "Dare to Face the 'Strong Enemy': How Xi Jinping
Has Made the PLA Talk about the United States," *Sinocism*, March 4, 2021, https:
//sinocism.com/p/dare-to-face-the-strong-enemy-how?r=2e&utm_campaign=post
&utm_medium=web&utm_source=twitter&s=09.

Beckley, Michael, and Hal Brands. "The End of China's Rise," *Foreign Affairs*,
October 1, 2021, https://www.foreignaffairs.com/articles/china/2021-10-01/end
-chinas-rise.

Bhatnagar, Aryaman. "Is the EU's COVID-19 Response Losing Central and Eastern
Europe to China?" *World Politics Review*, May 8, 2020, www.worldpoliticsreview
.com/articles/28744/is-the-eu-s-covid-19-response-losing-central-and-eastern
-europe-to-china.

Bishop, Christopher W. "To Understand China's Aggressive Foreign Policy, Look
at Its Domestic Politics," Council on Foreign Relations, October 8, 2020, https://
www.cfr.org/blog/understand-chinas-aggressive-foreign-policy-look-its-domestic
-politics.

Blanchette, Jude. "Xi's Gamble: The Race to Consolidate Power and Stave Off
Disaster," *Foreign Affairs*, vol. 100, no. 4 (July–August 2021), pp. 10–19.

Bown, Chad P. "China Bought None of the Extra $200 Billion of Exports in
Trump's Trade Deal," *PIIE*, February 8, 2022, https://www.piie.com/blogs/realtime
-economic-issues-watch/china-bought-none-extra-200-billion-us-exports-trumps
-trade.

Bucksbaum, Philip H. et al. "Current US Policy on China: The Risk to Open
Science," *American Physical Society News*, August 9, 2021, https://www.aps.org/
publications/apsnews/updates/china-risk.cfm.

Butch, Taylor. "China in the Middle East: Iran's 'Belt and Road' Role," *Middle East
Quarterly*, Spring 2021, vol. 28, no. 2, https://www.meforum.org/62067/china
-middle-east-irans-belt-and-road-role.

Cai Xia. "The Party That Failed: An Insider Breaks with Beijing," *Foreign Affairs*,
vol. 100, no. 1 (January–February 2021), pp. 78–96.

Campbell, Kurt M., and Jake Sullivan. "Competition without Catastrophe: How
America Can Both Challenge and Coexist with China," *Foreign Affairs*, vol. 98,
no. 5 (September–October 2019), pp. 96–110.

Carrer, Gabriele. "Italian Alarm as China Eyes Port of Palermo," Center for European
Policy Analysis, December 6, 2021, https://cepa.org/italian-alarm-as-china-eyes
-port-of-palermo/.

Chausovsky, Eugene. "China Can't Carry the Russian Economy," *Foreign Policy*,
February 4, 2022, https://foreignpolicy.com/2022/02/04/china-russia-sanctions
-ukraine/.

Cheng, Yangyang. "Cancel Culture Isn't the Real Threat to Academic Freedom," *The Atlantic*, November 23, 2021, https://www.theatlantic.com/international/archive/2021/11/china-academic-freedom-cultural-revolution-cancel-culture/620777/.

Christensen, Thomas J. "There Will Not Be a New Cold War," *Foreign Affairs*, March 24, 2021, https://www.foreignaffairs.com/articles/united-states/2021-03-24/there-will-not-be-new-cold-war.

Clemens, Walter C. Jr. "Triangular Diplomacy in the Age of Putin, Xi and Trump," *Global Asia*, vol. 15, no. 1 (March 2020), https://www.globalasia.org/v15no1/feature/triangular-diplomacy-in-the-age-of-putin-xi-and-trump_walter-c-clemens-jr.

Cotton, Tom, Office of Senator. "Beat China: Targeted Decoupling and the Economic Long War," February 2021, https://www.cotton.senate.gov/imo/media/doc/210216_1700_China%20Report_FINAL.pdf.

Crowe, Jack. "Beware China's 'Investigation' into COVID's Origins," *The National Review*, March 25, 2021, https://www.nationalreview.com/2021/03/beware-chinas-internal-investigation-into-covids-origins/.

D'Eramo, Marco. "Our Daily Sanction," *New Left Review*, January 24, 2022, https://newleftreview.org/sidecar/posts/our-daily-sanction.

Das, Rup Narayan. "The Galwan Clash: A Landmark Change in India-China Relations," *Global Asia*, vol. 16, no. 2 (June 2021), pp. 78–85.

Denmark, Abraham, and Caitlin Talmadge. "Why China Wants More and Better Nukes," *Foreign Affairs*, November 19, 2021, https://www.foreignaffairs.com/articles/china/2021-11-19/why-china-wants-more-and-better-nukes.

Devlin, Kat, Laura Silver, and Christine Huang. "U.S. View of China Increasingly Negative Amid Coronavirus Outbreak," Pew Research Center, April 21, 2020, https://www.pewresearch.org/global/2020/04/21/u-s-views-of-china-increasingly-negative-amid-coronavirus-outbreak/.

Diamond, Larry, and Orville Schell. "Chinese Influence & American Interests: Promoting Constructive Vigilance," Hoover Institution and Asia Society, November 2018, https://www.hoover.org/research/chinas-influence-american-interests-promoting-constructive-vigilance.

Dollar, David. "Clear Skies over Asia's New Foreign Investment Landscape," *East Asia Forum*, May 2, 2021, https://www.eastasiaforum.org/2021/05/02/clear-skies-over-asias-new-foreign-investment-landscape/.

Dorfman, Zach. "Beijing Ransacked Data as U.S. Sources Went Dark in China," *Foreign Policy*, December 22, 2020, https://foreignpolicy.com/2020/12/22/china-us-data-intelligence-cybersecurity-xi-jinping/.

———. "Tech Giants Are Giving China a Vital Edge in Espionage," *Foreign Policy*, December 23, 2020, https://foreignpolicy.com/2020/12/23/china-tech-giants-process-stolen-data-spy-agencies/.

Esfandiary, Dina. "Iran's 'New' Partnership with China Is Just Business as Usual," *World Politics Review*, April 22, 2021, https://www.worldpoliticsreview.com/articles/29593/the-iran-china-deal-isn-t-all-that.

Fang, Songying, Xiaojun Li, and Adam Y. Liu. "Chinese Public Opinion about US-China Relations from Trump to Biden," *The Chinese Journal of International Politics*, 2022, https://doi.org/10.1093/cjip/poac001.

Fedasiuk, Ryan, and Emily Weinstein. "Beijing's Strategic Blueprint Is Changing as Tensions Grow," *Foreign Policy*, December 3, 2021, https://foreignpolicy.com /2021/12/03/china-strategic-blueprint-technology/.

Felbab-Brown, Vanda. "China and Synthetic Drugs Control: Fentanyl, Methamphetamines, and Precursors," Brookings Institution, March 2022, https://www.brookings.edu/research/china-and-synthetic-drugs-control -fentanyl-methamphetamines-and-precursors/.

Feng, Emily. "Rights Activist Xu Zhiyong Arrested in China amid Crackdown on Dissent," National Public Radio, February 17, 2020, www.npr.org/2020/02 /17/806584471/rights-activist-xu-zhiyong-arrested-in-china-amid-crackdown-on -dissent.

Feng, Tianli. "Bringing Evidence-Based Policy Change to Rural China," *Stanford Social Innovation Review*, Fall 2021, https://ssir.org/articles/entry/bringing_ evidence_based_policy_change_to_rural_china.

Fischer, Karin. "Chinese Scientists Feel a Chill under U.S. Investigation of Higher Ed's China Ties, a New Survey Shows," *Chronicle of Higher Education*, October 28, 2021, https://www.chronicle.com/article/chinese-scientists-feel-a-chill-under-u -s-investigation-of-higher-eds-china-ties-a-new-survey-shows.

————. "Do Colleges Need a Foreign Policy?" *Chronicle of Higher Education*, June 22, 2021, https://www.chronicle.com/article/do-colleges-need-a-foreign -policy.

————. "Has the Hunt for Chinese Spies Become a Witch Hunt?" *Chronicle of Higher Education*, August 11, 2021, https://www.chronicle.com/article/has-the -hunt-for-chinese-spies-become-a-witch-hunt.

Fiskesjö, Magnus. "Bulldozing Culture: China's Systematic Destruction of Uyghur Heritage Reveals Genocidal Intent," *Cultural Property News*, June 23, 2021, https: //culturalpropertynews.org/bulldozing-culture-chinas-systematic-destruction-of -uyghur-heritage-reveals-genocidal-intent/.

French, Howard W. "Can America Remain Preeminent?" *New York Review of Books*, April 29, 2021, https://www.nybooks.com/articles/2021/04/29/can-america-remain -preeminent/.

Fulda, Andreas. "Germany's China Policy of 'Change through Trade' Has Failed," RUSI (Royal United Services Institute), June 1, 2020, https://rusi.org/commentary /germanys-china-policy-change-through-trade-has-failed.

Fulda, Andreas, and David Missal. "German Academic Freedom Is Now Decided in Beijing," *Foreign Policy*, October 28, 2021, https://foreignpolicy.com/2021/10/28/ germany-china-censorship-universities-confucius-institute/.

Galston, William A. "A Momentous Shift in US Public Attitudes toward China," Brookings Institution, March 22, 2021, https://www.brookings.edu/blog/order -from-chaos/2021/03/22/a-momentous-shift-in-us-public-attitudes-toward-china/.

Gardner, Michael. "Germany Doubles Funding for China Studies, Collaboration," *University World News*, July 7, 2021, https://www.universityworldnews.com/post .php?story=20210707080823132.

Gerard, Bonnie. "Even Duterte Can't Get around the Thorn in China-Philippine Relations," *The Diplomat*, December 1, 2021, https://thediplomat.com/2021/12/ even-duterte-cant-get-around-the-thorn-in-china-philippine-relations/.

Gill, Bates, ed. *Meeting China's Military Challenge: Collective Responses of U.S. Allies and Security Partners* (Washington, DC: The National Bureau of Asian Research, January 2022).

Goddard, Stacie E. "The Outsiders: How the International System Can Still Check China and Russia," *Foreign Affairs*, May–June 2022, https://www.foreignaffairs .com/articles/ukraine/2022-04-06/china-russia-ukraine-international-system -outsiders.

Gordon, David F., Haoyu Tong, and Tabatha Anderson. "Beyond the Myths: Towards a Realistic Assessment of China's Belt and Road Initiative, the Security Dimension," International Institute for Strategic Studies, Report, September 2020, https://www .iiss.org/blogs/research-paper/2020/09/beyond-the-myths-of-the-bri.

Gowan, Richard. "China's Pragmatic Approach to UN Peacekeeping," Brookings Institution, September 14, 2020, https://www.brookings.edu/articles/chinas -pragmatic-approach-to-un-peacekeeping/.

Grassley, Chuck, Office of Senator. "News Releases: Grassley to Schools: Confucius Institutes Are Fronts for Chinese Propaganda; Just Ask FBI Mar 11, 2020."

Green, David. "The U.K.'s Incoherent China Strategy," *World Politics Review*, January 29, 2021, https://www.worldpoliticsreview.com/articles/29387/boris -johnson-s-approach-to-china-uk-relations-is-incoherent.

Greitens, Sheena Chestnut. "China: Two Key Questions," *Democracy*, no. 61 (Summer 2021), https://democracyjournal.org/magazine/61/china-two-key -questions/.

Grossman, Derek. "Duterte's Dalliance with China Is Over," *Foreign Policy*, November 2, 2021, https://foreignpolicy.com/2021/11/02/duterte-china-philippines -united-states-defense-military-geopolitics/.

Grubel, James. "ANU Helping to Reshape Australia's Ties to China," *ANU Reporter*, n.d., https://reporter.anu.edu.au/anu-helping-reshape-australia%E2%80%99s-ties -china.

Grunstein, Judah. "More 'Wolf Warrior' Diplomacy, Please," *World Politics Review*, March 24, 2021, https://www.worldpoliticsreview.com/articles/29517/wolf-warrior -diplomacy-and-the-us-china-relationship.

Gurtov, Mel. "Co-opted: The UN's Failed Mission to Xinjiang," June 16, 2022, https: //melgurtov.com/2022/06/16/post-341-co-opted-the-uns-misguided-mission-to -xinjiang.

———. "Downhill from the Summit for Democracy," December 19, 2021, https: //melgurtov.com/2021/12/19/post-321-downhill-from-the-summit-for-democracy/.

———. "The China Conundrum," *China-US Focus*, September 26, 2018, https:// www.chinausfocus.com/foreign-policy/the-china-conundrum.

_____. "The Uncertain Future of US-China Relations," *The Asia-Pacific Journal*, vol. 11, Issue 52, No. 1 (December 30, 2013), http://japanfocus.org/-Mel-Gurtov /4052.

_____. "What the End of 'America First' Might Mean for US Foreign Policy," *Global Asia*, vol. 16, no. 1 (March 2021), pp. 18–21.

Gurtov, Mel, and Mark Selden. "The Dangerous New US Consensus on China and the Future of US-China Relations," *The Asia-Pacific Journal*, August 1, 2019, https:// apjjf.org/2019/15/Gurtov-Selden.html.

Guterres, Antonio. Interview with the Associated Press, September 19, 2021, https: //thehill.com/policy/international/572978-un-chief-warns-of-potential-new-cold -war-between-us-china.

Hanemann, Thilo, Mark Witzke, Charlie Vest, Lauren Dudley, and Ryan Featherston. "An Outbound Investment Screening Regime for the United States?" Rhodium Group and National Committee on U.S.-China Relations, January 2022, https:// www.ncuscr.org/sites/default/files/page_attachments/NCUSCR_RHG_TWS_2022 _US_Outbound_Investment_1.26.22_FINAL.pdf.

Hass, Ryan. "How China Is Responding to Escalating Strategic Competition with the U.S.," *China Leadership Monitor*, March 1, 2021, https://www.prcleader.org/hass.

Hass, Ryan, Ryan McElveen, and Robert D. Williams, eds. *The Future of US Policy toward China: Recommendations for the Biden Administration* (Washington, DC: Brookings Institution and Yale Law School, November 2020), https://www .brookings.edu/wp-content/uploads/2020/11/Future-U.S.-policy-toward-China-v8 .pdf.

Hoffman, Aaron M. "A Conceptualization of Trust in International Relations," *European Journal of International Relations*, vol. 8, no. 3 (2002), pp. 375–401.

Hsiao, Russell. "Taiwanese Preference for Status Quo Remains Constant Even as Views Harden," *Global Taiwan Institute*, July 28, 2021, https://globaltaiwan.org /2021/07/vol-6-issue-15/#RussellHsiao07282021.

Hu Wei. "Possible Outcomes of the Russo-Ukraine War and China's Choice," U.S.-China Perception Monitor, March 12, 2022, https://uscnpm.org/2022/03/12/ hu-wei-russia-ukraine-war-china-choice/.

Huang, Yufan, and Deborah Brautigam. "Putting a Dollar Amount on China's Loans to the Developing World," *The Diplomat*, June 24, 2020, https://thediplomat.com /2020/06/putting-a-dollar-amount-on-chinas-loans-to-the-developing-world/.

Hufbauer, Gary Clyde, and Megan Hogan. "Security Not Economics Is Likely to Drive US Trade Engagement in Asia," *East Asia Forum*, January 9, 2022, https:// www.eastasiaforum.org/?p=568999.

Huntsman, John Jr. "Biden's China Relationship: The View from Utah," *Deseret News*, February 5, 2021.

Hvistendahl, Mara. "Journal Retracts Paper Based on DNA of Vulnerable Chinese Minorities," *The Intercept*, December 13, 2021, https://theintercept.com/2021/12 /13/china-uyghur-dna-human-genetics-retraction/.

_____. "Mass Resignations at Scientific Journal over Ethically Fraught China Genetics Papers," *The Intercept*, August 4, 2021, https://theintercept.com/2021/08 /04/dna-profiling-forensic-genetics-journal-resignations-china/.

Jay, Paul. "Biden's China Policy: A More Polite Trump—Amb. Chas Freeman," *The Analysis.news*, March 12, 2021, https://theanalysis.news/interviews/bidens-china -policy-a-more-polite-trump-amb-chas-freeman/.

Johnson, Keith. "How Europe Fell Out of Love with China," *Foreign Policy*, June 25, 2020, https://foreignpolicy.com/2020/06/25/china-europe-rival-strategic -competitor-huawei/.

Johnston, Alastair Iain. "The Failures of the 'Failure of Engagement' with China," *The Washington Quarterly*, vol. 42, no. 2 (Summer 2019), pp. 99–114.

Kafura, Craig, and Dina Smeltz. "Republicans and Democrats Split on China Policy," The Chicago Council on Global Affairs, December 10, 2021, https://www .thechicagocouncil.org/research/public-opinion-survey/republicans-and-democrats -split-china-policy.

Khatchadourian, Raffi. "Ghost Walls," *The New Yorker*, April 12, 2021, pp. 30–55.

Klare, Michael. "China, 2049: A Climate Disaster Zone, Not a Military Superpower," *TomDispatch*, August 24, 2021, https://tomdispatch.com/china-2049/.

Kristensen, Hans M., and Matt Korda. "Nuclear Notebook: Chinese Nuclear Forces, 2021," *Bulletin of the Atomic Scientists*, November 15, 2021, https://thebulletin.org /premium/2021-11/nuclear-notebook-chinese-nuclear-forces-2021/.

Kuik, Cheng-Chwee. "Introduction to the Special Issue," *Asian Perspective*, vol. 45, no. 2 (Spring 2021), pp. 255–76.

Kuo, Mercy A. "China in Afghanistan: How Beijing Engages the Taliban," *The Diplomat*, December 25, 2021, https://thediplomat.com/2021/12/china-in -afghanistan-how-beijing-engages-the-taliban/.

Kuttner, Robert. "The China Challenge," *The American Prospect*, September–October 2021, https://prospect.org/world/china-challenge/.

Lankov, Andrei. "Chinese Aid Strategy Hinders Goals on North Korea," *East Asia Forum*, December 30, 2021, https://www.eastasiaforum.org/2021/12/30/chinese -aid-strategy-hinders-goals-on-north-korea/.

Lewis, Robert. "After US Afghanistan Withdrawal Debacle, Huawei CFO Case May Be One Key to Reducing US-China Tensions," Paper, September 16, 2021, https://www.lexology.com/library/detail.aspx?g=0b90c84a-ed1f-4438-acf4 -44dbcfd70b15.

Lieberthal, Kenneth, and Wang Jisi. "Addressing U.S.-China Strategic Distrust," Brookings Institution, John L. Thornton China Center, No. 4 (March 2012).

Lieu, Ted, Representative. Press release, July 30, 2021.

Loh, Matthew. "Xi Jinping Forced 10,000 People Who Fled Overseas through an Operation Called 'Sky Net,' Says Human Rights NGO," *Business Insider*, January 19, 2022, https://www.businessinsider.com/china-forced-10000-fugitives-return -operation-sky-net-safeguard-defenders-2022-1.

Lu, Lee, Mel Gurtov, and Dale Cope. *Confucius Institutes in the U.S.: Final Report*, November 2020, https://www.ciuscenter.org/wp-content/uploads/Confucius -Institutes-in-the-U.S.-Final-Report-1.pdf.

Ma Xinyue. "China's Shifting Overseas Energy Footprint," *China Dialogue*, September 8, 2021, https://chinadialogue.net/en/energy/chinas-shifting-overseas -energy-footprint/.

Malik, Ammar A., Bradley Parks, Brooke Russell, Jiahui Lin, Katherine Walsh, Kyra Solomon,
Sheng Zhang, Thai-Binh Elston, and Seth Goodman. *Banking on the Belt and Road: Insights from a New Global Dataset of 13,427 Chinese Development Projects* (Williamsburg, VA: AidData at William & Mary, 2021).

Marnin, Julia. "China Tells U.S. to Stop Suppressing Its Rights and Interests, Help Wanted in Afghanistan," *Newsweek*, August 17, 2021, https://www.newsweek .com/china-tells-us-stop-suppressing-its-rights-interests-help-wanted-afghanistan -1620117.

Martinson, Ryan D., and Andrew S. Erickson. "Manila's Images Are Revealing the Secrets of China's Maritime Militia," *Foreign Policy*, April 19, 2021, https:// foreignpolicy.com/2021/04/19/manilas-images-are-revealing-the-secrets-of-chinas -maritime-militia/.

Matsuda, Yasuhiro. Interview by National Bureau of Asian Research, December 23, 2021, https://www.nbr.org/publication/the-2021-defense-white-paper-and-japans -taiwan-policy/.

Mauk, Ben. "Inside Xinjiang's Prison State," *The New Yorker*, February 26, 2021, https://www.newyorker.com/news/a-reporter-at-large/china-xinjiang-prison -state-uighur-detention-camps-prisoner-testimony.

Maxmen, Amy. "Scientists Struggle to Probe COVID's Origins amid Sparse Data from China," *Nature*, March 17, 2022, https://www.nature.com/articles/d41586 -022-00732-0.

Mayer, Jane. "How Right-Wing Billionaires Infiltrated Higher Education," *Chronicle of Higher Education*, February 2, 2016, https://www.chronicle.com/article/how -right-wing-billionaires-infiltrated-higher-education/.

McLaughlin, Timothy. "Why the U.S. Finally Called the Genocide in Myanmar a 'Genocide,'" *The Atlantic*, March 2022, https://www.theatlantic.com/international/ archive/2022/03/blinken-myanmar-genocide-rohingya-muslims/627124/.

McNeill, Sophie. "'They Don't Understand the Fear We Have,'" Human Rights Watch Report, June 30, 2021, https://www.hrw.org/report/2021/06/30/they-dont -understand-fear-we-have/how-chinas-long-reach-repression-undermines.

Mearsheimer, John J. "Joe Biden Must Embrace Liberal Nationalism to Lead America Forward," *The National Interest*, December 29, 2020, https://nationalinterest .org/feature/joe-biden-must-embrace-liberal-nationalism-lead-america-forward -174928.

————. "The Inevitable Rivalry: America, China, and the Tragedy of Great Power Politics," *Foreign Affairs*, vol. 100, no. 6 (September–December 2021), pp. 48–58.

Medeiros, Evan. "How to Craft a Durable China Strategy," *Foreign Affairs*, March 17, 2021, https://www.foreignaffairs.com/articles/united-states/2021-03-17/how -craft-durable-china-strategy#author-info.

Meng Weizhan. "Is China's IR Academic Community Becoming More Anti-American?" *Asian Perspective*, vol. 44 (2020), pp. 139–61.

Mize, Zoe. "China's Green Silk Road to Nuclear Power," IISS (International Institute for Strategic Studies), December 21, 2021, https://www.iiss.org/blogs/analysis /2021/12/chinas-green-silk-road-to-nuclear-power.

Mohan, C. Raja. "China's Two-Ocean Strategy Puts India in a Pincer," *Foreign Policy*, January 4, 2022, https://foreignpolicy.com/2022/01/04/india-china-ocean -geopolitics-sri-lanka-maldives-comoros/.

Niarchos, Nicolas. "Buried Dreams," *The New Yorker*, May 31, 2021, pp. 40–49.

NoiseCat, Julian Brave, and Thom Woodroofe. "The United States and China Need to Cooperate—for the Planet's Sake," *Foreign Policy*, February 4, 2021, https:// foreignpolicy.com/2021/02/04/united-states-china-climate-change-foreign-policy/.

Nye, Joseph S. Jr. "The End of Cyber-Anarchy?" *Foreign Affairs*, vol. 101, no. 1 (January–February 2022), pp. 32–42.

O'Brien, Robert. "The Chinese Communist Party's Ideology and Global Ambitions," June 26, 2020, https://trumpwhitehouse.archives.gov/briefings-statements/chinese -communist-partys-ideology-global-ambitions/.

O'Neill, Patrick Howell. "Chinese Hackers Posing as the UN Human Rights Council Are Attacking Uyghurs," *MIT Technology Review*, May 27, 2021, https:// www.technologyreview.com/2021/05/27/1025443/chinese-hackers-uyghur-united -nations/.

Pamilih, Julia. "Data: Chinese Research Partnerships with UK Universities," China Research Group, June 9, 2021, https://chinaresearchgroup.org/research/data -chinese-research-partnerships-with-uk-universities.

Pamilih, Julia, and Chris Cash. "The UK and China: Next Steps," China Research Group, September 2021, https://static1.squarespace.com/static /5f75a6c74b43624d99382ab6/t/61504b44c2965710d91a7bcd/1632652104633/ The+UK+and+China_+Next+Steps.pdf.

Panda, Rajaram. "Japan's Military Gets a Boost in Response to Threats from China and North Korea," *Global Asia*, vol. 16, no. 4 (December 2021), pp. 100–104.

Panichi, James. "Australia's 'Spartacus' Moment: Canberra Pushes Back at Beijing," *Global Asia*, vol. 16, no. 2 (June 2021), pp. 90–95.

Perry, Elizabeth. "Debating Maoism in Contemporary China: Reflections on Benjamin I. Schwartz, Chinese Communism and the Rise of Mao," *The Asia-Pacific Journal*, January 1, 2021, https://apjjf.org/2021/1/Perry.html.

Ratcliffe, John. "China Is National Security Threat No. 1," *Wall Street Journal*, December 3, 2020, https://www.wsj.com/articles/china-is-national-security-threat -no-1-11607019599.

Richardson, Sophie. "Thermo Fisher's Necessary, but Insufficient, Step in China," Human Rights Watch, https://www.hrw.org/news/2019/02/22/thermo-fishers -necessary-insufficient-step-china.

Rosen, Daniel H. "China's Economic Reckoning: The Price of Failed Reforms," *Foreign Affairs*, vol. 100, no. 4 (July–August 2021), pp. 20–29.

Rotella, Sebastian. "Even on U.S. Campuses, China Cracks Down on Students Who Speak Out," *ProPublica*, November 30, 2021, https://www.propublica.org/article/ even-on-us-campuses-china-cracks-down-on-students-who-speak-out.

Rudd, Kevin. "What Explains Xi's Pivot to the State?" Belfer Center, Harvard University, September 19, 2021, https://www.belfercenter.org/publication/what -explains-xis-pivot-state.

_____. "Why the Quad Alarms China," *Foreign Affairs*, August 6, 2021, https://www.foreignaffairs.com/articles/united-states/2021-08-06/why-quad-alarms-china.

Sarlin, Benji, and Sahil Kapur. "Why China May Be the Last Bipartisan Issue Left in Washington," NBC News, March 21, 2021, https://www.nbcnews.com/politics/congress/why-china-may-be-last-bipartisan-issue-left-washington-n1261407?cid=eml_nbn_20210322.

Sawa, Dale Berning. "Uyghur Civilisation in China Continues to Be Erased as Part of Chilling Mission," *The Art Newspaper*, November 3, 2020, https://www.theartnewspaper.com/2020/11/03/uyghur-civilisation-in-china-continues-to-be-erased-as-part-of-chilling-mission.

Schiff, Adam. "The World," September 30, 2020, https://www.pri.org/stories/2020-09-30/schiff-us-power-confront-hard-targets-china-has-really-atrophied.

Schuman, Michael. "China Isn't That Strategic," *The Atlantic*, July 1, 2021, https://theatlantic.com/international/archive/2021/07/china-communists-demographics/619312/.

Segal, Adam. "China Moves to Greater Self-reliance," *China Leadership Monitor*, December 1, 2021, https://www.prcleader.org/segal.

Seligsohn, Deborah. "The Rise and Fall of the US-China Health Relationship," *Asian Perspective*, vol. 45, no. 1 (Winter 2021), pp. 203–24.

Seo, Jungkun. "Strange Bedfellows and US China Policy in the Era of Polarized Politics," *The Korean Journal of Defense Analysis*, vol. 29, no. 1 (March 2017), pp. 47–69.

Sharma, Yojana. "Taiwan Fills Gap Left by Confucius Institute Closures," *University World News*, December 2, 2021, https://www.universityworldnews.com/post.php?story=20211202125025734.

Shidore, Sarang. "De-risking the India Relationship: An Action Agenda for the United States," Quincy Institute Brief No. 10, March 10, 2021, https://quincyinst.org/report/de-risking-the-india-relationship-an-action-agenda-for-the-united-states/?mc_cid=a0f34e4c69&mc_eid=a890eb89be.

Shirk, Susan L. "China in Xi's 'New Era': The Return to Personalistic Rule," *Journal of Democracy*, vol. 29, no. 2 (April 2018), https://muse.jhu.edu/article/690071.

Silver, Andrew. "Scientists in China Say US Government Crackdown Is Harming Collaborations," *Nature*, July 8, 2020, https://www.nature.com/articles/d41586-020-02015-y.

Silver, Laura. "China's International Image Remains Broadly Negative as Views of the U.S. Rebound," Pew Research Center, June 30, 2021, https://www.pewresearch.org/fact-tank/2021/06/30/chinas-international-image-remains-broadly-negative-as-views-of-the-u-s-rebound/.

Silver, Laura, Kat Devlin, and Christine Huang. "Large Majorities Say China Does Not Respect the Personal Freedoms of Its People," Pew Research Center, June 30, 2021, https://www.pewresearch.org/global/2021/06/30/large-majorities-say-china-does-not-respect-the-personal-freedoms-of-its-people/.

Snyder, Scott, and See-Won Byun. "China-Korea Relations: Economic Stabilization, End-of-War Declaration, and the Ongoing 'Joint Struggle,'" *Comparative Connections*, vol. 23, no. 3, pp. 107–16.

Sposato, William. "Taro Aso's Taiwan Slip Was Likely Deliberate," *Foreign Policy*, July 12, 2021, https://foreignpolicy.com/2021/07/12/taro-aso-taiwan-japan-china-policy/.

Starting, Rebecca, and Joanne Wallis. "Strategic Competition in Oceania," in Ashley J. Tellis, Alison Szalwinski, and Michael Wills, eds., *Navigating Tumultuous Times in the Indo-Pacific* (Seattle, WA: The National Bureau of Asian Research, 2022), https://www.nbr.org/wp-content/uploads/pdfs/publications/strategicasia2021-22_oceania_strating_wallis.pdf.

Subbaraman, Nidhi. "US Universities Call for Clearer Rules on Science Espionage amidst China Crackdown," *Nature*, April 6, 2021, https://www.nature.com/articles/d41586-021-00901-7.

Sullivan, Jake. "What Donald Trump and Dick Cheney Got Wrong about America," *The Atlantic*, January 2019, https://www.theatlantic.com/magazine/archive/2019/01/yes-america-can-still-lead-the-world/576427/.

Sun, Yun. "China's Strategic Assessment of the Ladakh Clash," *War on the Rocks*, June 19, 2020, warontherocks.com/2020/06/chinas-strategic-assessment-of-the-ladakh-clash/.

————. "The Domestic Controversy over China's Foreign Aid and the Implications for Africa." Brookings Institution, October 8, 2015, https://www.brookings.edu/blog/africa-in-focus/2015/10/08/the-domestic-controversy-over-chinas-foreign-aid-and-the-implications-for-africa/.

————. "FOCAC 2021: China's Retrenchment from Africa?" Brookings Institution, December 6, 2021, https://www.brookings.edu/blog/africa-in-focus/2021/12/06/focac-2021-chinas-retrenchment-from-africa/.

————. "Ukraine: China's Desired Endgame," *Carnegie*, March 22, 2022, https://www.stimson.org/2022/ukraine-china-endgame/.

Swaine, Michael D. "US Official Signals Stunning Shift in the Way We Interpret 'One China' Policy," *Responsible Statecraft*, December 10, 2021, https://responsiblestatecraft.org/2021/12/10/us-official-signals-stunning-shift-in-the-way-we-interpret-one-china-policy/.

————. "Chinese Views of U.S. Decline," *China Leadership Monitor*, September 1, 2021, https://www.prcleader.org/swaine-2.

————. "Recent Chinese Views on the Taiwan Issue," *China Leadership Monitor*, December 1, 2021, https://www.prcleader.org/swaine-3.

Tan, CK. "China Signals Shift on Ukraine as Russia Accused of Atrocities," *Nikkei Asia*, March 9, 2022, https://asia.nikkei.com/Politics/Ukraine-war/China-signals-shift-on-Ukraine-as-Russia-accused-of-atrocities.

Tan, Yeling. "How the WTO Changed China," *Foreign Affairs*, vol. 100, no. 2 (March–April 2021), pp. 90–102.

Thornton, Susan A. "Whither the Status Quo? A Cross–Taiwan Strait Trilateral Dialogue," National Committee on American Foreign Policy, December 2021, https:

//www.ncafp.org/2016/wp-content/uploads/2021/12/NCAFP-Cross-Strait-Trilat
-Report_2021_Final.pdf.

Tibet Watch (International Campaign for Tibet), Spring 2021.

Tong, Kurt. "Hong Kong and the Limits of Decoupling," *Foreign Affairs*, July 14, 2021, https://www.foreignaffairs.com/articles/asia/2021-07-14/hong-kong-and-limits-decoupling.

Ullah, Shakir et al. "Problems and Benefits of the China-Pakistan Economic Corridor (CPEC) for Local People in Pakistan: A Critical Review," *Asian Perspective*, vol. 45, no. 4 (Fall 2021), pp. 861–76.

Urbina, Ian. "The Smell of Money," *The New Yorker*, March 8, 2021, pp. 24–29.

Van Ness, Peter. "Hitting Reset on the Australia-China Relationship," *East Asia Forum*, February 2, 2022, https://www.eastasiaforum.org/2022/02/02/hitting-reset-on-the-australia-china-relationship/.

Wagner, Caroline. "Scrutiny of Chinese Researchers Threatens Innovation," *University World News*, January 30, 2021, https://www.universityworldnews.com/post.php?story=20210128141727753.

Wang Dong. "The Case for a New Engagement Consensus: A Chinese Vision of Global Order," *Foreign Affairs*, April 15, 2021, https://www.foreignaffairs.com/articles/china/2021-04-15/case-new-engagement-consensus.

Wang Jisi. "Inside China," *Global Asia*, June 10, 2010, https://www.globalasia.org/v5no2/cover/inside-china-a-note-from-the-guest-editor-wang-jisi_wang-jisi.

————. "The Plot against China? How Beijing Sees the New Washington Consensus," *Foreign Affairs*, vol. 100, no. 4 (July–August 2021), pp. 48–57.

————. "The Understanding Gap," *China-US Focus*, March 11, 2021, https://www.chinausfocus.com/foreign-policy/the-understanding-gap.

Wang, Christoph Nedopil. "China Belt and Road Initiative (BRI) Investment Report H1 2021," Green Finance and Development Center, July 21, 2021, https://greenfdc.org/china-belt-and-road-initiative-bri-investment-report-h1-2021/?cookie-state-change=1638536227352.

Weiss, Jessica Chen. "A World Safe for Autocracy? China's Rise and the Future of Global Politics," *Foreign Affairs*, vol. 98, no. 4 (July–August 2019), pp. 92–102.

Wertime, David. "'Not the World's Number One': Chinese Social Media Piles on the U.S.," *Politico*, May 4, 2020, www.politico.com/news/magazine/2020/05/04/china-america-struggle-disaster-221741.

Wike, Richard, Laura Silver, Janell Fetterolf, Christine Huang, and J. J. Moncus. "What People around the World Like—and Dislike—about American Society and Politics," Pew Research Center, November 1, 2021, https://www.pewresearch.org/global/2021/11/01/what-people-around-the-world-like-and-dislike-about-american-society-and-politics/.

Williams, Ian. "How China is Stoking Racial Tensions in the West," *The Spectator*, May 2, 2021, https://www.spectator.co.uk/article/how-china-is-stoking-racial-tensions-in-the-west.

Wong, Audrye. "How Not to Win Allies and Influence Geopolitics," *Foreign Affairs*, vol. 100, no. 3 (May–June 2001), pp. 44–53.

Woodrow Wilson Center. "Walking the Walk after the New U.S.-China Climate Declaration," January 13, 2021, webcast interview of Fan Dai, director of the California-China Climate Institute, https://www.wilsoncenter.org/event/walking-walk-after-new-us-china-climate-declaration.

Wright, Robin. "Russia and China Unveil a Pact against America and the West," *The New Yorker*, February 7, 2022, https://www.newyorker.com/news/daily-comment/russia-and-china-unveil-a-pact-against-america-and-the-west.

Wright, Thomas. "Democrats Need to Place China at the Center of Their Foreign Policy," Brookings Institution, May 15, 2019, https://www.brchinookings.edu/blog/order-from-chaos/2019/05/15/democrats-need-to-place-a-at-the-center-of-their-foreign-policy/.

Wyne, Ali. "Competition with China Shouldn't Dictate U.S. Foreign Policy," *World Politics Review*, February 25, 2021, https://www.worldpoliticsreview.com/articles/29450/competition-with-a-rising-china-shouldn-t-dictate-u-s-foreign-policy.

Wyne, Ali, and Ryan Hass. "China Diplomacy Is Limiting Its Own Ambitions," *Foreign Policy*, June 9, 2021, https://foreignpolicy.com/2021/06/09/china-wolf-war-diplomacy-foreign-policy/.

Xu Zeyu and Zhai Xiang. "The View from Beijing: America's 'Mirage' of Strength," *U.S.-China Perception Monitor*, August 9, 2021, https://uscnpm.org/2021/08/09/the-view-from-beijing-americas-mirage-of-strength/.

Xu Zhangrun. "Xi's China, the Handiwork of an Autocratic Roué," *New York Review of Books*, August 9, 2021, https://www.nybooks.com/daily/2021/08/09/xis-china-the-handiwork-of-an-autocratic-roue/?lp_txn_id=1269942.

Xu, Vicky Xiuzhong, James Leibold, and Daria Impiombato. *The Architecture of Repression*, Australian Strategic Policy Institute, October 2021, https://www.aspi.org.au/report/architecture-repression?__cf_chl_jschl_tk__=pmd_mj4ySTi65QZKxNen850h27K8CiUW.363UdjlQ8HQgi0-1634662284-0-gqNtZGzNAiWjcnBszQjR.

Yan Xuetong. "Becoming Strong: The New Chinese Foreign Policy," *Foreign Affairs*, vol. 100, no. 4 (July–August 2021), pp. 40–47.

Yang, Dali L. "The COVID-19 Pandemic and the Estrangement of US-China Relations," *Asian Perspective*, vol. 45, no. 1 (Winter 2001), p. 10.

Zakaria, Fareed. "The New China Scare: Why America Shouldn't Panic about Its Latest Challenger," *Foreign Affairs*, December 6, 2019, www.foreignaffairs.com/articles/china/2019-12-06/new-china-scare.

Zhao, Suisheng. "Top-level Design and Enlarged Diplomacy: Foreign and Security Policymaking in Xi Jinping's China," *Journal of Contemporary China*, 2022, DOI: 10.1080/10670564.2022.2052440.

GOVERNMENT AND OTHER OFFICIAL PUBLICATIONS

"Announcement of the Full Meeting of the 19th Central Committee, 6th CCP Plenum," Xinhua Net, November 11, 2021, http://www.news.cn/politics/2021-11/11/c_1128055386.htm.

Blinken, Antony J. "The Administration's Approach to the People's Republic of China," Speech at the George Washington University, US Department of State, Washington, DC, May 26, 2022, https://www.state.gov/the-administrations -approach-to-the-peoples-republic-of-china/.

China, Ministry of Foreign Affairs. "Ambassador Zhang Jun Exercises the Right to Reply in Response to the Statement Made by the Representative of the United States at the General Debate of the Third Committee," October 4, 2021, https:// www.fmprc.gov.cn/mfa_eng/wjb_663304/zwjg_665342/zwbd_665378/t1912680 .shtml.

_____. "Chinese President Xi Jinping Speaks with U.S. President Joseph Biden by Phone," https://www.fmprc.gov.cn/mfa_eng/zxxx_662805/t1906035.shtml.

_____. "President Xi Holds Virtual Meeting with US President Biden," November 16, 2021, https://www.fmprc.gov.cn/web/zyxw/t1919210.shtml.

_____. "State Councilor and Foreign Minister Wang Yi Gives Interview to Xinhua News Agency and China Media Group on International Situation and China's Diplomacy in 2021," December 30, 2021, https://www.mfa.gov.cn/mfa_eng/zxxx _662805/202112/t20211230_10477324.html.

_____. "Wang Yi Meets US Deputy Secretary of State Sherman," July 26, 2021, https://www.fmprc.gov.cn/web/wjbz_673089/zyhd_673091/t1895177.shtml.

_____. "Xi Jinping and US President Biden Hold Virtual Summit" (in Chinese), November 16, 2021, https://www.fmprc.gov.cn/web/zyxw/t1919210.shtml.

China, State Council Information Office. *Poverty Alleviation: China's Experience and Contribution*, April 2021, https://Xinhuanet.com/English/2021-04/06/c-139860414 .htm.

Clinton, Bill. *A National Security Strategy for a New Century*. Washington, DC: The White House, October 1998, https://www.whitehouse.gov/WH/EOP/NSC/html/ documents/nssr/pdf.

Congressional Research Service (CRS). "China's Naval Modernization: Implications for U.S. Navy Capabilities—Background and Issues for Congress" (Washington, DC: September 9, 2021), https://crsreports.congress.gov/product/pdf/RL/RL33153 /253.

Deng Xiaoping. *Fundamental Issues in Present-Day China*. Beijing: Foreign Languages Press, 1987.

Director of National Intelligence. *Annual Threat Assessment of the US Intelligence Community*, April 9, 2021, https://www.nytimes.com/interactive/2021/04/13/us/ annual-threat-assessment-report-pdf.html.

Embassy of the People's Republic of China in the United States of America. "Wang Yi: U.S.-Britain-Australia Nuclear Submarine Cooperation Poses Three Hidden Dangers," September 28, 2021, http://www.china-embassy.org/eng/zgyw/t1911163 .htm.

Japan, Ministry of Defense. *Defense of Japan 2021*, n.d., https://www.mod.go.jp/en/ publ/w_paper/index.html.

"Joint Announcement of the People's Republic of China and the Russian Federation on the New Era in International Relations and Global Sustainable Development" (中华人民共和国和俄罗斯联邦关于新时代国际关系和全球可持续发展的联

合声明), *Renmin Ribao*, February 22, 2022, http://politics.people.com.cn/n1/2022/0204/c1001-32345502.html.

New Zealand House of Representatives, Justice Committee. "Inquiry into the 2019 Local Elections and Liquor Licensing Trust Elections, and Recent Energy Trust Elections," July 2021, https://www.parliament.nz/resource/en-NZ/SCR_112173/ac056d5bfbb02d80f3171b435891330c1ff92bb7.

North Atlantic Treaty Organization. "Brussels Summit Communiqué," June 14, 2021, https://www.nato.int/cps/en/natohq/news_185000.htm.

Pence, Mike. "Remarks by Vice President Pence at the Frederic V. Malek Memorial Lecture," October 24, 2019, https://vn.usembassy.gov/remarks-by-vice-president-pence-at-the-frederic-v-malek-memorial-lecture.

Pompeo, Michael. "Communist China and the Free World's Future," Nixon Library, July 23, 2020, https://www.state.gov/communist-china-and-the-free-worlds-future/.

————. "The Chinese Communist Party on the American Campus," December 9, 2020, https://www.state.gov/the-chinese-communist-party-on-the-american-campus.

Price, Ned. Department Press Briefing, April 7, 2021, https://www.state.gov/briefings/department-press-briefing-april-7-2021/.

"Remarks by President Obama and President Xi of the People's Republic of China before Bilateral Meeting," September 6, 2013, www.whitehouse.gov/the-press-office/2013/09/06/remarks-president-obama-and-president-xi-peoples-republic-china-bilatera.

"Remarks of President Obama and President Xi Jinping of the People's Republic of China after Bilateral Meeting," June 8, 2013, www.whitehouse.gov/the-press-office/2013/06/08/remarks-president-obama-and-president-xi-jinping-peoples-republic-china-.

State Council Information Office of the PRC. "Fighting COVID-19: China in Action," June 2020, http://english.scio.gov.cn/whitepapers/2020-06/07/content_76135269.htm.

"Statement by President Xi Jinping at Virtual Event of Opening of the 73rd World Health Assembly, Fighting COVID-19 through Solidarity and Cooperation: Building a Global Community of Health for All," May 18, 2020, transcript.

United Kingdom. "Foreign Affairs Committee Publish Report: 'Never Again: The UK's Responsibility to Act on Atrocities in Xinjiang and Beyond,'" July 8, 2021, https://committees.parliament.uk/committee/78/foreign-affairs-committee/news/156425/fac-xinjiang-detention-camps-report-published-21-22/.

UN Development Programme. *Human Development Report 2020* (http://hdr.undp.org/en/content/download-data).

U.S.-China Economic and Security Review Commission. *2021 Annual Report to Congress*, https://www.uscc.gov/sites/default/files/2021-11/Chapter_1_Section_1--CCPs_Ambitions_and_Challenges_at_Its_Centennial.pdf.

————. *2021 Annual Report to Congress*, https://www.uscc.gov/sites/default/files/2021-11/Chapter_4--Dangerous_Period_for_Cross-Strait_Deterrence.pdf.

US Congress, Senate. 117th Cong., 1st Sess., "Strategic Competition Act of 2021," https://www.congress.gov/bill/117th-congress/senate-bill/1169.

US Department of Commerce. Press Release, "Commerce Department to Add Nine Chinese Entities Related to Human Rights Abuses in the Xinjiang Uighur Autonomous Region to the Entity List," May 22, 2020, www.commerce.gov/news /press-releases/2020/05/commerce-department-add-nine-chinese-entities-related -human-rights.

US Department of Defense. *Indo-Pacific Strategy Report: Preparedness, Partnerships, and Promoting a Networked Region*, June 1, 2019, https://media.defense.gov/2019 /Jul/01/2002152311/-1/-1/1/DEPARTMENT-OF-DEFENSE-INDO-PACIFIC -STRATEGY-REPORT-2019.PDF.

US Department of Justice. "Information about the Department of Justice's China Initiative and a Compilation of China-Related Prosecutions since 2018," June 14, 2021, https://www.justice.gov/nsd/information-about-department-justice-s-china -initiative-and-compilation-china-related.

US National Intelligence Council. "Foreign Threats to the 2020 US Federal Elections," March 16, 2021, https://www.dni.gov/files/ODNI/documents/assessments/ICA -declass-16MAR21.pdf.

————. "Global Trends 2040: A More Contested World," March 2021, https:// www.dni.gov/files/ODNI/documents/assessments/GlobalTrends_2040.pdf.

US National Security Council. "National Security Strategy," February 2015, https: //obamawhitehouse.archives.gov/sites/default/files/docs/2015_national_security _strategy_2.pdf.

————. "U.S. Strategic Framework for the Indo-Pacific," n.d., https:// trumpwhitehouse.archives.gov/wp-content/uploads/2021/01/IPS-Final-Declass .pdf.

US Office of the Secretary of Defense. *Military and Security Developments Involving the People's Republic of China 2021: Annual Report to Congress* (Washington, DC: Department of Defense, 2021).

US Office of the Secretary of State, Policy Planning Staff. *The Elements of the China Challenge*, November 2020, https://www.state.gov/wp-content/uploads/2020/11 /20-02832-Elements-of-China-Challenge-508.pdf.

United States Trade Representative. "2021 Report to Congress on China's WTO Compliance," February 2022, https://ustr.gov/sites/default/files/enforcement/WTO /2021%20USTR%20Report%20to%20Congress%20on%20China's%20WTO %20Compliance.pdf.

————. "Remarks as Prepared for Delivery of Ambassador Katherine Tai Outlining the Biden-Harris Administration's 'New Approach to the U.S.-China Trade Relationship,'" October 4, 2021, https://ustr.gov/about-us/policy-offices /press-office/press-releases/2021/october/remarks-prepared-delivery-ambassador -katherine-tai-outlining-biden-harris-administrations-new.

"The Video Meeting Is Another Instance in China-US Relations of the Two Countries' Leaders Piloting the Ship by Rudder at a Critical Moment" (in Chinese), November 16, 2021, http://world.people.com.cn/n1/2021/1116/c1002-32284196.html.

The White House. "President Biden and G7 Leaders Launch Build Back Better (B3W) Partnership," June 12, 2021, https://www.whitehouse.gov/briefing-room/ statements-releases/2021/06/12/fact-sheet-president-biden-and-g7-leaders-launch -build-back-better-world-b3w-partnership/.

————. "Readout of President Joseph R. Biden Call with President Xi Jinping of the People's Republic of China," September 9, 2021, https://www.whitehouse.gov/ briefing-room/statements-releases/2021/09/09/readout-of-president-joseph-r-biden -jr-call-with-president-xi-jinping-of-the-peoples-republic-of-china/.

————. *Indo-Pacific Strategy of the United States* (Washington, DC: February 2022), https://www.whitehouse.gov/wp-content/uploads/2022/02/U.S.-Indo -Pacific-Strategy.pdf.

————. *Interim National Security Strategic Guidance* (March 2021), https://www .whitehouse.gov/wp-content/uploads/2021/03/NSC-1v2.pdf.

————. "United States Strategic Approach to the People's Republic of China," www .whitehouse.gov/U.S.-Strategic-Approach-to-The-Peoples-Republic-of-China -Report-5.20.20(1).pdf.

Xi Jinping. "Keynote Speech by President Xi Jinping at Extraordinary China-Africa Summit on Solidarity against COVID-19," Xinhuanet, June 18, 2020, http://www .xinhuanet.com/english/2020-06/18/c_139147084.htm.

————. "Speech at a Ceremony Marking the Centenary of the Communist Party of China," July 1, 2021, http://en.people.cn/n3/2021/0701/c90000-9867483.html.

NONGOVERNMENTAL REPORTS

American Anthropological Association. "The Assault on Indigenous Peoples in Northwest China Must End," February 26, 2020, www.americananthro.org/ ParticipateAndAdvocate/AdvocacyDetail.aspx?ItemNumber=25500.

BP. "Statistical Review of World Energy, 2021: China's Energy Market in 2020," https: //www.bp.com/content/dam/bp/business-sites/en/global/corporate/pdfs/energy -economics/statistical-review/bp-stats-review-2021-china-insights.pdf.

"CGTN Sanctioned on Multiple Counts for Airing Forced Confessions," *Safeguard Defenders*, August 26, 2021, https://safeguarddefenders.com/en/blog/cgtn -sanctioned-multiple-counts-airing-forced-confessions.

Committee to Protect Journalists. "Number of Journalists behind Bars Reaches Global High," December 13, 2021, https://cpj.org/reports/2021/12/number-of -journalists-behind-bars-reaches-global-high/.

"Direct Investment Position of the United States in China from 2000 to 2020," *Statista*, https://www.statista.com/statistics/188629/united-states-direct -investments-in-china-since-2000/.

Eurostat. "China-EU International Trade in Goods Statistics," March 2021, https://ec .europa.eu/eurostat/statistics-explained/index.php?title=China-EU_-_international _trade_in_goods_statistics.

Fair Labor Association. "FLA Statement on Sourcing in China," December 3, 2020, https://www.fairlabor.org/blog/entry/fla-statement-sourcing-china#.X -jNTiLcdZE.twitter.

Lowy Institute. *Asia Power Index 2021 Edition*, https://power.lowyinstitute.org/data/ economic-relationships/regional-trade-relations/primary-trade-partner/.

"The Latest on Southeast Asia," Center for Strategic and International Studies, July 22, 2021, https://www.csis.org/blogs/latest-southeast-asia/latest-southeast-asia -july-22-2021.

"UN: Unprecedented Joint Call for China to End Xinjiang Abuses," Human Rights Watch, July 10, 2019, www.hrw.org/news/2019/07/10/un-unprecedented-joint-call -china-end-xinjiang-abuses.

United States Institute of Peace, Myanmar Study Group. "Anatomy of the Military Coup and Recommendations for U.S. Response," February 1, 2022, https://www .usip.org/publications/2022/02/myanmar-study-group-final-report.

World Nuclear Association. "Nuclear Power in China," January 2022, https:// world-nuclear.org/information-library/country-profiles/countries-a-f/china-nuclear -power.aspx.

NEWSPAPERS AND OTHER NEWS SOURCES

(Consult the notes for specific articles.)
Aljazeera
Asia Times
BBC News
Bloomberg
CBC News (Ottawa)
China Daily (Beijing)
China Times (Beijing)
CNN
Daily Mail (London)
Financial Times (London)
The Globe and Mail (Toronto)
The Guardian (US edition)
Hankyoreh (Seoul)
Korea Herald (Seoul)
National Public Radio
NBC News
New York Times
Newsroom (New Zealand)
Nikkei Asia (Tokyo)
Renmin Ribao (People's Daily, Beijing)
Reuters
RTHK News (Hong Kong)
South China Morning Post (Hong Kong)

Straits Times (Singapore)
Sydney Morning Herald
Taiwan News
Voice of America
Wall Street Journal
Washington Post
Xinhua (Beijing)
Yahoo! News

Index